Cadences

Writers on other titles by Anne M Scriven

'I have read, loved and bought for others ...'
— Sophie Dahl on *Learning to Listen: Life and a Nervous Dog*

*'A vivid and entertaining tour of the eccentric customers — and staff — of
Scotland's most beguiling bookshop.'*
— Margaret Elphinstone on *Provenance: Tales from a Bookshop*

Cadences
Notes from an Ordinary Life

Anne M Scriven

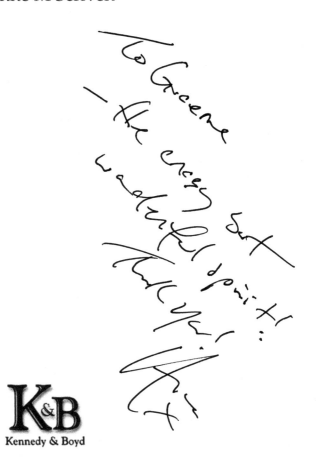

K&B
Kennedy & Boyd

Kennedy & Boyd
an imprint of
Zeticula Ltd
Unit 13,
196 Rose Street,
Edinburgh,
EH2 4AT

http://www.kennedyandboyd.co.uk
admin@kennedyandboyd.co.uk

First published 2017:
Text and Photographs Copyright © Anne M. Scriven 2017
ISBN 978-1-84921-168-0

For Aunt Clemmy who understood

Cadence: Latin, cadentia, 'a falling'. A melodic or harmonic configuration that creates a sense of resolution.

Let us record the atoms as they fall upon the mind in the order in which they fall, let us trace the pattern, however disconnected and incoherent in appearance, which each sight or incident scores upon the consciousness. Let us not take it for granted that life exists more fully in what is commonly thought big than in what is commonly thought small.

— Virginia Woolf, 'Modern Fiction', (1919)

A note on the text

Laced throughout this book are the occasional Scots words or phrases that may be unfamiliar to some readers. To help sort out the ensuing stramash in the mind of such people there is a glossary provided at the end of my blethers.

Acknowledgements

Howwood Parish Church Ladies' Guild
— *for reminding me of another rhythm*
Anne MacLean
— *for unlocking the language of music*
Rachel Poolman
— *for understanding the needs of strangers*
Ian Jack
— *for kind validation*
Margaret Elphinstone
— *for reliable continuity*
Renfrewshire Tapestry Group
— *for pausing stitching*
The FMDM community of Ladywell Convent, Godalming
— *for sharing of archival memory*
My extended family
— *for being the source and sustainers of stories*
Colum
— *for being my blood critic and perfect listener*
Sam
—*for your way of seeing*
Kennedy & Boyd
— *for patience with fictitious deadlines*
Peter McCormack
— *for an intelligent gaze*
Desmond
— *for unfailing belief that my next title
will be a long-awaited bestseller*

x

Contents

To see rightly

There once was a very little boy, whom I knew so very very well, who sat in his high chair one winter evening waiting for his dinner to appear on the plastic tray in front of him. His gaze wandered round the small kitchen and then up to the window and then out through the glass. Delight broke out on his face and danced in his eyes as he raised a dimpled finger to point and say *'Wass tha?!'* I turned in the direction of where he was looking and saw the moon. The moon sitting just above the rooftop of the block of flats opposite ours. A bright silver orb, suspended by magic, smiling down at my son. He smiled his best smile back, entranced and captivated, his face reflecting sheer joy, his fish fingers forgotten. I lifted him out of his high-chair into my arms, pulled the blind up further, turned off the kitchen light and we gave that moon a long long look. I had seen many moons by this time, but it took a little toddler to remind me of the miracle that it is and so worthy of our stopping and of our gazing.

This book is made up of such focused gazings. Gazings at the familiar. That which we often overlook just because it is the stuff of everyday life. It is therefore a bit of a risk. Books about the everyday are, as a general rule, not the stuff of sensation. Writing about everyday life can easily be judged as boring and lacking in *oomph* or, as the Scots has it, *smeddum*. As Virginia Woolf astutely noted in her famous extended essay *A Room of One's Own* (1929):

> This book is an important book, the critic assumes, because it deals with war. This is an insignificant book because it deals with the feelings of women in a drawing-room.

What such critics miss of course is that those same women may be aware of the movement of nations while quietly taking tea, choosing to follow their normal daily rhythm because such rhythms are what hold society together. The essays here, measures from my daily life as I experience them, therefore focus on the ordinary but are mindful of wider happenings.

Some of the stories that form this book are reflective of situations political, both local and global. To live in today's Scotland is to live in a country that is awake to politics. Politics which impact on our daily lives. It is a highly charged time. I don't offer a definitive response — an impossible task anyway for such a shifting spectrum — nor in-depth polemic on any contemporary concerns. Aware of the problematics of locating writing in a fixed calendar date, I aim mostly for the long view rather than the immediate. But neither do I write from a position of neutrality. No writing ever does if you look at it hard enough.

If anything, the inherent difficulty in the construction of this book was where to stop. As time went on and my senses were honed to be on constant alert for the jewels of the moment spilling out around me, and knowing that everywhere there is detail, I had to decide which to write about and which to let alone. To attempt to inscribe the whole would render me insane and there is wisdom in the belief that less is more.

This book has also had the added grace of being shaped by some serious swings in tempo that spun around people I hold dear. It is also mindful of some special people who, like my toddler son, caused me to be attentive to the myriad experiences, episodes, events and emotions playing out around me. It would be easy to compress each occurrence with the conclusion that it has been a sair fecht — each successive transition asking some significant effort from me. For a writer however, all is material and difficult things are part of life. Each brings its own insights, its own pace, its own story. And, interspersed between each exigent situation were many moments of joy in the ordinary, that would not be negated. I have thus written of the light and the dark because that is what a writer does, that is the task given, and is our natural response to the varying cadences of life.

In the beginning was the Word

To be a writer is, I jalouse, to be a mercenary being. There are some rare beings, granted, who do not prostrate themselves on the altar of publicity and availability. There are some writers whose complete disinterest in meeting their readership ironically adds a definite allure to their hidden profile. Elena Ferrante springs to mind. An Italian (assuredly) female (arguably) writer (definitely) who says in the (translated) version of *Frantumaglia: A Writer's Journey* (2016) — an (alleged) collection of autobiographical fragments — that connecting a writer with their writing is a pointless desire. The marks on the page are all that should matter. Roland Barthes, he of the 'Death of the Author' argument surely applauds from his grave. A writer that is confessional, or a readership that is interested in meeting the person who created the words, are thus ridiculous to some of us. I am not that sophisticated and doubt I ever will be. I wonder how Ferrante did it. Is it really possible in this day and age to simply send off a manuscript to a publisher and, if lucky enough to be accepted, then refuse to do one jot of marketing because you perceive your job as being done? Maybe it is. Don't misread me here. Ferrante, or whatever her real name may be, is a superb writer. Having borrowed the first of her Neapolitan Quartet from our local library I went back within a week to request the next three volumes. I am a fan. I remain however intrigued at her overt stance to be out of the public glare. This isn't an impulse born from the kind of modesty that once rendered many a woman writer shy of visiting the public office of their publishers — women who requested a male relative or friend to be an intermediary or who received the publisher in the privacy of their own home and away from all that nasty place of noise and ink. The persona created in

Ferrante's letters and emails doesn't suggest a shrinking violet but quite the reverse. No, this is a writer in the driving seat of her career. There have been speculations as to the real identity of Ferrante — in 2016 an Italian journalist, Claudio Gatti, believed he had unmasked her as being Anita Raja, a translator for the same publisher who produces Ferrante's books. If this is the truth, and as yet there is no surety, then it answers my question of how she did it. Having the ear of a quality publisher during your day job is really useful. You don't have to do the agent thing, the crawling letter thing, the anything thing. You just pass him/her the manuscript and let your words stand or fall. Then you go home and get on with writing the next book.

Alas, I am not in that bracket. I cannot afford anonymity — beguiling in its aestheticism though it is. So, when a parish church ladies' guild in rural Renfrewshire asked me if I would come and read from my books and chat with them, I said, without hesitation, that it would be my pleasure. As our old car slugged along, with the heater up full blast to de-ice the windscreen on a biting January evening, I thought of the title on some sheet music I had come across earlier that day in the bookshop where I work — a song, popular in the 1920s, 'When It's Night-time in Italy, It's Wednesday Over Here'. Ferrante's controlled urbanity and mystery, her accounts of the hot and violent passions of Naples and complex relationships exist in a world far away from mine. I shivered into my fleece-lined coat and knew that I would happily trade the secrets of my writer's life for the price of a hot cup of tea.

I was right to accept the invitation. They were a great audience. Actually, if I am honest they were one of the best audiences I have read to. No one looked bored, no one went out for a fag halfway through, no one was riffling through paper working out what they would read from when I had shut up, no one stared out of the window. Instead they listened with intent, laughed where I hoped people will laugh, nodded their heads when agreement was required, adjusted their faces in accord with whatever I was harping on about, and gave me a hearty applause when I wound up. Gloriously hot tea with some scrumptious home-baking was my heavenly reward. I mean, really, a listening audience who then bought my books and also gave me tea and cake — what's not to like? Anonymity be damned.

Talk done, books sold, tea consumed, cake munched and a tour of the historical old church adjoining the hall accorded, the women then resumed their seats. There was a dash through some housekeeping stuff as to who was picking up who for the next meeting and who was doing what and when. Then the page number of the closing hymn was given out.

I flicked through the hymn book in my hand and my eye fell on the old hymn 'What A Friend We Have In Jesus'. I'm not quite sure how I know this hymn. It's not in the usual repertoire of the Catholic church — the denomination that I was formed in. I wonder if it is because of the use of the word 'Jesus'? For some esoteric reason, and any of you theologians or anthropologists reading this can perhaps elucidate, the hymns in the Catholic stockpile are often those which use 'Christ' or 'Our Lord' instead of the more familiar 'Jesus'. Or, if not that, is it the jolly *oompah oompah* rhythm reminiscent of and favoured by the Sally Army, which precludes it from the top ten favs in Catholic assemblies? I don't remember ever singing it in church while I was growing up. I must know it from watching *Songs of Praise* or from the brilliant 'beach missions' which me and my brothers and sister would skoot along to every morning during our Summer holidays in Millport on the Isle of Cumbrae. Anyway, wherever I have heard 'What a Friend We Have in Jesus', heard it I have, to the extent that I also know the tune. What I hadn't known before was who wrote it. While the Guild leader waited for the recalcitrant CD player to stop buzzing and get into gear, I stared at the name beside the lines. 'Joseph M Scriven'. In Scots Gaelic, the word *co-thuiteamas* has the meaning 'a falling together' which contains a different quality than the English *co-incidence*. It is suggestive of a greater plan rather than a random happening. I called out to the leader asking her if they had deliberately chosen this hymn because of the author? She glanced down at her book, giggled, then said to the assembled women:

'Anne has just asked if we chose this hymn because she was reading to us this evening. We didn't, but it just shows how the good Lord works.' Turning to me she then asked, 'Is Joseph Scriven a forebear?'

'Not that I know of, but I'll take the royalties if they're going,' I quipped.

'Ah, you were meant to come this evening,' assures a Guild member.

The CD player, having been given an assertive thump, began to play. We all stood up (why do Presbyterians always stand to sing?) and, with great zest, pitched into the verses. As we sang I reflected on the words.

The tune is a bit too singalong-with-Jesus for my taste, the words are sentimental, are simplistic, are all those other things that more avant-garde minds would abhor, and yet ... and yet ... they have a wisdom. A wisdom that reminds us of the basic belief of all Christians, that the teachings of Christ can be central to our lives. Can be in our lives both as a reference point, a refuge and many other things besides. I often forget that. I am no longer a faithful member of the Catholic church. I am probably now in the camp of 'the occasional attender' that some may name as 'lapsed' — a coinage which always makes me think of the tipsy leaning Tower of Pisa or of a wilted stick of celery. Daft name it is. I prefer to think of myself as someone whose philosophy was shaped by Catholicism but who then found light in other thoughts, other teachings, other praxes which have given me, I hope, a tolerance of all faith beliefs. I take what is useful and healthy from each that I have come across and leave aside that which is not. Occasionally, without seeking it, as in that hall in rural Renfrewshire on a bitter January evening, I am reminded of what Christianity has to offer, despite it being a religion which has fallen from favour in an increasingly secular world.

As I had been explaining to the listening assembly at the outset of my spiel, at that juncture in our lives my husband and I were poised on the lip of a new venture. Two short months from the date of that evening — Colum was set to leave his reliable and long-standing employment as an IT manager, and embark on a totally different path. At least hoping to embark. Colum's dream was to open a day care centre for dogs. As a trained and experienced Dog Listener who follows the Amichien Bonding method as founded by Jan Fennell, Colum had worked towards this dream for some time. The problem was that he needed land. Three acres for rent would suffice. He knew exactly what he could and would do with it. Land was, unfortunately, shy to be found. I tend to be a bit of a worrier and the thought of Colum giving up the job that had kept us solvent for so many years and finding nothing to replace it, was gnawing at my inner peace. I was more than fully behind his dream. I wanted it for him. I knew if he could just find some land and realise his dream then many dogs and their owners would benefit from Colum's skills. Being but human, I still worried. I had been speaking to too many people who are also worriers and who were worrying for me. As a writer, the money I bring in is hardly worth me filling in an annual tax return —

Elena Ferrante I am not — and thus the worrier part of me was currently in high ascendancy. All of this was in my mind as I sang Joseph M Scriven's words, words that he had penned in 1855 in his new home of Canada for his ill mother back in Ireland, words which went on to give comfort and reassurance for generations of anxious people, words which have remained popular and have been recorded by artists such as Ella Fitzgerald, Aretha Franklin, Tina Turner:

Have we trials and temptations?
Is there trouble anywhere?
We should never be discouraged —
Take it to the Lord in prayer.
Can we find a friend so faithful
Who will all our sorrows share?
Jesus knows our every weakness;
Take it to the Lord in prayer.

I wouldn't call my worries 'sorrows'. No, they are not 'sorrows'. Neither are they 'afflictions' or anything so Victorian. They are just worries. Worries stem from casting my mind too far into the future and fretting that it wouldn't be the future I wanted it to be. Busy with these thoughts and busy with all the other furies that fill my head and my days, I had forgotten about the power of prayer, of trust, of anything else you prefer to call it, that provides tranquility of mind and heart.

Driving home in the sub-zero temperature, my book boxes considerable lighter, my writer's ego bolstered by how well the reading had gone, I mused on the evening's events and how a nudge in the right direction comes from the most unexpected sources. Not only had the church gig reminded me of higher laws at work but it had also called back my creative self which had disappeared, smothered and disenchanted with the materialistic marketing side of a writer's job. I sat at my desk until long past midnight scribbling down words. Ladies of the Guild, I am indebted to you and I don't mind confessing that. Of course, when I am famous, hidden in a cloud of workable secrecy, with the literary paparazzi on my heels, I may have to deny it was really me.

Early Contemplation

Being open to something Other was something partly taught me by my Dad when I was but a bit bairn. Whether he deliberately wanted to teach this or whether it was more a matter of doing what came naturally, I am unsure. Dad died some years ago so I can't ask him, but I suspect he would question the question. In all possibility, he was sharing something with his children that he derived pleasure from and probably would be loath to interrogate it any further than that. I am talking here about how I was taught to listen. To listen to the ways of silence. To discover how to be in silence. To feel its presence, its unmappable perimeters, its strength and its intelligence. To read it not as absence but as presence. How did Dad do such an extensive teaching? By doing something very close to my heart — making tea.

Tea itself, is I am sure, a harbinger, a vehicle of the profound, a portal to the wells of peace that are within our grasp. The cynical among you will say that it is because it is a drug. True, it is. But, come on, it's just a teensy-weensy one. And, we are assured, it is full of antioxidants that are extolled as excellent for our bodies. My favourite tipple is green tea – there's just something about it that hits all the right spots especially when accompanied by lemon polenta cake or crispy vegetable samosas or Thai dishes or just good old ryvita with marmalade. I am in danger here of penning a hagiography to tea which would take me right off point so, suffice it to say, I think tea good stuff.

Tea is in particular good stuff when, as a young lass, you have puffed and complained your way up to the highest cairn in the Campsie Fells – a range of volcanic hills set to the north of Glasgow and a hop, skip and jump from where I grew up. A keen hillwalker all of his adult life, my dad, an east-end of Glasgow man, loved these fells. Like many a Glaswegian before him, Dad appreciated the veritable lung that the countryside around the city offered to its dwellers. When, as a parent of a young family, he got the chance to move out of the city under the 'Glasgow Overspill' scheme and settle in Kirkintilloch, he and mum grabbed the chance. My brothers and sister and I thereafter spent many a day with our parents tramping up from the Clachan of Campsie from the bus terminal, on up to the high car park on the Crow Road — an Anglicisation of the Gaelic *Crodh* (cattle) just as Campsie is a corruption of the far more enchanting Gaelic *cam* (crooked) and *sith* (fairy) thus Crooked Fairy Hill. The origin of the name was, sadly, appropriate when the RAF aircraft, 'Fairey Firefly' crashed close to the summit of the fells in January 1950 killing both airmen. I rambled over the Campsie many years after this event, but nevertheless remember Dad pointing out the rusted pieces of plane wreckage as we climbed to the first cairn, and finally to the Meikle Bin (mixture of Scots for *large* and the Gaelic *beinn* / *high hill*). Sometimes we would opt for the alternative walk, or slog as it really was, up the Fin Glen (possibly from the Gaelic, *fionn*, meaning *fine* or *fair*), to the trig point of Earl's Seat (named after the Earl of Lennox whose lands once extended to the south side of the Campsie Fells). As we went along Dad would encourage our flagging legs and grumbles with the assurance that we would 'drum up' at the top of the hill which was always 'just round the next corner.' Our hearts pumping, our muscles protesting, we would somehow get there, fling ourselves on the ground and wait for our reward.

Dad would then swing his large saggy canvas backpack off his shoulders, delve into its depths and get out the small primus stove and a kettle filled by him with water from a burn, and begin to make us a life-saving infusion. All of us drank tea, even the youngest of us was given 'dinky tea' – weak tea with a big slosh of milk and a teaspoon of white sugar – (don't judge us, it was the seventies, we didn't know the evils of sugar then). As the water slowly heated it made a desperate puffing sound as if the effort of heating the water was almost beyond its capabilities. Then, just a few moments from boiling point, Dad would say 'Now ... get ready to listen.' At these words those of us gazing listlessly at the view, would flop back onto the scrubby ground, to stare at the sky.

As Dad turned the valve to extinguish the flame, an immense wash of very different sounds sluiced our senses — the cry of a peesweep which had been circling unnoticed high above, or a rare hawk (which has the far more imaginative name *Willie-whip-the-wind* in Scots); the industrious buzzing of a cleg wondering which victim to lurch onto next; the pleasant tickles of wind rippling the heather or wild grass level with our ears; the breathing of the person next to us as they watched the scudding clouds move and shift shape. We would stay like this for some minutes until the most impatient or thirsty of us would ask, 'Is the tea ready?' and the peesweep and rustling grasses were forgotten as we all sat up ready for the delectable drink. After we had swilled our brew – which always had random tea-leaves floating in it as Dad spurned any such nonsense as teabags in favour of the good loose stuff – and had munched on a marmite sandwich or two (the influence of an English mum), Dad would pull out his 'moothie' and accompanied by the groaning of us kids, play some tunes. Byron's 'Lachin Y Gair' (did many of you know Byron was Scottish-born?) and Hanley's 'Scotland The Brave', figuring prominently in his favoured repertoire. Then, for an encore, requested or not, he would recite the opening lines of Walter Scott's 'The Lay of the Last Minstrel', Canto VI, (1805):

Breathes there the man, with soul so dead,
Who never to himself hath said,
This is my own, my native land!'

Legacy of the Romantic sensibility though it might have been, the feeling and passion for his country was genuine. A passion he passed on to all of us kids, despite our high embarrassment if any other walker should happen to be in earshot. Literary pieces recited and the countryside honoured, we would then gather up the cups, the milk bottle, the tub of sugar, teaspoons, and any paper wrappings, while Dad cited some lines of the walker's code:

Leave no trace of your wayside meal
No paper bag, no scattered orange peel,

[…]
Let no one say, and say it to your shame,
That all was beauty here, until you came.

There are more lines to this verse — a verse that remains anonymous — but I don't remember Dad ever quoting them. Perhaps these lines were enough, particularly as emphasis was always laid on the final 'you'. Thus, ensuring we had left no trace but our breath and flattened heather, off we would go, the lactic acid in our legs making its presence known in our stiffened legs as we stumbled our way downwards, back to the timetabled bus far below and *Dr Who* on the telly later.

Sometimes we would stop at Jamie Wright's Well, a drinking well fashioned in 1900 into the rock face, found high up on the Crow Road. The spring water, reputedly discovered by Jamie Wright, a local fisherman, was naturally filtered off the hillside. Clear and wondrously fresh, we were unhesitating in our drinking of it. Again, there were lyrical words associated with this — extracts from a ten-stanza poem by a local poet, James MacIntosh Slimmon, entitled 'The Packman's Salutation to The Mountain Well' published in his collected works *The Dead Planet and Other Poems* (1898). Any connection between Slimmon and Jamie Wright remains obscure. Slimmon certainly knew the Campsies judging from another of his poems, 'Campsie Fells' and from the explanatory note on 'The Packman's Salutation' making clear that the focus of the poem is that of Jamie Wright's well. And there is no doubt that the words, chiselled in to the commemorative granite slab at the well, are still apt:

[…]
Hail to your dimplin', wimplin' drop,
Clear, caller, caul'.
That bids the drouthy traveller stop,
And tak' his fill.
Hail to your heart-reviving tipple,
Enticing sale wi' twinkilin' ripple,
Thou crystal milk frae Nature's nipple,
Wee Mountain Well!

[...]
Born of the whirlin' wintry flake
Of Arctic shower!
When charging storms the welkin rake
And scrudge the bower,
You joukit frae the furious blast
And seepin' doon the mountain past,
Till here my craig you weet at last;
Sine ower the stour.

As an adult I came to understand that these walks, these 'drum ups' were not just cheap and pleasant activities to do with a young family on a shoe-string economy, but were lessons for life. For what Dad taught us four children was the praxis of appreciation of the simple and of contemplation. The ability to stop what we were doing, what we were hurtling towards, what we were expecting, and listen to and note that which was already going on around us. That's quite a gift for a parent to give a child. A sustainable, sound and soul-enhancing legacy.

Solvitur Ambulando

It is the simplest of things. One foot in front of the other. One foot in front of the other. Stopping when you get where you wanted to go or stopping when you've had enough. When other forms of exercise prove too taxing or awkward for whatever reason, we still have this one. We need not necessarily think of it as exercise but just how we get from one place to the other without the use of wheels.

Before sitting down to write this chapter I took one of our dogs out. I wanted to get a decent writing session under my belt but my head wasn't quite ready to begin. It needed air and Jenna, our pretty red and white collie, needed a pee. Perfect synchrony. Aware I would lose precious time and the day would slip away as it has a habit of doing if not kept under tight control, I decided a street walk with a bit of grassy ground would suffice. The day was cool but dry and fairly mild. I needed only a light jacket and trainers — the ground not being particularly soggy. It was a pleasant beginning and I thought for the hundredth time how fortunate I was that my work routine didn't include hurtling along a motorway in a tin bubble, second-guessing the traffic.

To Jenna, however, any walk is not a walk at all. It is a hunt. I can see herself gearing up her adrenaline as I clip on her lead and we cross the doorstep. Being married to a Dog Listener who has trained me to 'Think Dog', I wait a few minutes until she has calmed herself. When she wants to bound up the steps to the street, I refuse to move. She's an intelligent lass so gets the message quickly. I'm in charge, not her. I will lead the hunt even though she suspects I am not quite as up for it as her. I am not thinking of the projected fifteen or twenty-minute slow amble around the area as a hunt, it isn't as vital as that to me. We get food from shops and are occasionally blessed with a homegrown gift from generous friends — so I have no need to hunt anything. Neither does Jenna as we also buy her dog food from the local pet shop. But instinct is instinct and, to her, a walk will always be a hunt. Thus, on every walk I have to remember that she is thinking of the same activity in a very different light than I am. If I see another dog approaching, I cross the street or divert Jenna thus protecting her from possible danger of an invading pack. If a refuse lorry rattles past I make sure I am on the outside of the pavement shielding her. If something stresses her, such as the mean-looking cat glaring from the gatepost of a neighbour's house, I move into 'Stop, Start, Change Direction' mode until she is focused on me. It doesn't always go to plan. Quite often a well-meaning person will approach her and bend down to say hallo to her. In human behaviour they're just following their desire to clap an attractive dog (for English speakers, the Scots word 'clap' means 'to pet' in this context — although I have to say that our Jenna is worthy of putting your hands together for). In dog terms, however, such an action is an invasion of space and a more anxious dog will often back away or snap, then be reprimanded and told to 'Be nice!' As Colum teaches, we have to think how we feel when another person comes too close to us without invite, how we unconsciously step back, as we feel uncomfortable with the proximity. It is similar with dogs. Some dogs will tolerate it. Others won't. A good leader should protect their dog and ask the person either to ignore the dog or call it over. That way the dog has a choice and isn't forced into anything. I'm saying all of this because what might seem like a tiddly walk out into the street can actually be a much larger thing.

This morning though the street is quiet. We circulate around the area for a while until Jenna has downloaded all she needs to download. I enjoy the greenness of the large trees in our street, the light breeze that doesn't upset the mildness of the day, the lush swathe of grass leading to the park. I then spy a black Labrador with its perpetually grumpy owner, in a side street, off-lead and heading our way. Jenna hasn't as yet noticed but I pick up the pace and we get back to the safety of our front door without any unnecessary altercation. Jen is happy and content and so am I.

Sometimes I take a stroll around the streets in the evening. I don't tend to take a dog with me when I do this. For reasons already outlined when I am out with a dog, I have to keep my wits about me and make the dog's needs my priority. It's harder work and sometimes, as Miss Lavish commands Lucy Honeychurch to do in Forster's *Room with a View* (1908), I simply want to drift. When drifting you can let your mind wander. Wander over the events of the day, wander over snatches of conversation uttered or overheard; promises to be planned and scheduled; actions to be taken or discarded; threads of words read and waiting to be written down. When my mind has tired of all of that I begin to take note. I note the shape and state of gardens. The sad sterile decision of mono-blocking, the environmental disaster of plastic grass (yuk), gardens joyous in a chaos of colour and vitality and those which haven't yet made up their mind what they want to be. I pass children playing and dreepin over walls or fences; adults putting out the bins and warning the children they have only five minutes more for play; a lamp suddenly illuminating a room inside a house; a visitor making their way down a path to their car and turning back to wave; a tired woman carrying bags of shopping to a front door; a driving instructor car with an anxious learner negotiating a difficult reverse park; a half-empty bus rattling along. Each is its own vignette. Each activity wrapped up in itself. As Woolf realises in her essay 'Street Haunting' (1930):

> Into each of these lives one could penetrate a little way, far enough to give oneself the illusion that one is not tethered to a single mind, but can put on briefly for a few minutes the bodies and minds of others.

I think of the literary figure of the flâneur — the saunterer, the boulevardier, what in Scotland we name the stravaiger. The unhurried person, taking in their surroundings, affixing images, sifting what they encounter measuredly, without attachment. Having no particular destination or purpose but that of letting their feet lead through the tangle of streets and of the deliberate refusal of busyness.

The term 'the flâneur' was first explored and brought to prominence in 19th century France by Charles Baudelaire who characterised this leisured figure as 'the incognito observer' who fades into the crowd, in his essay 'The Painter of Modern Life' (1863). Some decades later, (c.1930s), Walter Benjamin in various essays, rescued the appraisal of Baudelaire as a late-Romantic dreamer by developing Baudelaire's concept of *flanerie* to argue that the walker was more than an idler but an important tool for the interpretation of modern culture. Both Baudelaire and Benjamin presume it a given that the walker is male. Fictional characters who deliberately walk the city — as found in the writing of Edgar Allen Poe, Robert Louis Stevenson, Arthur Conan Doyle, Joseph Conrad, E M Forster, T S Eliot, James Joyce — are all male. To be fair to them, at their era of history, it was unusual for a woman, of privileged class, to walk the streets unaccompanied and unprotected, unless they were about charitable work. The relationship of women to spectatorship was therefore a problematic one. The figure of the flâneur was a figure of anonymity. A woman, walking alone, could not always have that. As Woolf has Sara Pargiter relate in her novel *The Years* (1937):

> I can remember being told by a woman — a very beautiful woman
> — [...] when she went into Regents Park to have an ice, at one of
> the one little tables under the trees, [...] the eyes, she said, came
> through every leaf like the darts of the sun; and her ice was melted.

There were women who famously attempted to resist this restriction of movement. Women who refused to be bound by the public / private divide. There were also women who had to be quiet about their activity. George Sand (pseudonym of the French novelist Aurore Dupin, 1804–76), roamed Paris, unmolested, by disguising herself as a cigar-smoking young man. Vita Sackville-West, (1892-1962), also dressed as a young man, (re-naming herself as 'Julian') and in the posthumously published *Portrait of a Marriage* (1973), delights in the fact that had she met her own mother while strolling down Piccadilly, she would not be recognised by her.

The freedom to step out of the house and walk around my local environ is something I have never really questioned. Walking to the shops and cafes in town, to the train station, to the doctor, dentist, pharmacy, pet shop, library, art centre, town hall, houses of friends, bookshop or countless other destinations, is normal for me. Unless it is throwing down very wet pelters or I need the car for transporting heavy things, or the distance is too great, I prefer to walk. It wasn't until a friend from the U.S. was on an extended stay that I realised walking to an obtainable destination wasn't normal for all of the world. Our friend was a large lady — both in spirit and in body. After only a few weeks in Scotland she reported that she had lost almost a stone in weight. She wasn't eating any less but the major difference was that she was walking. In her home of Cleveland, Ohio, her car sat at the end of her pathway. A car which took her everywhere, even to a five-minute destination. There were few pavements (sorry, *sidewalks*) around her neighbourhood but, even if there were, it was deemed that something must be wrong if you were seen walking on them — particularly without a dog or not clad in jogging gear. While staying with us, our friend used public transport and walked to and from it. Simple unconscious exercise that has a life-enhancing impact.

In her ground-breaking study *Flâneuse*, (2016), Laura Elkin recounts how her formative family home in suburban Long Island was also bereft of pedestrians and thus, she realises in later years when she rejoices in walking around New York, Paris, Tokyo, Venice and London, that the lack of allowance for pedestrians ultimately means a lack of freedom. When your choices are determined by the town planners who have designed the locale around that of car users, individual freedom of movement is indeed compromised. Thus, Elkin feels 'let loose' on encountering her first experience of living in a European city which she can explore on foot, taking the twists and turns it offers at whim, on impulse, finding out the variety existing around corners, along small streets, twisting alleyways all inaccessible to the cumbersome car.

Solvitur ambulando — (Latin, *it is solved by walking*) — was a phrase and philosophy understood by Thoreau. In his essay 'Walking' (1851) Thoreau states that he 'cannot preserve his health and spirits' unless he walks for some hours each day 'absolutely free from all wordly engagements'. I presume he does mean *wordly* as against *worldly* as my spell-checker wishes to insist upon. And we should also presume that Thoreau was blessed with people, probably women, at home doing all that needed to be done there, thus allowing him freedom to roam outside at will. But I take his point. Walking is good for you on both the corporeal and psychological level. He advises though that when walking 'you must walk like a camel which is said to be the only beast which ruminates while walking'. Presumably his premise rests on the Arabic belief that 'the soul travels at the speed of a camel' — the accuracy of this coming into play when an airplane deposits our bodies in a country far far away from our home, and our souls are still with the last conversation we had that morning in our own kitchens by the kettle. Pace is everything. Pace matters to us as humans no matter how much we pretend it doesn't.

As Thoreau elucidates in 'Walking':

> I have met with but one or two persons in the course of my life who understood the art of Walking, that is, of taking walks, who had a genius, so to speak, for sauntering; which word is beautifully derived from idle people who roved about the country, in the middle ages, and asked charity, under pretence of going à la sainte terre, to the holy land, till the children exclaimed, 'There goes a *sainte-terrer*', a saunterer — a holy-lander. [...] Some, however, would derive the word from *sans terre*, without land or a home, which, therefore, in the good sense, will mean, having no particular home, but equally at home everywhere. For this is the secret of successful sauntering.

Such walking then is greatly different, in intent, from the determined forward tilt of the 'power walker' seen pounding our streets at times. I have to confess I find this a comical concept. Why do we name it as such? Why don't we just name it 'a swift walk'. A swift walk where we can still chat with our pal — at their side, not two steps in front and shouting backwards — and go at a steady gait that simultaneously steadies our spirits and purifies our sluggish arteries. Is it because unless we are seen to be actively *using* the walk as exercise — and making sure we electronically 'Map my Walk' — then it is not productive and thus not commendable?

What then of the walk of the retreatant, the contemplative, the quiet stroller of a monastery garden or cloister? Or the deliberate focused walk of the mindful practitioner? The stilling down of extraneous thoughts as the walker concentrates on slowly transferring weight from one foot to the other. Has this a value in our modern day? The answer is, of course, an affirmative. When our breathing is regular and the heart is at peace, our minds unhurried, we are adding to the balance of peace not just in ourselves but in our immediate environment and ultimately in the world. That, surely, is estimable.

Walking, sauntering, stravaiging — or whatever you name it — offers thinking time. And it informs writing. Letting phrases, possibilities of subject, shape themselves at the front of my mind which I will quickly scribble down on return before I will lose them. This is common to writers. In her posthumously-published *Moments of Being,* Woolf describes how '... one day walking round Tavistock Square I made up, as I sometimes make up my books, *To the Lighthouse,* in a great, apparently involuntary act.' Wish that I could do that. I have never returned with a novel in my head, more just a line or so or a possible thread of an idea — or a realisation that I have quoted Woolf too many times in one chapter.

And I doubt that my walking is in quite the same vein as Rousseau who remarks in his *Confessions*: 'I can only meditate when I am walking. When I stop, I cease to think; my mind only works with my legs'. Walking for me is not the sole catalyst for literary creation. For, in all honesty, when I roam around the pavements and parks and pathways of our town, I am not conscious of anything so elevated as believing myself a flâneuse. I simply just enjoy it.

To be a pilgrim

Thoreau, viewed walking in the wild terrain as a self-reflexive spiritual act that does much to teach you about yourself and reclaim aspects of yourself that have, for one reason or another, been left aside. Many years ago, probably more than he would care to work out, Colum walked across Spain following in the footsteps of St Ignatius, traversing the 500 kilometres from Loyola in the west to Manresa in the east. He remembers how his body at first deeply protested at the new regime imposed on it, how the first mile of the morning in the early days was painful, how exhausted he and his companion were, but then how their bodies adjusted, how they got used to waking in the early morning and walking some 15 to 20 kilometres before resting in the shade to wait for the midday heat to subside, how they then picked up their packs and walked another 15 kilometres or so until they had to seek a bed for the night, either in a Jesuit community or on some suitable ground underneath the stars. He has spoken of how life became very simple as their needs were simple. Enough food and water to sustain them as their bodies directed, somewhere to rest while the noon day sun scorched the land and somewhere to sleep, in safety, until it was time to walk again. He has spoken of how he grew to love being out in the quiet of the countryside and almost resented populated towns when they had to enter them. And, in Thoreauvian style, has spoken of how such a long long walk allows the mind to get in touch with itself.

I haven't attempted anything as impressive. And, in self-condemnatory honesty, I don't think I would want to. I know this because of my experience of attempting the St Cuthbert's Way. The St Cuthbert's Way, an attainable 62-mile route bridging the Scottish town of Melrose and the English Holy Island of Lindisfarne. It sounded do-able, fairly easy, indeed rather pleasant. A nice amble along country tracks, open fields, woodland paths. I should have read the guide book a little more closely. In particular, I should have read where it says something like '*Path climbs steeply up from Melrose onto the Eildon Hills where it gets more steep and more steep and more steep until your shoulders ache from the unimaginable weight that is your backpack and your legs turn to jelly as your boots sink into muddy mud. And you still haven't got to the summit. And you've only just begun the whole damn walk.*' But I didn't. I left that to Colum and carried on with my nice fantasy.

By the end of Day One I was wondering if I would ever get my legs back into working order and what a piercing block of wood was doing in each one them. And I wondered if it had been a sensible thing to sign up to a long distance walk a short while after I had been in hospital with a gynae complaint which had weakened my defences, dictated that I follow a course of medication that made me feel strange, and left me open to the beginning of a cold. A cold which steadily got worse as I sweated up those Mountains of Mordor (misprinted in the guide book as The Eildon Hills) and got throughly damp from the persistent rain the same afternoon. Daft it was really. Really daft. But sometimes in life an equally daft self says 'Och, it'll be fine. It'll be good to do something different. Don't be a wimp. Give it a go.'

I carried on in giving it a go into the middle of Day Two when I had to call a taxi from a very quiet pub in a one-horse settlement — that had stopped serving hot food just an hour before we got there — to take me and my shivering body to the next village where we had booked a B&B. A nice wee settlement with a cute cafe that I sat in looking every inch the long-distance walker with my walking trousers, thick socks, kagoul, base-layers, fleece, hat, buff, gloves, boots and pole. I chatted with a group of sturdy church people who were doing the same walk as an annual pilgrimage and sleeping on community hall floors each night without guarantee of a hot shower. Hardy and cheery folk who, the next day, Day Three, came across me waiting for yet another taxi in yet another middle of nowhere and gave me warm sugary coffee and sympathy. On I went to the next town and to the generous hearted owners of a B&B

who collected me from the high street, showed me to a warm room, with kettle, with bath, with bed. The B&B who asked if I wanted paracetamol, and bought me a warm pastry as they reckoned I might like it with my hot honey and lemon, and said they would also collect Colum should he need it.

Day Four I gave in and got the bus. Got the bus with a group of local ladies all destined for a day's shopping, who looked curiously as the white-faced woman huddled in their midst, sniffing, coughing, looking awful. I took refuge in Anwick in the wonderful secondhand bookshop, that has warm fires and hot soup and books. There I whiled away some hours while waiting for another bus to take me to a stop near our next B&B — a farm steading slightly off the beaten track which my stuffed head hadn't quite managed to retain the information of exactly where it was. The divine laws were fortunately gracious and when I stepped off the bus, stressing that I had little clue where to go next, Colum was sitting waiting for me with a large grin on his face and his GPS phone which directed us straight to the farmhouse.

It was that evening that I realised Colum and I were on different pilgrimages. His was to do the walk as designated. One foot in front of the other, rejoicing in the rhythm of walking, the fresh fresh air, the adventure, the linking with other walkers, time to think and reflect. All that is usual for a narrative of the long-distance trekker. Mine was to know the sense of slight desperation, slight displacement, to appreciate that the word 'pilgrimage' has the word 'grim' hidden in it, and to feel like a failure. Once I verbalised this, Colum decided we'd call it a day and go home. He was within sight of the Holy Isle. It was just across the water. Just a matter of a few miles but, being the kind of man he is, decided that was a walk for another time.

My experience then of long-distance walking hasn't been the best. The timing was all wrong I suppose. My body wasn't up for it. And because of that my spirit wasn't up for it either. I am not a pathetic kind of person really. I have been a road-runner for years — I will bore you with that later — so physical exertion is not particularly scary for me. At this particular moment in time I should however have listened to my body telling me to take a rest, get my gynae thing sorted once and for all, and only then put on my walking boots and pull on my pack. Learning to accept where you are with things, learning to listen when your body has other needs, is key. If I was but perfect, oh how smooth life would be.

On the upside, and so to rescue this chapter from gloom, I must tell you that my misery did result in an unexpected gift close to my heart. Colum had kept a daily on-line blog going throughout our trip. When he reported that I was finding the going tough and was becoming increasingly glum, my cousin, Ronnie — short for Veronica, her full name only used by her mum when her daughter was in for a telling-off — posted in reply: 'Think she deserves another tea set.' My cousin alluded to a time, many years ago, when I was but a wee four-year-old lass who had had her tonsils out. Shortly afterwards my mum had gone off for a short holiday to her sister in Yorkshire as Mum had miscarried a baby and was in sore need of some time out. My Aunt Betty, a Glasgow aunt, was looking after me and my sister. First night in her charge I decided to haemorrhage. Was rushed to hospital in a blue-light-flashing ambulance. Everything eventually calmed down and I was mending by the time my aunt came back in to visit me the next afternoon. She said she saw this wee shilpit looking lass in a big hospital bed and her heart went out to me.

'Is there a toy you would like?' she asked. 'Any toy? Anything?'

A small and sore voice mumbled, 'Could I have a .... a ... tea set ... please?'

She told me many years later that, right at that moment, she would have given me a thousand such sets. Anyway, the next afternoon she walked up the ward and handed me the most wonderful tea set. It was blue plastic, had four cups, four saucers, milk jug, sugar bowl, teaspoons and a big teapot. I loved it. The hospital ward and its strange ways with strange people in starched uniforms, was forgotten as I sat up and played and played with this thing of comfort for hours. My cousin, who replied to Colum's blog, remembered the night of the ambulance dash to hospital, remembered the story of her mum's question, remembered my reported answer and subsequent joy when the pretty present was laid on my hospital bed. I'm not sure if I had told Colum about that snippet of personal history or not, but he somehow knew the detail.

Day Five, having caught a bus back to Melrose, retrieved our car (why did we ever leave it?), and driven some miles north, we stopped at Lauder for a cheer-up refreshment. The coffee shop in Lauder is also a delightful showcase for local artisans. I had spied a most arty ceramic set of cups and saucers and teapot on one of their display shelves. Knowing it was quality with a probable equivalent price and mindful of all the cash we had spent in B&Bs that week, I thought it exquisite but left the set where it was. As we got into the car an hour later, Colum handed me a bulging bag.

'Here, this is for you,' he said grinning, watching my face closely.

It was the teacups, the saucers and the teapot I had just admired. I may be much much older and experienced in the ways of the world than that wee girl in a big clanky hospital ward who had just had a very scary time, but what delighted me then delights me still. We drove home with me looking forward to shedding my backpack, mud-clad boots and cumbersome gear, and reaching for our own kettle and playing with my new tea set.

For the time being therefore, I will leave sustained arduous treks to other souls, and apart from random woodland, moorland or seashore walks inside of a day, content myself to my saunters around the streets. Saunters that can be surprised by sudden sights — such as the clusters of crab apples jiggling above my head as I walked by a piece of ground augmenting a grey slabbed pavement next to a depressed looking nightclub, on my walk home from the university library yesterday. A handful of apples spilling onto the pavement causing me to look up to search for whence they had sprung from, and to smile at the cheeky trees.

Insula Sacra

For centuries pilgrims have recognised Lindisfarne, the tiny yet tenacious and ancient outpost of Christianity, as their goal, their endpoint, their place of arrival and completion. In 1984, Magnus Magnusson — he of 'I've started so I'll finish' catchphrase — published a scholarly account of the history, natural environment, archaeology and people connected to 'The Cradle Island.' Colum spotted this volume amongst the secondhand books for sale in that arty cafe in Lauder. I have it by me as I write this and am determined not to shelve it until I have read it right through or at least a good way through. It feels like a book one should read in one's lifetime. Tastefully illustrated and elegantly written, not quite to the standard of the intricate *Book of Kells* produced by Columba's monks who went on to establish the monastic settlement on Lindisfarne, but one's life is surely made a little brighter by the reading of Magnusson's volume. Perhaps you think I should have read it assiduously before writing this chapter. Well, that's a worthy viewpoint. And yet, and yet ... when I think about my experience of Lindisfarne it is not peppered with erudite facts, figures, fissures or indeed fishes of the island. Instead, when I go to that part of my memory which holds what I saw and experienced in Lindisfarne, there is little there to do with academic illumination but much to do with pattern.

If you have read this far you will already know that Colum and I had hoped to do the full 62 miles of the St Cuthbert's Way which crosses the border running between Scotland and England. And you also know that as circumstances weren't the most favourable — the weather, the arduous terrain and my rather fragile body not being the best mix — we called it quits earlier than planned. As the miles truckled by, various friends left encouraging comments on Colum's on-line blog, many of them saying that they felt they were with him in spirit. Not all of these friends are overtly interested in either religion or spirituality but somehow the walk we were doing caught their imagination and each morning, afternoon and evening, and sometimes in the night, they would leave reflections and appreciations. When it became clear that it was downright idiotic for me to continue and Colum gave up thoughts of reaching Lindisfarne, he posted up that he had learned that the pilgrimage 'ultimately was about journey and not the finish.'

Some months later we embarked on a road trip which encompassed a drive from our home in the west of Scotland, down to the northwest of England, then way down to the south of England, round its bottom, then a snaky line up the east coast to Northumbria. We were doing this road trip, or rather the 'Friends and Family Tour', really just because we could. There were friends and family to visit. Friends and family whom we had promised, for far too long, that we would visit. That summer we did them all in one fell swoop. 1,000 miles later we found ourselves back at the lovely B&B that is Fenham Farm, Fenwick. Arriving there around 9pm we threw our cases into the room, pulled on some more layers of clothing — it being considerably cooler than the south of England — and went out for a walk.

We went down a farm track towards the estuary which separates the mainland from the island of Lindisfarne. The track we were on petered out after a bit but it was sufficient for us to see the headlights of some cars slowly making their way back over the causeway. Just a few miles from where we stood, rested Lindisfarne. Majestic, still and alluring. A red light intermittently flashed from it like a guiding beacon, steady and assuring. I thought of Fitzgerald's character, Jay Gatsby, whom his narrator, Nick Carraway, witnesses stretching his arm out towards a green light at the end of the dock where his first and only love, Daisy, lives. The light symbolising a tantalising dream of fulfilment to Gatsby's yearning heart.

Lindisfarne hadn't gone away and neither had Colum's desire to complete his pilgrimage to it. We were heading home the next day. We had had a lovely holiday, seen the people we wanted to see, done the things we wanted to do — all except one. So near and yet so far. The tide timetable for the next day didn't seem to offer too much space for walking to the island and back again. And we didn't want to rush it. We wanted to make our arrival on Lindisfarne a befitting one, unhurried and in tune with the spirit of pilgrimage. Once again Colum said 'I think we should come back another time. Make a definite trip and do it properly.' Tired from lots and lots of driving on unfamiliar roads and feeling the pull of home, I concurred. Yes, another time would be better. We'd do it as it should be done then. Sometime.

Sleep, however, has a way of soothing out and making clear. I woke around 7am. Listened to the silence around the building. Thought of the delicious air outside and got up. This would be my last chance of untrammelled country roads and fresh fresh air before getting home and returning to zig-zagging around our town's streets.

'What are you doing?' said a sleep befuddled voice.

'Going for a run.'

The curled-up shape in the bed that was Colum, uncurled itself.

'Hmmm. Running. Do you mind if I go for a walk instead?'

'Not at all,' I chirruped, twisting my wayward hair into a hairband. Empty these roads may be but I didn't want to cause critical comment from any curious rabbits or random car.

We agreed to meet at breakfast at 8.45 prompt — this B&B has a 'breakfast award' and you would be foolish to miss it — and went our separate ways.

I returned a half hour later full of endorphins and joie-de-vivre. Dived in the shower, collected up as many of my scattered things as possible, stuffed them into bags and made my way over to the breakfast room at precisely 8.45.

Helping myself to a bowl of melon, pomegranate and grapefruit pieces, a dash of raspberries, brambles, a sprinkling of pumpkin seeds and a drizzle of local honey — having ordered local gluten-free sausages, grilled tomato and mushrooms to follow with a possible option on a tasty croissant or two — the door opened and a slightly dishevelled Colum came in. He grabbed the room key, winked at me and disappeared. I had already ordered him the full bhuna for breakfast, as I somehow suspected that that would be his choice, so had bought him some time. He appeared seven minutes later, showered, cleanly clad and with a huge grin on his face.

'Did it,' he said.

'Um ...' I said. 'Did what exactly?'

'Got to the causeway. Did the last bit of the walk before the Pilgrims' Path. Yes!'

An hour later, satisfied in mind and body, we drove away from the B&B. I was behind the wheel and Colum was setting the GPS on his phone for the route home. Mindful of those curious rabbits I was driving slowly. This allowed my eyes to dart every few seconds to the estuary and the dark shape of Lindisfarne. Shortly after we had begun our road trip we had heard of the final journey of a friend's dad. I had decided that when we got to Lindisfarne I would light a candle somewhere and say a prayer for her grieving heart. But we weren't going to Lindisfarne that day. Or, were we ...

'How long would it take to drive over to Lindisfarne?' I asked Colum.

'Not long at all. Why, do you want to go?'

'Well, am thinking that I would like to fulfil my promise to pray for someone. If we drive over that would give us time to potter about a bit and then get off the island before the turn of the tide.'

Colum was silent for a bit then said: 'How would you feel if I walked it?'

'Fine. I've had my exercise for the day. I would just like to go there.'

'Howsabout you drop me at the causeway. I'll change into walking dods, follow the Pilgrims' Path and meet you over there somewhere.'

Fortified with backpack, kagoul, extra sweater, bottle of water, some boiled sweets and old sandals — seawater isn't kind to good walking boots — Colum set off over the mudflats. I, meanwhile, drove over the narrow causeway road which the sea had just retreated from. As I drove I noticed how busy it seemed. Lots of people walking as well as quite an amount of cars. Twenty minutes later I was parking the car in a large field outside of the village of Lindisfarne and seemed to be parking it alongside another hundred or so vehicles. I paid the £4.40 for the day's parking and set off towards the village.

People. People everywhere. People of all ages, all shapes, all tongues. I got into the village. There was a queue for the loos. I joined it. I felt as if I was on a massive bus trip. Was this really the quiet mystical island that so many had spoken about and written of? I then followed the swathes of people swarming through the village. Perhaps they would all suddenly veer off and gather in some humungous hall. They didn't. I reminded myself that they had as much right to be here as I did. I further reminded myself that I was there for two reasons — to allow Colum to finally finish his pilgrimage and to remember a grieving person. Best calm down then and just go with the flow.

I passed along a cobbled street with low-slung shops dotted along it. One of these looked like it sold quality crafts. Conscious that Colum was literally achieving a landmark that day I went inside in search of something relevant to give him on arrival. I thought it would be nice to get a ceramic image of the St Cuthbert cross — the same symbol which guides and directs the pilgrims from gateposts, fences, walls and trees all along the route. There were a few in the shop but they weren't ceramic and the asking price was around £50. Bit too much for our budget. I looked around some more and my eye fell on a wee ashet. It had a roughly-shaped yet pleasing lug, was painted in a fusion of hazy blues, browns and purples and embedded in the front was the Celtic sign of the Trinity. I turned it upside down to look at the markings. *Made in Ireland. Colm de Ris*. Ok, so not an overt St Cuthbert thing but still relevant considering the historical connection between St Cuthbert and St Colm (or the Latin, *Columba*). A scant synopsis of their story comprises: In 563 AD the exiled Columba rowed the 12 miles with his twelve companions from Antrim, Northern Ireland and landed briefly in Southend, the most southern tip of Scotland's Kintyre peninsula, and from there travelled on to the island of Iona where he founded his monastery. A century later, Aidan, a monk from the monastery in Iona, spear-headed an outreach team and set up a similar religious settlement in Lindisfarne in 635 AD (a kind of monastic brand chain when one thinks about it, these chaps obviously knew a thing or two about marketing). Legend has it that a young man named Cuthbert while watching over a sheep flock, witnessed a vision of the soul of Aidan being carried to heaven on the night of Aidan's death in 651 AD. This vision prompted the young man to enter the monastery of Melrose, a satellite of Lindisfarne, as a novice. He went on to be the personage of St Cuthbert. My Colum is named after St Columba — or St Colmcille as his Irish father would have said — thus I concluded that the nicely crafted bowl in my hand was a suitable medallion for the victorious St Cuthbert's Way pilgrim. I paid the £15, satisfied with my choice and left the shop thinking that a cafe with a pot of tea would now be a good plan.

Alas (a word, fittingly, from the Latin *lassus* meaning *misery*), everyone else seemed to have the same yearn for a cuppa and there were clumps of thirsty people around the various cafes. I wandered about a bit more thinking that perhaps I could at least fulfil my prayer intention and seek out the old church of St Mary which my mum had told me about. Mum liked this church and had gone there on the day that I was undergoing some explorative surgery to sort out my gynae problem. She told me that she had focussed her prayer on my healing. Thanks also to some skilful medical action by an experienced consultant whose hand, we could argue, was guided by divine influence, here I was today strong and well. Mum's prayer appeared to have got through. The Almighty however had other ideas about a suitable venue for my prayer that day. Walking along a winding street which I thought might take me to St Mary's, I passed alongside a low wall surrounding an old church. A sign hung next to the gate proclaiming it was 'St Cuthbert's Centre' and in the stewardship of the United Reformed Church. It seemed quiet and, being in no hurry to find St Mary's, I found myself walking through the gate and up the slabbed pathway towards the open door. A woman was in the porch sorting out a pile of hymn books. She turned and smiled as I came in. She was wearing jeans, a pink fleece and a blue clerical shirt and collar. I smiled back and, as she didn't seem worried by my presence, I continued on inside.

There was some gentle music playing from somewhere and the atmosphere of serenity pervaded my senses. Here was peace. Blessed peace. And not another soul here. I stood for a moment taking in what was happening. The 'church' was in actual fact a large open space which had been cleared of pews and the usual associated furnishings. Artfully constructed areas of colour and texture were the chosen substitutions. I moved towards the first one, the lovely music continuing to wash over me like a playful wave. There was a kind of 'tree' with shapes of stained glass hanging from it instead of leaves. A notice said: 'If you write the name of someone on a sticky note and paste it on the tree our community will pray for them.' I picked up the offered pen, wrote 'For my friend, who grieves' and stuck it on a shining blue square of glass. Then, an impulse made me tear off another sticky note, and write 'For Colum, who waits on God's plan.' I stuck this on a twinkling green leaf shape and thought of my man trekking over the muddy flats.

Adjacent to the 'tree' was a table set up with strips of rough cotton. One strip was embroidered and looked like a finished piece. Another unhemmed piece was laid out next to a big box of buttons and some cards of thread. There were two sewing needles tucked into the cloth. A small notice invited: 'Feel free to do some stitches, sew on a button in memory of someone you have loved and lost.' Well, why not? I pulled off my backpack, dumped it on the floor and sat down.

My dad was a tailor. I grew up seeing half-finished suit jackets, padded and basted, swinging from coat-hangers dangling from the living room curtain poles. I saw Dad whump out yards of cloth on our living room table. I heard his big tailor scissors make that crunching sound as they cut through the cloth. I saw him measure inside and outside legs, shoulders and waists of people who came to him saying 'Tommy, I wondered if you could make me up a suit with this?' And Dad would sometimes sigh when they had gone saying 'This stuff is rubbish to work with,' but would nevertheless get out the large tin that held his sewing things and begin the process of making a suit. Dad made all our school blazers, our kilts and velvet waistcoats for our highland dancing displays, bow-ties for the boys for particular occasions, suits for Mum that prompted everyone who met her to think our family were wealthy, and skirts and jackets and trousers for me and my three siblings. Sewing was embedded in my earliest memories. Dad didn't have a shop but instead was employed by Glasgow Corporation as the resident tailor in a former poorhouse which became a home for elderly and homeless men. Here he worked long long shifts in his workshop and, looking back, I am sure that the last thing he really wanted to do, when home, was any more sewing. But sew he did. We weren't a wealthy family and we needed his skills to cover — literally — our own sartorial requirements. As I grew older though I realised that Dad was really more of a man's tailor. One day in a Gym session in school I wondered why I couldn't run very well in the crisp new white cotton shorts Dad had made for me. They felt far too stiff and restrictive. I must have told my mum and perhaps that was when it was decided that my sister and I should go to sewing classes. Dad had forgotten that growing girls might have developing hips. To Mrs Woollen's sewing classes we therefore went and learned how to set a sleeve, do a french seam, pin darts, set box or knife pleats and smock a neckline. All highly useful stuff until the clothing industry changed and it became both cheaper and easier just to buy our clothes. I have forgotten much of what I learned in those classes, but what I haven't forgotten is the soothing rhythmic feel of hand stitching.

I unpicked one of the needles, threaded it with some of the pretty blue thread lying around, chose a small wooden heart-shaped button and sewed it onto the cloth, remembering to wind the thread under the button before finishing and tie the end off neatly. I thought of my dear dad and my eyesight blurred as tears rolled down my cheeks. I don't know why I cried. Perhaps I was tired — we had driven a huge distance recently, slept in many different beds, spoken with and visited lots of people — but it could just have been that what I found at that table, in the action of simple sewing, was real and touched precious memories, or it was that I felt the beauty of the action and the prayerful stillness of the moment.

I heard the minister come in and go out again. I liked her non-intrusive nature. She must be used to seeing people interact with the installation. I sniffed and wiped my tears away. Re-tucked the needle back into the cloth for the next person to use and moved over to another area.

As I moved about the space I became aware that everything was about grief, about loss and how fabric, thread, wool, painting, writing and naming enabled the process of healing to begin. I stopped at another little 'tree' that invited you to hang a coloured bead in memory of a loved one. I chose a deep purple bead and a pink one — the purple for our son,

James, who never came to birth and the pink one for our little girl, Ruah Beag, who also died in my womb at 26 weeks and whom I delivered and said goodbye to in the same afternoon. Two little spirits that I so wish could have stayed with us. I kissed each tiny bead, threaded them together and hung them on a branch.

There were one or two areas arranged for reading and reflecting and another that had a rocking chair with a shawl laid over it. The booklet beside it — written by a Ruth Sprague — explained that she had knitted this 'grief shawl' when in deep sorrow and how the simple act of knitting had helped her in her worst moments. Ruth wrote that it was in some ways easier for the Victorians who wore black for some months, or even years, after a death. Observers therefore knew, without having to guess or enquire, that you were in mourning and due respect and allowance were given. For Ruth, this grief shawl, was instead of widow's weeds. What an excellent idea. Helpful, practical and spiritual all at the same time. I ran my hand over the plush wool feeling its depth of comfort.

Phew. That was an unexpectedly intense half hour. My phone had buzzed some minutes previously. I knew it would be Colum but hadn't wanted to answer it as visitors had been politely requested to turn off their phones on entering the Centre. I moved towards the entrance, saw some postcards connected to the 'exhibition', chose three of them, put some money in the honesty box and went out into the light.

The minister and another woman were sitting on wooden benches just outside the porch. I walked a few steps down the path then turned back towards them.

'Thanks. That was really good.'

'You're welcome,' said the minister.

I liked her non-pushy nature. No opening gambits to find out who I was and why I had engaged with the installations inside her church. Just simple acceptance of a stranger who had wandered in and was now wandering out.

Turning my phone back on, I noted a text from Colum saying he would be with me soon. I walked a few more yards down the street passing St Aidan's Winery, home to the apparently famous Lindisfarne Mead and Preserves. I was mildly tempted to see what was on offer there but, remembering my odysseying husband and that he may not be ultra-keen on checking out the local curios in preference to a cup of tea somewhere, I pressed on towards the ancient St Mary's Chapel, or as the sign correctly informed me, 'Parish Church of St Mary the Virgin'. To be honest I was only directing my feet there so I could say to anyone interested that I had done so. It could also prove worth the effort. I like old buildings and the stories they tell. This church, reputed to stand on the site of St Aidan's original monastery, should surely speak to my researcher's curiosity.

On entering the church though I saw that me and another hoach of folk, had had the same idea. If there had been any tranquillity here it had departed just after the causeway had opened up. Cameras clicked, people shifted, murmurs abounded, guides guided, information leaflets fluttered. I walked past the startling and peculiar life-sized carving of six J K Rowling dementor-styled chaps carrying a coffin. Gloomy didn't cover it. Why is 'holy' or 'sacred' or 'solemnity' so often equated with 'miserable'? It's not actually in the same semantic field. Really, it's not. And one would think that after all that enlightened teaching from St Cuthbert, those who were taking him to his place of final rest should have had a deep confidence that their beloved brother had already gone to Glory. Perhaps they had just been told that the usual heartening sup of mead wasn't happening at the purvey. Well we all have our sorrows to bear. I left the disconsolate lads to it and walked up to the high altar. My phone chose this moment to sing out its cheeky cheery piano rift. *Ta ra ra tum. Ta ra ra tum. Ta ra ra tum te tum te tum ...* Oh, Lordy Lord. Embarrassing or what? I crammed it deep in my pocket where it finished its signature tune, then did a kind of slow glide down the nave to the door, wriggled my way through the clutches of tourists and escaped into the churchyard. I extracted my phone from the wadding of tissues in my pocket, and listened to a voicemail from Colum asking where I was.

I pressed Colum's number and, after a moment, heard a very crackly voice say: 'Hi ... you ... really busy ... where...'

'Sorry. Can't hear you. What?' I replied.

He offered more disconnected words.

'Still can't hear you. Text me!' I kind of yelled.

Silence followed. I walked on towards the centre of the village. Finding each other in this throng might be a tad difficult. My phone went again.

'Can you hear me? The signal seems stronger. Where should I meet you?' said a much clearer Colum voice.

'Right here,' I replied, walking up to him.

As I suspected, a mug of tea was high on the list of Colum's preferences. Here again the Spirit took charge and I found myself walking him towards the St Cuthbert's Centre. There was no cafe at the centre but I knew he would relate to the quiet there and that need was, I judged, probably jostling for attention in Colum's being. Finishing a pilgrimage isn't something you do every day and requires a little marking, a little time of reflection. The minister was still sitting outside with her friend when we came back in the gateway.

'I had to bring him back to see what you have here,' I explained.

'Excellent,' she said, 'this is Ruth, the artist behind what is inside.'

She gestured towards her friend.

'Really?' I said 'Well, I found it very moving. Thanks for creating it.'

Ruth also smiled and said 'I'm really glad you like it. I was hoping that it would touch people.'

'It will certainly do that,' I assured.

Colum had already gone inside. I joined him. Showed him the prayer tree, the remembrance tree, the cloth with the sewn-on buttons, the grief shawl, the cards, the pictures. He liked them all but either the thought of tea was over-shadowing the impact or he had already worked or walked through his own thoughts and prayers. An image of the minister and her friend sitting outside returned to me — they were holding mugs filled with some kind of steaming brew. Well, if you don't ask …

Five minutes later Colum and I were happily ensconced on the benches with the minister, Rachel as we now knew her, and Ruth, the artist. And, in our hands, were large mugs of tea. Hurrah! In true spirit of the gospels Rachel had allowed us to use her kettle and tea bags. We returned the favour by offering round our gluten-free biscuits and chocolate. Another woman had joined the merry crew as the water was warming. This turned out to be Tessa, a Roman Catholic religious sister, who had been stationed on the island for some years. I thought it a good sign that the United Reformed Minister, the RC sister and an artist were obviously at ease in the practice of sharing a cuppa together. And how lovely it was sitting with them. The talk turned to pilgrimage, to prayer, to loss and what it meant to be eternal. Just the run of the mill subjects for a Tuesday morning. We also spoke of how popular the island was and Rachel and Tessa told us of how they had learned 'to meet people where they are' and how they had observed that even though some people came with the express purpose of making money from some business on the island, that 'the island has a way of rubbing off on them'. I suspected that there must be times that they would just like to close their doors and hide from it all but was grateful that today, in the lovely sunshine, they were happy to share of themselves to two strangers.

We didn't do any more touristy things after that. I gave Colum the glazed ashet which he loved — or at least said he did. And we did pop by the RC church of St Aidan where we saw the intricate hanging that Tessa had created, entitled 'A Moment in Time'. And I did stand for a moment in that same church and send out a prayer that the passing of my friend's dad would be peaceful and graceful. Our respective missions thus fulfilled, we then walked most contentedly back to our car, now twelve rows deep in the field, and drove off the island. There were, I am sure, lots of other sights we could have seen, lots of other historical attractions and walks to be tempted by, but somehow what we had experienced there was sufficient unto our spirits.

Écriture

Writers are often asked why they write. For me it is quite simple. There are words inside of me that want to get out. Margaret Elphinstone, the historical novelist, said to me once that writers suffer from a compulsion, a kind of mental illness, because there is something in them that cannot be stilled and it will not cease from agitating, until written down. Another Margaret — Margaret Drabble — echoes this in her genre-crossing memoir *The Pattern in the Carpet: A Personal History with Jigsaws* (2009), where she also views her lifelong draw to the blending of words as an incurable illness, which can simultaneously be a therapy and a perturbation. Too much writing, she says, can make you ill. I can't say I have ever reached that point, nor expect to.

Writing can be its own release, its own purpose, its own end. Many people think that publication is the end. That is only the public end. The private end is the actual act of writing. I, like all other writers, feel out of kilter with myself if I haven't been writing. I am attuned with my deepest self when I have time and space to write. For the last two hours I have been writing, thinking, writing. I took a break to hang some washing out in the garden. As I did so I thought about what I was writing. When I came in I made some coffee, spilled half the bag out onto the floor, swept it up, considered getting the hoover out to finish the job, but didn't because, once out, knew I would hoover more yardage than just the coffee grounds. Took the cafetière of coffee to my desk. Moved the armchair to the window so I could look out over the rusting leaves on the trees in our garden and out towards the long low line of the Campsie Fells. Picked up Anne Lamott's book *Bird By Bird: Some Instructions on the Writing Life*, (1994), and opened it at random. I found her speaking of how there is a scene from the 1981 film *Chariots of Fire* that, as we all know, was based on the life of the Olympic runner, Eric Liddell. His sister is worried for him and feels that he is straying from God's ways by the distraction of running. He answers that he will eventually join her at their church mission in China but first he will train for the Olympics, with all his heart and might, because God had made him fast. As Anne Lamott concludes, writers have also been born fast — fast with words — but we need to keep up the practice, give time to our craft, nurture it and protect it from all that would distract. Although few of us will reach the literary equivalent of Olympic standard or accolade, the training itself will be worth the doing.

There are times when it feels like my mind is dredging a residue of treacle. It is heavy, unwilling to engage. It wants to dodge the work, bargains that it could do a long session soon that will make up for today's lack of attention. Or it gets drawn into other non-writing concerns. Since I have begun this writing session my computer has alerted me to three new emails, two text messages and one voicemail — none of which, I discover, are connected to the writing of this book and one of which asked that I act on something as the sender couldn't because he was 'at work'. The dogs have also, loudly, alerted me to the delivery of a package and to the bin men and to the possibility of marauding invaders. Sam, our mid-twenties and athletic son, has slithered in and out of the room I work in to borrow my yoga mat then returned a while later to rummage in a cupboard for a packet of pasta. Colum has been in to check on the state of the ink cartridges in the printer, to tell me of how he got on at the dentist and then, slightly more worryingly, to ask if I have a neighbour's phone number as their house alarm is going off. All smallish interruptions, nothing major, and all just components of a writing day at home.

I recently listened to James Robertson reading from his book *365 Stories*, which, he told us, he worked at every day. Every day, for three hundred and sixty-five consecutive days, 'Just to see if I could do it'. When he said this, I, rightly or wrongly, presumed that he must have a room of his own. A room dedicated to his work where the pressures of the rest of life were forestalled and refused entry. And he must have a helpmate who shields him from all callers-in, who also does the cooking, the cleaning and all that daily paraphernalia. Or, in full awareness that that probably sounds sexist and James Robertson doesn't strike me as such, maybe he is capable of just shutting off and getting down to writing no matter what other distractions may present themselves. He is perhaps just disciplined. Oh, that word needs a capital **D** — in bold. But does such discipline require the support of distancing? And are towers required? In Dodi Smith's enchanting novel, *I Capture The Castle*, (1948), Cassandra the youngest daughter, literally locks her writer-blocked father up in Belmont Tower to force him to confront and purge himself of his demons and thus begin to write again. Then there's Uncle Quentin, that mad-scientist explosive-tempered character in Enid Blyton's *Famous Five* series, who seems to spend his life in his study (unless being kidnapped and held hostage) or is occupied building himself a tower on Kirrin Island, to conduct his experiments in peace. Isolation from the ordinary, the *lingua franca*, appears key.

Well, key for some. The review section of *The Guardian* published on a Saturday, currently carries a feature — 'My Working Day' — written by individual contemporary writers. My reading of this feature each week results in me either casting it aside feeling guilty and gloomy or, more rarely, nodding with agreement and feeling reassured. Michael Bond's description of his writing day — he who brought the wonderful Paddington to us and he whom the literary world has recently lost — outlines a consistently steady regularity, unceasing even on Christmas Day. This left me wondering who it was then who was peeling the spuds, chopping the veg, basting the turkey and setting the table, while he was cocooned in his study. I was also jealous both of his success and dedication. So it goes with many a writer's outline of their working day. Occasionally though there is a writer — mostly female — such as Tessa Hadley, who has to make room for other parts of their lives. Hadley describes the differing rhythms that she finds herself in that are shaped by what else is going on in her family life. How her writerly self has sometimes to take a back seat, watching and waiting till there is space for her. And, in almost complete contradiction to the preferred norm of a separate room, Hadley writes on a little table in her bedroom, as she thinks a dedicated study could cut her off from what sparks her writing. Jane Austen, who famously wrote in a corner of the sitting room in her family's Hampshire parsonage, would, I imagine, have concurred with this belief. And Cassandra, of Smith's *I Capture the Castle* seems to find sitting with her feet in the kitchen sink most conducive to stimulation of the creative juices — the result of which, I suspect, is far more readable than whatever her father eventually produced.

Perhaps what it comes down to is what Alan Bennett states in his essay 'Staring Out of The Window' published in his autobiographical *Untold Stories*, (2005). Bennett discusses how a writer only feels they are worthy of the title when actually writing. Reading, researching, observing and thinking are, to possibly coin a phrase, *para*-writing. Writing that is not quite the real thing. Or is that too purist an approach? I spent over a decade writing about other people's writing — it's what you do in academia. If writing is to be judged on effort then the furious endeavour that was the scripting of lecture notes, handouts and conference papers not to mention publications, must surely qualify. And yet, and yet, I know what Bennett is getting at. It was only when I left academia and 'found my voice' did I feel that I was finally really writing. Really chiselling out my own words from the multi-layered rock of life that is all around. Sometimes to see the faint form lying just below the conscious you have to get rid of what is blocking your vision. As Natalie Goldberg wisely advocates in her *Writing Down the Bones* (ed. 2005), sometimes it is necessary to sit down and write what is already running through my head. Just write it out, and by clearing out all that loose gravel, that flimflam, discover that there is an idea, an image, a seam of thought emerging that has been buried underneath all the detritus.

Excavation is worth the doing. Here I am continually grateful for my academic training. Interest in discovering buried roots remains with me. I like nothing better, for example, than discovering the origins and journey of a word. Such as that word 'discipline' which I have used in this chapter. It's not always considered a nice word. It has connotations of harshness, rigour and cruelty. When misunderstood it can be a relentless and destructive master. The Oxford English Dictionary tells us that the word comes from the Middle English sense of 'mortification by scourging oneself'. Not too pleasant a practice then and not one I want to sign up to. If we dig deeper we find the Old French meaning of 'instruction or knowledge'. Even further back is the Latin *discipulus* which denotes 'learner'. If you are a learner you are in a place of humility (itself an interesting word, the Latin, *humilis,* meaning *low,* which can also be translated as *of the earth* or *rooted*). As a learner, you are in a state of openness, of willingness to learn, to put aside that which you thought you knew, or be receptive to that which you have never known. By being disciplined, by doing something that continually stretches or demands effort, we are entering a gateway to a higher state of being. If we practice the piano we will recognise the notes as they are meant to be recognised and we will (possibly) delight ourselves and our listeners. If we do our physio exercises as the therapist instructed us, our stressed ligaments will get strong and heal. If we lift our feet up off the ground and practice turning the pedals and balancing, we will know the blissful joy of cycling. And if we make ourselves sit down on a regular basis and write out the thoughts in our heads we should become better writers.

Discipline. Rigour. Single-mindedness. All useful and often necessary praxes. Occasionally though there comes an acute awareness of words floating on the surface of my mind, for which I forsake all else to reach in, pull them out and land them on paper or screen. And it is almost effortless. Almost.

Prayer of Protest

Four minutes. Surely that cannot be effective? Surely it should be at least ten times as long? Surely there should be more words, more music, more planned silence, more, more, well more ... rubric? Time, though, as we all experience, is relative. Who is to say that four minutes is less potent than a far greater span — especially within the context of prayer.

This questioning reminds me of a scene from my son's primary school days. Sam, a shy child, had been instructed by his teacher to choose a poem by Burns, learn it by heart and recite it to the full class in preparation for the school's annual Burns comp. Unlike his adult self, who would have gleefully fastened on to the comic possibilities of such a stage performance, Sam's seven-year-old heart quaked at the prospect. To help him out I suggested he recite Burns' two stanza poem 'Extempore' which, for those of you unacquainted with the corpus of our Bard, goes:

> *O why the deuce should I repine,*
> *And be an ill foreboder?*
> *I'm twenty-three, and five feet nine,*
> *I'll go and be a sodger!*
>
> *I gat some gear wi' mickle care,*
> *I held it weel thegither;*
> *But now it's gane, and something mair –*
> *I'll go and be a sodger!*

Short, punchy and just the dab for our timid boy. His teacher however, not being quite the authority on Burns she thought she was, was put off her stride at Sam's recitation of this poem the next afternoon. He probably galloped through it so to return to the safety of his seat as soon as possible and let the glare of the spotlight shine on some other miserable kid. To his way of thinking he had fulfilled the requirement. Task done. That should have been the end of the matter. Allegedly however, after a brief silence, his teacher pronounced: 'That can't possibly be Burns, it's too short!'

Sam came home from school his heart in his boots, worried that he would have to learn something much more irksome and go through the whole trial again. Such situations however are where mothers come in. Unfortunately for his teacher I was at the time doing a post-graduate diploma in literature and we had reached the stage in one of our classes where we were delving into the delights of the minimalist poets — William Carlos Williams et al — and this had led on to further study of the tightly controlled syllabic structure of Japanese Haiku. I was also quite well versed in Scottish Literature. Pushing up my sleeves, I seized pen and paper ('twas the days before email), and wrote Sam's teacher a letter. It was the epistolary equivalent of a shot between the eyes. Her inane judgement that Sam's chosen poem was a false contender was thus decisively returned and dismissed.

Surprisingly — not — Sam didn't win the competition. That laurel went to some kid who spouted the four lined, two stanzas and double chorus of Burns' 'My Heart's in the Highlands'. The performer had obvious zero understanding of what it was actually about, but did remember to stamp his feet at an apparently appropriate moment of pathos. I wondered as I listened if I should raise my hand and say 'Eh, don't want to put a spanner in the works (LOL) but Burns, as was his want, cribbed the first verse from a much older source and added on the next, so can we really claim it as a true Burnsian text?' I didn't though. I had already won a private victory and saved the honour of my son who, to this day, will happily recite 'Extempore' to all and sundry with great gusto every 25th of January whether they want to hear it or not.

So, shortness does not necessarily connote irrelevance or ineffectiveness. Instead, as any decent teacher of writing will stress, brevity can be far more powerful and dynamic than a rambling, directionless, boring, repetitive, dull, never-ending, never-getting-to-the-point … collection of words. And it is the same with prayer.

I found it so the afternoon I stood with a cluster of other people outside the gates of Faslane, the home of Britain's nuclear weapon store. It was the 70th anniversary of the atrocity that were the attacks on Hiroshima and Nagasaki. Across Scotland, people were gathering to mark their recognition of the anniversary and to register their desire that such horrific happening would never happen again in their name. Faslane lies some twenty-five miles from our front door. It exists in an area of outstanding natural beauty, lying on the eastern shore of Gare Loch (*An Gearrh Loch* in Gaelic, meaning *the short loch*) in Argyll. Well, it was outstanding before the advent of Her Majesty's Naval Base and its Armaments Depot in the 1960s. Nowadays, should you drive along an outer perimeter of the base, you will be confronted by a line of ugly, ugly, ugly buildings inside ugly ugly ugly steel fencing with roles of twisted wire mesh on top and intermittent poles with cameras. (Completely transgressing Scotland's legal decision that walkers have right to roam provided no damage is inflicted.) The message reverberating from the outer edges of Faslane being an aggressive 'STAY OUT… OR ELSE …' So, it's an unpleasant spot and not one that makes my heart sing.

Neither does it make the hearts of any of the small group of people, gathered there that Saturday afternoon, sing either. All of them, including me, would far rather be doing something else. Something far nicer and less worrying. Something that wasn't about standing up to a massive global and sinister network that believes the threat of violence is the only way to control and temper countries. Faslane, should you be unaware, is where the UK holds more than 225 nuclear warheads – each warhead having an explosive power eight times (!) that of the bomb dropped on Hiroshima. Hiroshima, where the US on 6th August 1945, dropped an atomic bomb on the city killing over 180,000 people and three days later doing the same to Nagasaki where an estimated 100,000 people died. The vast majority of Japanese people killed were civilian men, women and children. Those who died instantly were the lucky ones. Others perished more slowly suffering the unimaginable pain of burns and radiation. As I write this our UK government, that is the Westminster-led government, not our devolved Scottish parliament, has plans to spend over 100 billion – yes, *biiiilllllioonnnn* – replacing the Trident nuclear programme. Stupid beyond words when we need every penny of that amount to invest in health care and education and not in an outdated way of being, which, even if you had been duped into thinking that we need such 'defence', has in reality only succeeded in making us a sitting target for lunatics.

So, despite the lure of far more pleasing Saturday afternoon occupations, here I was, with Colum and other folk, at the black north gate of Faslane. The other people were members of the Catholic Worker movement. Founded in the early 1930s by the incredible Dorothy Day – no relation to Doris as far as I am aware — she was an editor, women's rights activist, anti-war activist, journalist and writer. Dorothy Day tackled issues of social justice through the prism of the Catholic church and this movement still has a loyal, and apparently untiring, following. I say untiring as this small band of members which seemed to be the core of the existing Catholic Workers in the west of Scotland, had been turning up at the gates of Faslane once a month for the past two years despite the dire vagaries of our weather pattern. This was only my second time at the prayer witness and I really don't know how many more I am willing to sign up to. This is where one's faith gets put to the test. It's all fine and nice sending out a bit prayer in a nice setting — a scented retreat house garden, a quiet and architecturally stunning church – but the non-aesthetic concrete pavement and space outside of a nuclear armaments store asks a little more effort, a little more resolution, a little more faith. Particularly when the prayers are accompanied by a lurking and surveilling military police car and CCTV cameras.

So, what's the point? What's the point of a few people turning up once a month for a quiet, non-flag waving, non-slogan shouting, non-confrontational witness? Many might say there is little point. Having been there twice, having joined in the prayer by reading out some of the prepared scripture passages, having sung along any of the lines of 'Salve Regina' that I can remember from my childhood, having hung-out with the Catholic Workers and felt their spirit and commitment to a gospel of faith-in-action, I say there is every point. Yes, it is a drop in a vast ocean. Yes, it could be viewed as a total waste of time and a futile attempt to dissuade an entrenched establishment to rethink its policies. Yes, the brief minutes of prayer once a month could be read as too weak an action to have any effect.

But.

A wee word that. Three letters. Three letters with the ability to turn around a sentence, redirect an argument, offer another perspective. But. Our prayer on that Saturday afternoon has the same force and effectiveness as that sma' sma' word. Who is to know what impact that apparently insignificant group has on someone keeping an eye on the camera? On a police officer watching from a slight distance? On the driver or passengers of the cars driving past? On anyone listening to the on-line recording of the prayer? On any of our friends and family who ask what we did on Saturday? On anyone reading this? Probably we will never know. Just as we will never really know how prayer itself functions. All those intangible utterances spoken, sung or sent silently out from spaces of darkness, century after century, arising from the best intentions of the human heart, must, surely, be a force for good. As Dorothy Day wrote in her diaries which were sealed until twenty-five years after her death and then published under the title *The Duty of Delight* (2008), activism and the contemplative life must go hand-in-hand. Taking courage from the teachings of St Thérèse of Lisieux, she reminds herself that when apathy surrounds and small acts of protest seem irrelevant, a petition for greater faith is required and, with it, an assurance that a greater power who will do the rest. We can *but* try.

Perhaps in similar spirit to the beliefs of Dorothy Day, Rebecca Solnit re-released her own polemic *Hope in the Dark* (2004 rpt., 2016). Rebecca Solnit did so because her message, her words — composed initially when the US invaded Iraq — hold up through our present tumultuous time. In the 2016 edition she stresses that what we do to make the world a better place does matter, but we may not know at the time that it has mattered. She asserts that both optimism and pessimism can be useless positions — as both can be excuses not to act. Total optimists work from the naive premise that all shall be well without their doing anything, and the pessimist believes if we are all going to hell in a handcart, then there is no point in protesting. Neither position is useful. What Rebecca Solnit espouses is a belief *in* the belief that what you are doing will have an impact, will have an effect and thus is grounded in hope. A hope which is both practical and powerful. Furthermore, she draws attention to how we already, and almost naturally, act for good in the world. Most of us live in a capitalist society but most of us simultaneously and unconsciously do daily acts of anti-capitalism. Whenever we care and commit to someone or something, for absolutely no financial payment, and do so out of love, concern or principle — visiting a sick relative, forsaking a career climb to bring up a child, taking someone to hospital, gifting produce from your garden, giving useful and skilled advice, providing a reference or testimonial, baking for a charity event, giving a home to a rescued dog, and countless other seemingly invisible unpaid acts — we are, in effect, resisting the narrative of greed and private profit.

Small acts are therefore immensely powerful. This reminds me of a story sent to us by our American friend, Kent, who when travelling the world, found himself up Everest when the 7.9 magnitude earthquake happened killing more than 8,500 people and destroying 500,000 homes. Kent survived unharmed but, seeing first-hand the devastation all around him, asked his Facebook friends to help him help one Nepalese family who had lost everything. Kent is a wise chap and, possibly to pre-empt those whose response might be something along the lines of what was the point of helping just one family in the face of so much disaster, he told the story of the boy with the starfish. The story goes thus ... *A man came across a young boy walking along the tide-line. The beach was littered with swathes of starfish who had been stranded ashore by a storm. Starfish will die if left out of the water for too long. The man watched the boy slowly and steadfastly tossing starfish back into the water. He walked up to the boy and said 'What's the point of doing that? There are hundreds. You can't change this situation. You can't make a difference'. In reply the boy took hold of another stranded starfish and tossed it back into the sea. 'Saved that one. Made a difference to that one,' he said.*

I was a Stranger

My mind is disturbed. The tiny body of a drowned child has been washed ashore. The image pulsates around the world. I see it on Facebook once, twice, three, four times. Different angles but the same tragic reality. I scroll on when next it appears. There is only so much piercing of the soul one can take. But I see it. There at the corner of my mind, just a flicker removed from everything else.

The wave of awakening began late yesterday. Something snapped in the minds of us safe and secure. Perhaps it was the power of that little dead body. That innocence incarnate. Enough it said. Enough. It is time to say Enough. We put a poster in our kitchen window which says *Refugees Welcome Here*. We take a Selfie with us holding a copy of the poster and put it on the Facebook pages that we manage. We sign the on-line petition. We share the First Minister of our country saying the UK response has so far been shameful and that she is calling an emergency cross-party conference. We share postings from other pressure groups. Then we go and have a meal with friends.

The food is colourful, thoughtful and delectable but my stomach has a swell of unease in it. We talk of what is happening and the too slow response. 'It is because we all have too much,' says our friend and they fill the boot of our car with books they don't need nor want, that they are giving freely to the bookshop. Later, as I get into bed I wonder if any of the refugees have a book.

Colum puts a tea light in our window underneath the poster. A light to guide the travellers. He goes to bed. I sit for a while in the soft dark watching the dance of the tiny flame. I think of the women holding children in the tossing and terrifying expanse of a wide wide sea. I hope they are braver than I. Wonder if my thoughts will give a particle of relief. Wonder if prayer works.

Around 2am I go back to the kitchen and blow the tea light out. I do not want to lose our house.

In the real morning, the poster is still in the window. I worry that a shambolic crowd of people will knock our door and ask for admittance. Does 'Here' really mean *here*? My stomach lurches again. Snatches of worn quotations and expressions swill around my mind: *For evil to triumph it is important that good people do nothing ... I was a stranger and you let me in ... For whatsoever you did to the least of my people you did unto me ... They came for the Jews, I did nothing ... Come away in!* Resting on her mop, the sleep-deprived wee wifie in my brain goes '*Jeeees*, ye've done it now.' My fingers itch to take the poster down. I leave it.

We take the bootfull of books to the bookshop. Offload them, banter with the owner and staff member on duty. Talk of Amazon sales, the diminished stock of tea in the kitchen, a local poetry anthology and who is covering the shop next week. Colum drives off to meet Mhairi Black MP meeting the local Fairtrade workers. I walk to the university library via a coffee shop. As I wait for my de-caff soya cappuchino with a delicate custard pastry to accompany — we have so much to thank the Italians for – I check Facebook. Mistake. A Syrian father is breaking his heart. The sound is off, even so, the anguish of his body movements penetrates my senses.

I put my phone away and glance around. The table next to me has three people at it. Two men speaking in English accents. One young woman with a sallow skin and splendid dark hair that does not grow locally. They talk of academic things. Strangers in my land. Strangers studying and at peace in my land. As I sip my coffee I see Mhairi Black walk past. No cameras. No entourage. Just a young local woman making a difference. Spending most of her week elsewhere, in a parliament, city and country she would rather not be in. Today helping raise the profile of an organisation in her own town that helps people stay in their own land.

In the foyer of the library there are books with a sign *Help Yourself!* Ah, the annual clear out. I tweak two paperbacks out of the slanting pile. Two Virago Classics – Elizabeth Von Arnim's *The Adventures of Elizabeth in*

Rügen and Mrs Oliphant's *Miss Marjoribanks.* The first I have read before. I may already have it at home, but it is free and could help me sleep. The other I know I have. But Mrs Oliphant was the focus of my long PhD journey, I cannot walk past her and the bookshop will benefit from this copy. Elizabeth Von Arnim. Born Mary Annette Beauchamp in Australia, moved to London, England, with her family. When grown she married a German widower, Count Henning August von Armin-Schlagenthin. She was a migrant as was her cousin Katherine Mansfield. And Oliphant. Margaret Oliphant Wilson Oliphant. Born in Wallyford, on the outskirts of Edinburgh, to Scottish parents. Moved to Liverpool at the age of 10, married a cousin (hence the repeated surname), spent most of her adult life in London with various episodes abroad. Another migrant.

I go up the library stairs to the second floor. The term has not yet started. The desks and computer terminals are quiet. I find my usual spot, a few desks distance from anyone else. Leave my coat there. Go and collect an Oxford edition Thesaurus. Pull my netbook out of my backpack and plug it in. Free power. Deposit the books from the table downstairs, on the desk. Gift. All is gift.

I hear a student nearby begin to talk on the phone. Arabic? No … Spanish. I quash my impulse to get up, poke my head around the bookshelf between he and I and fling an assertive *Wheeesht!* his way. His voice is low. I do not understand what he is saying. Perhaps it is a child calling him. He is far from home. I tell my mind that it will have to thole it. Stop being so precious. There is room enough here for more than me and my way of being.

Tending the Garden

We do not have a perfect garden. Three huge lime trees overshadow much of the garden and the newly sprung-up tree, which we think may be an alder, is contributing to the increasing shade. The grassy area is stubbly and has potholes at various intervals thanks to Jenna and her bouts of digging. The quince bushes struggle to fight off the Rose of Sharon and an invasive fern, the lemon balm has fallen over and needs tied onto a supporting pole, the assertive stalks of ornamental grass have edged out the campanula to the extent that it seems to have given up the fight to appear this year, the round slabs that should lead footsteps around the bee and butterfly patch are covered with moss or have sunk out of sight. The buddleia needs pruned as it has now pushed a metre over the fence into our neighbour's garden. The soil around lots of plants is asking for a hoe, the same soil needs fed, the brick path needs swept and freed from creeping grass poking its way through and the hedge needs trimmed. But there is a wooden sign hitched onto the rusty iron gate underneath the archway of rampant honeysuckle and clematis, which instructs us to 'Love Your Garden'. And we do.

Our back garden is our place of refuge. It is where I go in my mind which is marked 'Safe and Secure and Home'. The bench, which needs a good scrubbing, is where I sit and think and slowly let go of anxieties, large and small. It is where I remind myself of the important stuff, the real stuff. So, despite also noticing what needs doing in the garden, jobs that will not be completed inside a day, other things impress upon my mind. When my mind has begun to settle and I let go of whatever is bugging me, I notice the peace that lingers in this space. I notice the resident robin and blethering blue-tits that hop onto the bird-feeder in hope of a bit of food, or their pals who cavort in the high branches of the lime trees. I notice the scent from the naughty buddleia and the sudden appearance of a butterfly on its flower. I notice the bees furiously gathering nectar from the Rose of Sharon or the lavender heads. I notice the breeze as it wafts past my senses, clearing and cooling my thoughts.

To understand a garden is to understand regulation. Not regulation as in the laying down of rigid rules but as in rhythmic turning. The best evocation of this I have come across is that inscribed in the beautiful and erudite account of the creation of a garden as found in Katherine Swift's *The Morville Hours* (2008). There is something so measured and thus so tranquil about the description of the finding, planning, planting and tending the garden of an old dower house in Shropshire. There is both breadth and depth in her story of how her garden came to be. Even when things get difficult, like a summer drought which deeply challenges her thirsting plants, or when painful family memories intrude, her description is still unhurried and accepting of the way of nature. Accompanying her plans for her garden is a deep awareness and connectedness to the history of the area and, in particular, to the period when the Morville Priory housed Benedictine monks from the twelfth century to the sixteenth century. It was the nearby Cluniac priory of Much Wenlock which, I discovered in later research, sent thirteen monks to be the founding community of a new priory in my town of Paisley. Walter fitz Alan, High Steward of Scotland, originally a Shropshire man who came north at the request of King David I — was highly instrumental in the installation of the monks in 1163. The Paisley priory was built on the site of an old Celtic church founded by St Mirin in the sixth century. Then, in 1245, the priory was elevated to that of an Abbey and dedicated to the Virgin Mary, St. James of Compostella, St. Mirin and St. Milburga — the venerated seventh-century Abbess of Wenlock. A nice connection I hadn't expected.

Cluniac monasticism was governed by a set of rules based on the Rule of St Benedict — although with added modifications. The Rule of St Benedict operates from the premise of the near continuous praise of God with devotions being recited or sung seven times of day — known as the Canonical Hours. There were actually eight hours but the first two,

Matins and Lauds, were sung one after the other in the middle of the night. Prime was timed for dawn, then Tierce, Sext and None during the daylight hours, with Vespers and Compline concluding the day's prayer. Swift's book, *The Morville Hours*, recognises the connection of such ordering with that of a nature and the arc of the agricultural year, but also as having something to teach our twenty-first century rushed way of being which is so often off-balance, overloaded and lacking in moderation. Her book is a reminder of an ancient ordering that offers an alternative timing to that of our modern-day understanding.

Nowhere in Swift's *Morville Hours* is neatness spoken of. Nowhere is it lauded. Neatness has nothing to do with perfection. It is just neatness. Perfection is a far wider, intangible, almost indefinable concept. By its very essence, perfection cannot be defined for it depends on who is doing the beholding, who is judging. As Dickon and Mary in Frances Hodgson Burnett's 1911 classic *The Secret Garden*, agree about their plan to bring the old forgotten and locked-up garden back to life:

'I wouldn't want to make it look like a gardener's garden, all clipped an' spick an' span, would you?' he said. 'It's nicer like this with things runnin' wild, an' swingin' an' catchin' hold of each other.'
'Don't let us make it tidy,' said Mary anxiously. 'It wouldn't seem like a secret garden if it was tidy.'

Magic and tidiness don't work well together — unless of course you are Mary Poppins — and certainly not in an old garden where there is a possibility of '*a fountain o' roses*' come Summer.

Stories of gardens, principally those with old brick walls, are a bit of a personal penchant. It is perhaps to do with how they offer something other than the usual pressing demands of our everyday living. Old gardens seem to ooze peace, serenity and 'nowness'. It is as if the old fired clay and time-honoured plants enfold around the senses of the person who enters there and offers the invitation: 'Stay awhile, why don't you?' Some of this chapter has been written in my own garden. As any of you who work from home will know, and know so so well, at home you can be prey to lots of interruption. Other concerns which have nothing to do with the focus of your work. Concerns which can ensure that my spirit will be well and truly jangling if I get caught up in them. Often, too often, my desk has notes pinned around it to remember to do this and to do that. There are notes stuck to the fridge and notes around the hall telephone. Too many notes. This is when I retreat to a library or to the garden. We have a small shed in the back garden, which B&Q describe as a 'Summer House'. It probably just about makes it into the lowest rung of the category but it's just the thing for a frazzled writer looking for a refuge. Scribbling away, my eyes every few lines or so drift out to the surrounding garden as I search for the appropriate word or description. Away from the hub of the house and all its associated issues, my mind is free to dive in to that well of thought that we all carry around but often have little space to explore. Is it any wonder that Roald Dahl wrote all of his marvellous books in a wee hut in his garden? He, I believe though, had the good sense to have an electric heater in it. I have an old shawl which doesn't quite insulate to the same degree.

Another garden has given me asylum in the past. Our town has a 'Peace Garden' in a secluded corner of a public park — named because of its dedication to world harmony. Near the entrance to the garden there is a 'Peace Pole' which, in various languages, details the message 'Let Peace Prevail on Earth'. Every 6th August local people gather here to remember the atrocity that was Hiroshima and to express their belief that peace is the only workable option between nations. This message is reinforced by the plaque on the outside wall which commemorates the opening of the garden in 1988 by, the then, Monsignor Bruce Kent, a Catholic priest and CND activist. The founding premise of the garden was already a positive one but, to be honest, I loved it not because of its politics or wider message but just simply because of what it gave me. For the first ten years of our son's life we lived in a tiny flat where you would have been hard pushed to swing that metaphorical cat. The local park then was our solace, or necessary escape from continual attempts to tidy and sort the flat in the hope of finding another ten centimetres of space. I particularly loved the Peace Garden which, in the days before cuts to Council budgets, was meticulously cared for by a clutch of thoughtful gardeners — (if anyone knows the correct collective noun for such gardeners please do inform me.) I was very tired in Sam's early years as many new parents are, but I do reserve the right to claim I was more tired than the rest as our offspring didn't sleep the night until he was the ripe old age of three. There was therefore many a time I would push the stalwart Silver Cross buggy, with my fractious child on board, the twenty minute walk up to the park. The repetitive trundling rhythm of the pram would invariably send Sam off to sleep and I would make my way to the Peace Garden, find an unoccupied bench, put the brake on the pram, tuck the blankets more securely round my sleeping son, sit down, stick my foot next to a wheel so I would feel if it moved, pull out a book and when, after a few minutes, find that the words made no sense, I would lay it down, rest my head back and let my eyes drift over the pathways and flower beds till they blurred and my eyelids met.

I have no need of the Peace Garden now. Our son is grown, we live in a very different house and have our own secluded garden. It doesn't have an old brick wall around it but it is a peace garden in its own right. This morning as I picked the brambles nosing their way through the hedge, I could still hear residual drifts of voices floating on the air that belong to a recent gathering of friends. The weather this summer has not been anything like a scorcher. Cool, wet and temperate probably covers it. I am not complaining though. My land is green and healthy even though a bit soggy and the farmers are complaining. And, while other countries around the globe have watched its forested areas go on fire, its earth become cracked and brown and their garden plants wither in the heat, my country has remained its beautiful self. True there are a lack of butterflies this year but the bees are as busy as usual (as are the bloomin' slugs) and the bird community seem to be doing their usual thing.

It was therefore only after some hesitation that we decided to put up the awning which attaches to our 'Summer House'. As Colum stretched the tight canvas shape around the roof frame of 'The Far Pavilion', as he has dubbed it, he realised that the last person to fold away the awning had been his dad. Edmond died, very suddenly, some years ago and some of his possessions with his neat handwriting instructing of the correct way to use something, have found their way to Colum. Colum has inherited his dad's love of proper care of things. Our large family-sized tent is thus each year taken down, precisely, neatly, brushed, cleaned, tied, and packed away in line with Colum's directives. This always takes any impromptu helpers by surprise. On our camping holiday Colum is a relaxed free spirit, happy to do little the first week and even less the second. Campers who get to know him, who share a cup of tea, a glass of wine, a blether, a game of football or cards and many a laugh, all judge him as an easy-going chap, unhurried and unworried. They are then rather puzzled on the day of our departure from the campsite to find their offer of help utilised as in a military operation. Given exact instructions as to what to do and when to do it they wonder if they actually know the real man at all. Inherited genes are laid far down in the psyche I guess. And I thank Edmond's influence each year we put up the tent and find it dry, neatly folded with everything in order.

Back in the garden, the awning fitted to our wee shed looks quite classy. Chairs arranged, plastic camping table covered with a lace cloth, twinkling glasses and a tray of crackers and home-made veggie pâté, it all looks rather festive. And to the garden came all our visitors.

'It's like *Midsummer Night's Dream*,' said one.

'Stand at the gate, under the archway, while I take a photo,' said another.

'Oooooh, this is lovely,' said someone else.

Open Garden standard it may not be, but our garden still seemed to please. The trees, plants, bushes and pathways all roused themselves to be on their best behaviour, give of their best selves. The combination of soothing green punctuated by the incredible bright orange of the recently flowered crocosmia, the late flowering purple clematis — don't ask me the variety — the pretty maple tree in its large pot, the majestic trees, the bee-clustered Roses of Sharon, the old rusty chiminea and scattered railway sleepers, the finely tall fennel and, almost as tall, decorative grasses in the raised bed with its low granite wall, the wooden bench sitting snugly under the wild rose and privet 'umbrella' and the jasmine slowly curling its way up the side of the shed — all worked together to welcome our friends and say: 'Sit awhile, breathe us in and be happy.' The chilled fizzy wine, brought by some thoughtful person, probably did something to mellow folks out too.

Reading this back I wonder if it falls within the compass of Rebecca West's tart comment in her review 'Notes on Novels', (*New Statesman,* 1921), about the tedious type of women who simper alluringly about their gardens as if they were having a veritable affair with their delphiniums. West said this though as a snide attack on Elizabeth von Arnim, an enthusiastic gardener who wrote about such, but who was also West's rival for the attentions of H G Wells. I think we can thus interpret her comment as that of a hurt woman and perhaps I should also emphatically say that our garden contains no such self-conscious flower as a delphinium.

Vulnerable Climate

The Met office has issued a 'yellow' warning and have had great fun cranking up expectations of an approaching storm, which is trundling its way towards us. 'Storm Abigail' it is dubbed. Wonder who the Abigail was that unconsciously gifted her name — an ex of the meteorologist in charge, I jalouse. On checking the derivation of the name, I see that 'Abigail' is originally Hebrew and means *father rejoiced*, and, apparently, it later became a popular term for the lady's maid. Don't think that happened in Scotland though. Love how some writers take as universal something that happened in their neck of the woods, without checking if it actually had significance elsewhere. And I can't quite see the connection with the 'father rejoicing' bit either. Perhaps all they went on was the final syllable of Abi*gail*, or is that too prosaic even for the chaps in the Met Office? In Scotland, however, we tend to name it as we see it. The last storm to hit Scotland was promptly reduced to the excellent name 'Hurricane Bawbag'. I will leave it to you to work that one out.

So, with the concept in my mind that a storm is a-comin' I have just had a happy hour in our back garden. I initially went there to make use of the wonderful wind and peg out some soggy towels to dance in it for at least an hour. Once there I noticed that the tall ornamental grasses which grow under the bird feeder in the bee and butterfly patch were looking decidedly sad and spent. Having pegged out the towels I then pulled on my damp-feeling gardening gloves which I keep in the shed. It was the work of three minutes to secateur down the limp rods and pile them up at the back fence. I then saw that the slates that normally sit between the plants so to keep weeds at bay and also allow a designated standing spot when filling the bird feeder, were totally covered in mushy leaves. I got the rake out and set to. An hour later I felt the first warning drops of rain. The towels had had a happy frolic on the whirly-gig and it seemed wise to bung them back into the washing basket, toss the secateurs and rake back in their usual nooks, entice Jenna to come with the reward of a polo-mint and head back up towards the house.

I had such a tranquil hour. No, the sun wasn't anywhere to be seen. A snug woolly hat pulled firmly over my ears, a neoprene fleece-lined jacket well zipped up, and chunky socks stuffed into my wellies were all necessary to keep me warm, but my senses were aired out and cleansed, my lungs were full of reviving air and even my eye-sight felt clearer. As I worked around the garden I thought that it seemed no time whatsoever since our friends' gathering, the various mornings I had taken my first cup of green tea to the garden and perched on the low wall at the outset of the day, our lunches, afternoon teas and wine-sipping evenings that had peppered our summer and autumn even though the temps weren't much to comment on.

Now the garden wants to sleep. It has turned in on itself and is retreating back into the dark earth. There isn't much for we humans to do but trim the shrivelled-up leaves of the maple tree, gather up the mounds of squelchy leaves strewn all over the garden, cut-back the rampant wooden arms of the buddleia, clip the roses right down while rejoicing in the discovery of the last delicate bloom, trim and tie-up the stiff stalks of the fennel plant which still wave bravely at the heavy sky, take the copper-ribbons out of the frond-less pots of hostas that the slugs got to despite the efforts of the bands, stack them together in the best sheltered spot, close-up the shed, throw a prayer heavenward that the storm won't fell any of the soughing lime trees and return to the house. The limp lemon-balm has given its all and needs tidying and I would like to think I will gather up the rose-hips and do something virtuous and useful with them. But I shall do neither jobs today. The garden has told me to go inside and stop fussing. It will survive. And, underground, it is still busy. As the thirteenth-century Persian poet and Sufi mystic, Rumi, advised:

And don't think the garden loses its ecstasy in winter. It's quiet, but the roots are down there riotous.

Well, as storms go, Storm Abigail was a bit of a damp squib. Very damp and very dreich with bouts of thumping rain and cavorting wind but she never quite came up to full hissy-fit level. Not that I am complaining. I was ok. I was snugly and smugly inside, looking out at the furious darkness and enjoyed being so. 'Tis true I was happier when my loved ones got home from their respective pursuits. By then the living room wood-burning fire was happily flickering, curtains were drawn, a hot dinner was prepared and home was the best place to be.

The next morning we notice that the temperature has dropped. *Wow, it's Baltic!* texts Sam mid-cycle to his work. I look out of the window and see that the Campsie Fells are dusted with snow. Winter is at our doorstep.

Thinking of the weather it occurs to me that, for the majority of us in this part of the world — i.e. the west of Scotland — the weather is often more of a nuisance, an inconvenience, but rarely feels life-threatening. We are told when bad weather is approaching, we see it through and we expect it to end. What we don't expect is the kind of weather when the winds are frighteningly high so that buildings collapse and people die. It has happened, very sadly, out in the western Hebrides, where the wind has had full play and has claimed lives, but in the more sheltered belt where I live, we are more or less protected from the full force. I wonder though if this will always be the case. We know our weather pattern is changing, we know strange things are occurring which tell us that the planet is upset. Our time of complacency is surely over.

Paris is soon to host a World Climate Summit. Hundreds of influential people from all around the globe will congregate, meet and speak and hopefully form some kind of workable plan to reduce carbon emissions. They are aiming for a legally binding global agreement. One hopes therefore that (a) the agreement will be what the planet needs it to be and (b) that all nations will abide by it. High hopes. May it not be just a talking shop where more damage has been created by the carbon emissions created by the flying-in of various high-powered officials. Still, it is a start. Possibly too late but it is a serious stab to address what must be the prime item on any government's agenda, i.e. care of the very earth we walk on. I say that, but of course, it's not the prime item. It should be, but it's not. It's not the prime concern because to care for the earth is to ask people to change. To change what they are doing or not doing. It requires effort and we don't always like that.

To be strictly honest I didn't actually know the Summit was occurring until recently. Colum and I had gone up to Findhorn for a few days in part celebration of our Silver Wedding anniversary. As is our want, we went along to the Taizé prayer gathering on Sunday morning run by members of the Findhorn community. The venue for the gathering was Newbold House, a lovely old Victorian manor house in Forres, Moray. In the middle of the large front room where everyone gathered, someone had built an artistic centrepiece composed of wood, flowers and lavish leaves which immediately focused the mind as to the environmental and aesthetic importances of our natural world. The session began and a member of the Findhorn community, led us in a circle dance. They are so skilled at this. Simple walking-pace movement where people sing easy refrains while linking hands with each other. Simple but so effective. From there we progressed to song and prayer that the approaching Summit would be a step toward healing the earth as we learned to live lighter on it.

As is usual in these gatherings, the room was full of all nationalities. Interestingly, I seemed to be the only Scot there judging by the various voices and accents I heard. Why this is so is a question I haven't yet found an answer for. A glib answer would be to say that Scots are not your natural dance-around-flowers kind of race. That's it's all a bit too out-there and 1960s hippy culture for us. I counter this argument by thinking of our rich history of folklore and folk belief practices, from a vanished age, which involved and honoured the natural world. There was, for example, the ceremony of walking three times, sunwise, around a cairn, altar, bonfire, house or church, for luck — known in Scots Gaelic as *deiseil*. Or, anti-clockwise, *tuaithiuil*, (or *widdershins* in Scots), to invoke bad luck, evil. You only need dip into Alexander Carmichael's *Carmina Gadelica*, (1900), an impressive collection of blessings, songs, chants and thanksgivings, gathered from his travels around the highlands and islands, or F Marian McNeill's *The Silver Bough* (1956), or Margaret Bennett's *Scottish Customs from the Cradle to the Grave* (1993), to note how all parts of life were once accepted as being interwoven with spirituality. Perhaps that's the rub. New Age thinking isn't of great attraction to us because we already have a bedrock of former traditions lurking below our present-day beliefs. We have no need for a Californian-based guru to teach us about the inter-connectedness of life and our natural environment. That said, we do need reminders. And I, despite being a thrawn Scot, enjoy much of what the Findhorn Foundation has to offer. As Rumi would caution: 'There are a thousand ways to kneel and kiss the earth.'

So we can all do a bit. Few of us will physically be in Paris at the Summit. Some of us may send petitions to our governments, some of us may join the Green Party or lobby our own parties about this issue. Some of us may decide to use our car less, to recycle more conscientiously, to buy less, to grow more and a hundred thousand small but meaningful actions may be the result. As the Scots language has it: 'Mony a mickle maks a muckle'. Together great things could happen. We are but stewards of the earth, it is not ours to do what we like with — much as some global companies might short-sightedly believe that. No, it is ours to look after, to respect and treasure. As Mary Lennox says in a film version of Hodgson's *The Secret Garden,* (1993), 'If you look the right way, you can see that the whole world is a garden.'

An Eye for an Eye — Really?

Tragically, it was not the Climate Change Summit in Paris that caught the world's attention but a fatal evening of terrorist attacks across the city which killed over a hundred people. The responsibility for the attacks was claimed by ISIS — which, you will hardly need me to delineate — is an ideology and radical militant group seeking supremacy in the world. Its origins are complex and its methods are brutal and merciless. The Paris attacks appear to have been a response to France's intervention in Syria. I don't wish to give space to ISIS any more than saying they are a horrible worrying presence in the world. What I have been dwelling on though, as have many people, is the question of meeting force with force or violence with violence.

Yesterday evening a friend called round. We talked of what had happened in Paris. It was an obvious given that the shootings were wrong and the loss of innocent life also wrong but what was mostly concerning us was what should be the appropriate response? Possibly 'appropriate' isn't the correct word here. As I type this I think of a scene from *The Winslow Boy* by Terrence Rattigan (1946). The play, based on a celebrated legal case, is constructed around the expulsion of the young Ronnie Winslow from his private school — The Royal Naval College at Osborne. Ronnie stands accused of the crime of stealing and cashing a postal order belonging to another boy. Ronnie's father, Arthur, believes his son to be innocent and decides to clear his name. He engages the services of Sir Robert Morton KC. After a long and arduous struggle the name of Ronnie Winslow is cleared. Immediately after the court trial and in the final scene of the play, Sir Robert visits the Winslow home. Catherine Winslow, sister to Ronnie, a suffragette and highly intelligent young woman who has enjoyed sparring with Sir Robert, asks him why it was that he had wept at the verdict when he espoused that unemotional logic and behaviour were the only necessities for a successful outcome. After a moment's hesitation Sir Robert replies that he had wept because 'right' had been carried out. Catherine questions why he uses this word in favour of 'justice'. Sir Robert says that 'justice' is relatively easy to do, whereas 'right' is far harder.

Those grieving in Paris must be forgiven for wishing justice to be served on those who have bereft them of loved ones. Incredulously however, higher thinking is shaping the responses of some people. On Facebook there appeared a posting of a statement from a young husband whose wife was gunned down in the attacks. This husband's message to ISIS was 'I will not give you the gift of hating you'. And, despite his initial hardline statements of measures to be taken against jihadist terrorism, Françoise Hollande, the current President of France, two days later reaffirmed his commitment to take 30,000 Syrian refugees into his country, saying that it was a 'humanitarian duty'. There will be many who applaud his intention but there will also be many who abhor it. To my mind it is an illustration of true bravery and compassion in action.

I am, however, not living in Paris and yesterday as I made my way into Glasgow with a close friend to see Matthew Bourne's *Sleeping Beauty*, I was aware that we were attending a large gathering of people in a big city. I wasn't afraid but perhaps just slightly wary. Looking around the busy gathering there — mostly women of a certain age — it did seem a little ludicrous to believe we could be a target. But, why not? At this juncture, Britain is considering a bombardment of Syria. It could happen. We all still went to the theatre though because life, no matter what evil minds may conjure up, pushes through. We had bought our tickets. The ballet was happening and so we went. As President Hollande urged the scared and brittle citizens of Paris, city life is made up of an interweaving fabric in which theatres and concert halls and parks and cafes figure strongly. We cannot allow the fear of terrorism to shut these down.

As I watched the superb athletic and aesthetic movements of the ballet dancers, feasted my eyes on the detailed costumes and choreography, listened to Tchaikovsky's enchanting notes, I thought of how important a part that Art, in its broadest interpretation, has to play in the world.

Transcending nation and language it is capable of bringing balance to our base selves, reminding us that we are but part of an old and continuing story and it is not for us to decide when the story ends. Like the people of Paris, we have to opt for the continuation of the good things in life and not let fear dictate to us.

All of this does not detract though from the question of what would I do, how would I respond if one of my loved ones was killed or seriously injured by an intentional act of another? Would my higher self really kick in and opt for a peaceful non-violent response? Would I manage to quell the anger I would feel and not do a knee-jerk hostile retaliation? I like to think that I could at least attempt a peaceful return. In reality, I expect though that it is not until one is in such a dark circumstance that you can formulate an answer. During our recent conversation with our friend, we had mulled this over. We all agreed that evil must be stopped but questioned the possible methods of that. Is armed combat really the best the twenty-first century can come up with? Has it worked in the past? Was it worth the sacrifice of the thousands upon thousands of lives? Colum said he preferred to believe that non-violent resistance was the better way. He cited Gandhi and Mandela —two men with huge vision and open hearts who became world leaders and persuaded nations and generations to follow the ways of peace.

The gods however have a way of demonstrating just how difficult the peaceful way can be. On checking my coat in the cloakroom at the interval of the ballet, I couldn't find my scarf. There was a distinct nip in the weather and I was already chilled (— as in 'cold' not 'fine with it' as is now the confusing common usage). Our seats, in the highest part of the theatre, weren't in receipt of any rising warmth from the bulk of the audience below us and, as we were few in number up there, we weren't generating any useful body heat. I had been looking forward throughout the first act to retrieving my scarf from my coat and wrapping it around my stiffening neck and shoulders. My cloakroom coat proved, sadly, to be *sans* scarf. It was one minute to curtain-up for the second act and, thinking therefore that I would just have to do without, I returned to our seats. As the curtain rose I noted I felt decidedly cold. I thought I was silly not to find my scarf and wondered if I had left it in the ladies' loo. I clambered back up to the exit door again — to the slight questioning of the usher who told me, in a teacher tone, to 'Come back in quietly'. Why I would slam back in was beyond my comprehension, but I just nodded and went to the loo to search. No scarf revealed itself. I returned to my seat, step by dark step, holding on to the handrail for dear life. The second act trundled through — all great and entertaining and thoroughly worth our money — but by the time of the final bow I was more than cold. Action was needed.

The usher said that my scarf had still not turned up even after her radio-ing down to her colleagues in the ground floor cafe where we had had a cup of tea earlier. We went down there. I asked at the cafe. They said to go and ask at the Stage Door. Stage Door? Really? I asked another usher. He said to ask at the Stage Door. To the Stage Door we went. There were a handful of people already there. One young girl with an autograph book and another older couple. I buzzed the secure entry button. A rather harassed woman appeared. Ignoring me, she addressed the other people. One of them had apparently also mislaid a scarf.

'No, nothing found in the balcony.'

She went to shut the door.

'I've also lost a scarf. I was told to ask here,' I butted in.

'What colour and where did you lose it?'

'I don't know where I lost it, but it is red with swirls.'

'Where were you sitting?'

'Up in the gods.'

'A scarf was found but it wasn't found there.'

'But I was also in the foyer cafe and we walked up all the stairs through all the levels.'

'Nothing in the upper balcony was found.'

I felt myself getting annoyed. It was wintry outside. I had my scarf when I came in the building. I didn't have it now. I seriously doubted anyone would have nicked it. A scarf? And I wanted it back. Apart from needing it for warmth I had been given it by Colum on the morning of our Silver Wedding anniversary. He had bought it for me in the fair-trade shop. It wasn't my usual charity shop number. It was new and lovely and it was from him, especially for me. Just as I was thinking of getting more annoyed, a young man came up to the door whom I recognised as the boyfriend of a young woman who runs a writer's class in the bookshop. We had blethered with him briefly when we had first arrived at the theatre. I told him the scarf story. He went in and spoke to the snippy woman who had now retreated behind her glassed-in booth with the outside door firmly shut. After a moment or so he came back out and, rolling his eyes, said that the woman was a bit uptight as apparently lots of people were asking her questions at the same time. Well, yes. That could happen when a whole theatre turns out. However, sympathy aside, wasn't it her job to staff the Stage Door and deal with all that entailed?

'She gets like that,' he sighed. 'Tell you what, I'm off duty now but I'm back on later. If it doesn't turn up in the next ten minutes let me know. I'll do a search and, if I find it, I'll return it to the bookshop.'

I thanked him and he jogged off for some downtime in a peaceful cafe somewhere. I stood in the freezing air for another ten minutes being totally ignored by the woman inside the booth — the warm and heated booth. Inside. It was now also raining which didn't improve matters. The leading chap who played the Prince in the ballet came out. He smiled and momentarily hesitated, presumably thinking I was an autograph hunter. I just wanted my scarf. The young lass who had been waiting, edged forward and asked him for his signature. He signed her book and looked quizzically at me and my friend. She had the presence of mind to say 'Oh, you were very good. Well done.' I murmured something to the same effect. He grinned and walked off to join a group of young men waiting further down the road. I wondered what it must be like dancing your heart out then removing your costume and make-up, getting into normal clothes and leaving the theatre. Is it just a day's work? Having stood, many a time, waiting for my son at the end of a gruelling basketball game and observed his team mates triumphantly happy or moodily defeated, I thought how little difference there is between a sports athlete and a ballet dancer. Their physique is so similar. Guess the only difference would be the after-game or after-show chat … 'Did you see her miss the timing? Thought she was going to crash the whole corps-de-ballet!' as against 'That was definitely a foul, that ref was hopeless,' kind of comment.

Such musings distracted me for a minute or so until a passing wind made me shiver. I thought about pressing the buzzer again — and keep pressing it until Mrs Snippy moved herself and came back out. I thought about asking to speak to someone else like the manager and tell him that he needed to do some staff training with his Stage Door staff. I didn't do any of that even though I am more than capable of righteous anger and can stage quite a performance, punctuated by some choice and cutting words, should I opt to do so. Some residue of the conversation in our kitchen had come back to me and I realised that, right at that moment, in the cold in the street outside that door, I had a choice. Either flatten this woman with words and insist on speaking to the theatre manager, or trust that my scarf would be found and that my young friend would get it to me. Chilled to the bone, I pulled the collar of my coat higher up around my neck and and walked off to rejoin my friend who had gone off to do a spot of shopping. Maybe this could be read as cowardice but I don't think so. I opted for the peaceful route. Just wish I had opted for it a bit earlier and not stood in the raw street.

As the blood slowly edged its way back into my frozen bones, I thought about the unhelpful woman. She is probably on a minimum wage. Maybe she was working an extra shift. Maybe she was worried about something at home. Maybe some prima donna had annoyed her. When I thought about it there were lots of maybes. She still should have been more pleasant. She doesn't know me or my life either. Has no idea what I might have been facing that day. In the scale of things though, my life is a good one. I was going home to a warm house with food, ease and people who loved me. My scarf was precious on a sentimental level but not worth creating a full scale stooshie over and my coat collar was beginning to do a fairly good job at keeping my neck warm. I pulled my woolly hat firmer over my ears and and galloped on towards my friend and our arranged meeting place of the station where I reckoned I should have time to get a hot cup of green tea before the train was due.

Later that evening my mobile phone buzzed. It was my bookshop friend emailing me a photo of her boyfriend holding up a scarf. My scarf.

— *Is this it, Anne?*
— *Yes. Hurrah! Where did you find it?*
— *Under your seat in the theatre.*

Ah. Right. Hmmm. Under my seat. Glad I shelved the outraged customer scene.

Observing the Border

Trains. Trains are thinking places — at least this one is. I am on my way to Surrey in England and, at this moment, am enjoying the swathes of green fields, bundles of sheep, collations of houses, solitary stone-built farm steadings and twisting roads that lace the Borders. I am enjoying it all especially as, after Wigan Northwestern, I may have to relinquish this forward-facing seat with its entertaining window, and move back to my actual designated reserved seat — backwards facing with much less window. Fair is fair though. This seat may be the rightful one of some more needful body than I. I will give it up with a murmur but, in the meantime, shall continue to enjoy it.

Should the continuing tableaux afforded by the window begin to wane and lose my attention, I have other sources of entertainment. I have *The Scotsman* newspaper in my bag. I bought it in Central Station in Glasgow. I bought it for various reasons. It is a compact newspaper, changing in 2004 from being a broadsheet to the size it is now. Much easier to wield when on a busy train and mindful of elbow space. It is also not a stupid paper. It avoids sensation and aims for serious reporting. And I retain a curiosity about the paper because it was the newspaper of choice of my dad. When most other men would get *The Daily Record* or *Glasgow Herald* for amusement on the hour-long bus journey into their daily darg in the city, Dad would buy *The Scotsman.* I never quite appreciated how different this was, even though I knew we had to ask for it at the local newsagent as it wasn't out on the shelves. Dad was a convinced Scottish Nationalist when most men around were staunch Labour voters and as *The Scotsman*, at its inception in 1817, had stated its intention to be a paper committed to 'impartiality, firmness and independence', Dad must have decided that it still merited his readership. This is why I occasionally buy it and scan its columns, hoping that it is now perhaps swinging back to its original ethos. Regrettably they now interpret 'independence' in lower-case. In the still rather raw 2014 Referendum, *The Scotsman* came out as a strong 'No' voice — or, more accurately, 'No, *theenk* you' seeing as they are an Edinburgh based establishment. Dad would have been very disappointed in their decision.

While silently harrumphing at its political palimpsest, I continued to scan today's offerings of what is going wrong and what is going right in the world. As usual, the weighting is with the former. Gloomy reading indeed but it does provide an accompaniment, of sorts, to the overpriced cup of green tea I bought in a concourse cafe and carried onto the train. To be sipping a cuppa of choice while on a train slowly making its way out of Central Station is one of my most favourite things — (raindrops on roses are, I accede, a close contender). When I was teaching in two of Glasgow's universities I would look forward to the moment when I had successfully completed my teaching quota, with all the associated bits of fussy admin required, and was on the train home. With a restorative hot cup of tea in hand, I would happily sit and let my eyes glide up to the Grade A listed elegant Victorian roof of Central Station and how it then gives way to the bridge over the Clyde and the kaleidoscope of weathers that provide a backdrop to the city's skyline. I am deeply fond and loyal to this city and indeed of the west of Scotland. It is home and many of the people I most care about live here. If truth be told, I would rather not be on this train even though it is the right thing to be doing. I utter a silent word or two to my special ones as we cross the Clyde then settle down with my newspaper and tea.

I also have two books. One is Colm Tóibín's novel, *Nora Webster*, published in 2014. It is the choice for this month's read of a book group which I am still an occasional attender of. The other is the perhaps unwise choice of Stuart Kelly's study *Scott-land: The Man Who Invented a Nation* (2011). I am not particularly a Walter Scott scholar, nor enthusiast, but at the Wigtown Book Festival a short while previously, I had enjoyed a literary joust with Stuart Kelly while being interviewed by him, live on radio, about my book *Provenance*. Looking around our local library on my return home from a recent bookshop shift — I hear your surprise but the library still has tempting volumes to satisfy my bibliophile acquisitiveness — I had come across Kelly's volume. The introduction reminded me of his bold stabs of critique and I had borrowed it in the hope of being once more entertained by his verbosity and also perhaps learn a little more about Scott, a landmark literary figure who did so much to construct a particular understanding of Scottishness. I had had little time to get to dive into its pages before I was called south and, being unsure of exactly when I would return home, I thought that I would defend myself from the scary abyss of a book space and take a lengthy chewable tome with me. The 'unwise' aspect of my choice is that Kelly's book is in hardback and is weighing down my bag. I am of the philosophy though that books are worth the lugging.

Kelly's *Scott-land* was published in 2010. It is therefore more cognisant of a Scotland that was settling down to its new Parliament with powers devolved from Westminster, following a long campaign for a Scottish Assembly. If you are reading this outside of Scotland, or are new to Scotland, I should perhaps explain that governance in Scotland is a bit complicated. Our educational and legal systems have remained autonomous despite the Union of Crowns, when James VI of Scotland became James I of Britain in 1603, and the Union of Parliaments in 1707. Two vital infrastructures that were never signed away. And, significantly, the monarch of Great Britain and Northern Ireland, isn't the head of the Church of Scotland. The concept of Divine Right holds no sway north of the border but instead the *A Claim of Right for Scotland* (1989), resting on *The Claim of Right Act* (1689) which limited the power of the monarch, recognises the sovereignty of the Scottish people. In common parlance, the Court, the Kirk and the Schule have endured in Scotland when all else disappeared to London and a Westminster administration. Things have moved on apace politically in Scotland since the appearance of Kelly's volume. I wondered as I opened its pages if he would have written a different book about one of Scotland's greatest literary figures — a figure who balanced and inscribed the paradoxical position of nationalist unionist — in the light of the 2014 Independence Referendum and all the narratives that stirred up.

Toíbín and Kelly — an Irish writer of fiction with truth in his imaginings and a Scottish writer of biographical and social critique. Both writers interested in borders, in identity, what makes us who we are and how we still have a choice despite the weight of our histories. Newspaper scanned, I held both books in my hands. Which to choose?

I like the writing of Toíbín. He is, one of the few male authors (in my humble opinion) who can actually write women and write them convincingly. He gets what we are interested in and refuses to opt for the Angel or Monster characterisation so beloved by Dickens and so many male writers. I heard Toíbín recently on *Desert Island Discs* where he confessed that as a child he was surrounded by women whom he would innocently eavesdrop on for hours — the women never suspecting that he was listening — and therefore he caught the tone and concerns of the women.

Toíbín and Kelly are vastly different storytellers as far apart perhaps as Toíbín and Scott. Toíbín writes for us today. Walter Scott wrote in a time when there was no TV, no radio, no Waterstones, Amazon, Apple, Facebook, Google or something called The Internet (dear Lord, how did they operate?). Scott was fond of quoting advice from *Don Quixote*, 'Patience, cousin, and shuffle the cards,' which tells us more about Scott than Cervantes' character. The pace of life in the early nineteenth century was completely different. News and information came slowly. Readers had more headspace to digest, to ruminate, to consider, to ponder. The printed word, especially that in a bound book form, was a luxury. The innovative idea of affordable paperbacks hadn't yet happened. Personal owned copies of his novels were for the moneyed. If very lucky, lower classes could get occasional access by other means. In Margaret Oliphant's novel *Kirsteen* (1890), for example, the narrator describes how the benevolent owner of a London dressmaking business encourages her tired workers by reading aloud to them as they sewed late into the night:

> She read in the first instance stories out of the *Ladies' Museum* and kindred works, which were about as absurd as stories could be, but being continued from week to week, kept up a certain interest among the girls to know what happened to Ellen as an example

of youthful indiscretion, or Emily as a victim of parental cruelty. What a jump it was when Miss Jean brought in with triumphant delight a book called *Waverley; or 'Tis Sixty Years Since*, I can scarcely venture to describe.

In contrast to this slow-moving scene, the published word today is pitted against all else that competes for our attention. We are used to almost instant access to information through virtual mediums, our mobile phones attached to our person pelt us with detail upon detail throughout our day and sometimes our night, insistent and pushy television screens in pubs, cafes, train and bus stations tell us what is making news headlines, whether we want to know or not. Kindle editions of *Waverley* can be had for pennies — or for no pennies but just postage — on Amazon. The entire corpus of Scott's novels can be downloaded, for free, on Project Gutenberg.

I choose Kelly's book. It's a library book and I may need to return it soon if another reader wants it. I read for some ten pages or so which takes longer than it should as I keep lifting my head to look out of the window and think other thoughts. Perhaps I should apply some of my own advice that I used to issue when undergraduate students were required to read a novel by Walter Scott: *Begin reading / keep reading / ignore Scott showing off his legal knowledge / keep ignoring it / keep reading / stay sitting resisting all temptation to chuck the book out the window / keep resisting and keep reading until an hour is up / Scott will now have stopped showing off and the real story has begun / it'll be a good story and worth the initial pain / now reward yourself with a cup of coffee and a chocolate biscuit / sit back down and pick up the book again / the worst is over / you're into it / enjoy.*

No. That's unfair. My flichterin thoughts will simply not be contended by others' words. I put both books and newspaper back in my bag. I cannot blame my lack of attention on technological overload nor the furious pace of modern life. More like emotional overload. My aunt is ill. My elderly mum has already made the long journey down to the south of England and is in need of some assistance to make the long journey back again. I have had to shelve what I had planned for the next few days, throw some clothes in a suitcase, and get on a train. This trip was an unexpected one. By rights I should be at home at my desk writing. This isn't a designated 'quiet carriage' but it is hushed nonetheless. Perfect for thought forming and word choosing. I am aware that I should savour and make use of the quiet, hurtling as we are towards noise. London. Always an assault on the senses — at least the jolt across the city on the underground is. I resolve to set my mental dial to *Patient* and thus cope with it all. My gaze wanders back to the window and the tantalising country lanes, fields and trees arrayed in their Autumnal colours. I wish I was moving towards a different place of arrival. I wish I was travelling to a place where woolly socks, wellies, big jumpers and cosy coats are what is needed. Ah me, that would be nice. It is, unfortunately, the stuff of fantasy.

There is a sudden carfuffle. Oxenholme arrivals are disconcerted to find that their reserved seats already have an elderly woman and a businessman in them. Watching the interaction I think it a wise plan for me to move back to my 'proper' seat before I too am unceremoniously ousted. It doesn't ever wash why you are in someone else's seat. They don't care. They are too new onto the train to realise that they could jiggle their seat options too. One always feels like a bit of a spectacle to all the other settled passengers when you join a train. The elderly lady and the business man move to the other side of the table. They keep it all amicable. The new couple hoist their backpacks onto the luggage rack above, take off their outer gear and stuff it up there too, then with a sigh, sit down — trying all the time not to look at the people occupying the seats at the other side of the shared table. When they are more or less settled, I get up with my assortment of belongings and move back a few rows. I could explain to them why I am moving but guess they will work it out.

Now travelling backwards, the sense of leaving something is impressed on me. I think of Karine Polwart, the traditional singer-songwriter, and her song 'We're All Leaving' recorded on her album *Traces* (2012). The refrain runs around my mind. I am now in England, not Scotland. It is a different country try, as some might, to say that we are the same — that we are all British, that there are no real differences. Scott has often been viewed as arguing for the Union in his novels. Other critics, such as Edwin Muir, have read Scott as being more inclined to accept the status quo, to accept what was already there. Douglas Gifford, in his essay 'Scott's *Waverley*' in the impressive but hefty anthology *Scottish Literature* (2002) that could also serve as a small footstool, questions if Scott decided to adopt the impartial position of disengaged observer because any deeper involvement led to personal hurt and division. On the other hand, Lockhart, Scott's son-in-law and biographer, counters this by inscribing the patriotic and nationalistic Scott in his *Memoirs of The Life of Sir Walter Scott* (1837 - 39). As Scott has Andrew Fairservice of his novel *Rob Roy* (1817) assert:

> That it was an unco change to hae Scotland's laws made in England, and that, for his share, he wadna for a' the herring-barrels in Glasgow, and a' the tobacco-casks to boot, hae gien up the riding o' the Scots Parliament, or sent awa' our crown, and our sword, and our sceptre, and Mons Meg, to be keepit by thae English pock-puddings in the Tower o' Lunnon. What wad Sir William Wallace, or auld Davie Lindsay, hae said to the Union, or them that made it?

All of these positions — Unionist, detached observer, passionate patriot and also the oscillating 'Mibbes Aye, Mibbes Naw' — were in evidence in the 2014 Scottish Indy Ref. It is futile to go into a discussion of a whole host of other factors that came winging into play around that time and in particular in the last week leading up to the vote. What's done is done. It is not irrevocable though. Scotland does not now stand where she did. Too much has happened since. Too many decisions have subsequently been taken for our nation that are in contradiction to our wishes. A new chapter with a whole new narrative is being constructed in Scotland. A new narrative where difference will be celebrated not ignored or denigrated. A new narrative where our culture, history, voice and hopes are not viewed as odd, unimportant or irrelevant, but as central, workable and normal.

Meanwhile, as this train moves steadily over the border and ever deeper into another land, a land with its own problems to solve, a land which is home to family members I hold dear, a land with its own language, accents and opinions, a land questioning its identity now that we are where we are, I remind myself to move my Scottish money to a different part of my purse. They will not be needed where I am going. In Glasgow's Central Station I deliberately paid for my newspaper and tea with a Scottish five-pound note as issued by The Clydesdale Bank. Such notes over the border are treated with suspicion or simple bafflement. The larger currency notes that I took from the ATM in the station — issued by The Bank of Scotland and The Royal Bank of Scotland — will also be problematic. They are ok on the train. The staff are used to them. They should be ok in London but my experience is that, once out of the metropolis, Scottish printed notes are viewed as unacceptable. If I do try to use them I expect to have to patiently wait until they are stared at, held up to the light and examined. Then I wait a bit more for someone to phone their supervisor or manager or head office to check they are legal. If feeling obstinate, and if I have time, I sometimes say, in an irritable tone, that we accept English notes in Scotland without quibble and ours are legal tender believe it or not. Memories of all the scare-mongering about Scotland losing the pound if we voted for independence now make me grimace. Which pound, exactly, was that? And em, it wasn't ever Westminster's to decide. However, chances are that I will just go and get some English notes from somewhere and avoid the frustration and rising annoyance.

It is in such small, yet highly telling detail, that the vehicles of cultural difference are found. In the opening chapter of Kelly's *Scott-land*, which I did manage to read and retain, Kelly notes how a traveller from London to Edinburgh may be initially forgiven for thinking that the British Isles are a homogeneity. Globalisation has seen to it that recognisable international shop chains, with their weel kent brands, pepper Waverley Station as does a large television screen raining *Sky News* upon all heads and sensitivities. Apart from some tacky tourist items of the tartan and shortbread tin variety, Kelly says that there is no particular visual indication that you are now in another country. This impression lasts until some verbal exchange is necessary and the language that is Scots makes its presence known. Or when distinctive bank notes are utilised without the merest hesitation. The awareness that this is *not England* impinges. It works both ways of course. This is evident to me in that the staff who joined the train at Preston have a very different accent and syntax to those who worked the first stretch of the route. Their voices are higher and have elongated vowel sounds. The new passengers are opening up a newspaper that is not *The Scotsman* or any other Scottish-based publication. They pass comments on the leading articles such as 'I see his nibs is being rather naughty again' instead of 'Och, that man's a pure eedjit' and ask each other if they would like 'a sandwich' and not 'a wee piece'.

It is borne in on me that I have crossed the border.

On the Wings of Endorphins

It is mid-December and a dreich afternoon. People hunch over their coat collars, pull their hoods tighter around their heads. But I, I am insulated from their misery. I am insulated from their misery because I am running. Oh, is there anything like it? Is there anything that can expand the heart — figuratively and actually — so life-givingly well? I breathe steadily, deeply, slightly stretch my gait into a long lopping style — at least I think it is long and lopping, it feels confident, happy, like an engine moving up and settling into fifth gear. I can maintain this for a while yet. I have hit 'the flow' and life is good. The rain is still drizzling I feel it on my face and hands, but I have stopped feeling any cold. A mile or so back I tugged my thick cotton buff off my neck and stuffed it into my jacket pocket along with my gloves. The vents in my jacket were zipped open a mile before that. I am running down the long road towards my end of the town, the hardest bit of the run done, the hills, apart from one, now scaled and over.

When I turned onto this road I had 'Panis Angelicus' sung by the Welsh-voiced Aled Jones on my iPod. When the opening bar was played I instinctively lifted my hand to touch the screen onto the next choice. Then I thought 'Why not? Why not run to a lyric that has as its title 'Bread of Angels'? Right at the moment I am flying with the Angels. They understand and are blowing me along, laughing. What of it, if it is wet, if for others, it feels dreary and the sky is darkening even though it is but three o'clock in the afternoon? There is joy and life to be had out in these streets.

The music changes to 'Si Tu Vois Ma Mère'. I skim past the people holding shopping bags, waiting at the bus stop, frowning into the wind. It is true what they say — change your perspective and everything changes.

I am rejoicing in being alive, in feeling my muscles move in time with each other, in feeling my heart beat. I am in a bubble of happiness while on the same street as the people wondering where the bus has got to.

The music moves on to Jack Jones advising us to take life easy. I agree with him but for this hill I need a little more motivation. My wet hands take a moment to make an impression on my iPod screen but then an upbeat riff from Dave Stewart of The Eurthymics fills my head and I am pushing my arms, breathing in short sharp breaths and ... getting ... up ... this ... hill ...right ... to ... the ... top ... yeah! Crossing down and into the long straight road that is an extension of our own road, I run its length then turn, steady myself and jog slowly back to our end. The song now is 'Bonnie Glen Shee' sung in the rich mahogany tones of Jim Malcolm for whom singing in Scots is as natural as breath itself. I think how lucky I am to be here, to be part of this cool and wet land which has brought fire to my cheeks and life to my body and elevation to my senses. If that taxi wasn't sitting there with its window down to let the cigarette smoke out while on his ten-minute break, I think I might turn some twirls in the road. Instead I walk, lightly swinging my arms, to our front door, tug the key out of my pocket, turn it in the lock, close the door behind me. Sam calls down the stairs 'Good run?'

'Excellent,' I reply, beginning my stretches.

That, I must quickly say, was all a description of what can happen mid run, or towards the end of a run. It actually started with me looking out of the dining room window, the kitchen window, the bedroom window and chatting with myself: 'Those clouds have rain in them. Maybe I'll not bother. I mean, I can run at the weekend, can't I?' An image of a gruesomely wet Saturday or Sunday morning hoved into my head. There will be high temptation to stay in my jim-jams, slop about in my dressing-gown, munching toast and enjoying a pot of properly infused tea. Colum will be around and he will probably offer to take the dogs out. I can stay inside and enjoy doing so. And there are all those Christmas presents to be bought. I may decide to do that instead of going out for a run. Yes, I know I could do both, but this is me, not Mrs Totally-Dedicated-To-Fitness and so I will probably decide for the shopping and the visit to a cafe to read papers and drink yet more tea. I should therefore run today. In fact, right now before those nasty clouds get here.

'Just do it girl!' I say to myself.

Shivering, I pull off my warm layers and pull on what feels like damp running gear. My feet are like ice. I take my running socks downstairs and drape them on a radiator. They can have five minutes there while I faff about getting on my jacket, adjusting my iPod and watch and finding my keys and tissues. I think of the running wisdom which says something about 'The hardest part of running is getting yourself over the doorstep'. That is so very true.

Six minutes later I am out in the street. The warmed socks help a bit but my feet and now my ankles feel like two brittle bricks. I do some daft mincing steps along the street, conscious of a van parked halfway along and of what looks like an electric meter inspector moving between the houses. 'Look at the state of her,' I imagine they are saying. 'Middle-aged woman thinking she can run. Pathetic really.'

I turn up the hill. This is better. I can dig in a bit without worrying about slipping on leaves and the muck that a fortnight of rain accumulates. The hill then goes down and halfway I begin to feel my feet return to my body. I tell myself to relax and go with the run. My body will sort itself out. It really is cold though and the rain is beginning to make itself known. I am glad I have wound a buff around my neck. The cold is useful though. It makes me go faster.

A few streets later I turn into the park. The entrance also has a layer of compressed leaves. I slow down and cross it carefully. My mouth is full of gunk and I spit it out. I see the shape of a woman walking towards me. Probably thinks it disgusting to see a woman spit. Oh well, the rain will wash it away. The woman comes nearer then stops. I wait for her to voice her protest but she calls, 'Hi Anne!' It is my cousin. How nice. I stop, turn my watch and iPod off.

'Don't get cold,' she says, concerned.

We blether about a recent visit from her sister. We blether about my mum's teeth. And we blether about how good it is to get outside while there is still some daylight. I feel a shimmer of sub-zero air around my body, need to get going again. We quickly arrange a coffee date and go our separate ways. I am glad I chanced the rain and came out.

My cousin had also remembered that it was my dad's anniversary recently. He died some eleven years ago. I think about him as I run. I sometimes do this when running on my own. Once I heard his voice. This happened as I was pounding along in the 'gasp' stage of a 10k run on a very cold June evening down in Ardrossan — a small town on the west coast. I had got off on a fast start because it was so flipping freezing and my legs and arms were totally goose-bumped. It had taken the blood a while to get going in my veins and, by that time, I realised I was making excellent progress and definitely in line for a personal best. Adrenaline took over and I hammered round the course and towards the last kilometre. As I came up a path park which led back to the seafront I began to feel slightly queasy — a result both of my pace and rising excitement. Some months previous to this I had been ill. Very ill. Pancreatitis had followed a neglected gall bladder problem and I did the whole emergency blue lights and A&E scene. Thanks to some skilled doctors who diagnosed, operated on and patched me up, I mended. I had lost quite a bit of weight though due to my body's inability to cope with intake of fat and, on the evening of the Ardrossan 10k, I was still a very neat size. Being light can work for runners as you are not lugging around any excess body fat. Difficulty though is making sure you have enough stored energy to keep the legs moving. Anyway, it was all working for me in Ardrossan and I was feeling elated. So perhaps it was either falling blood sugar or the pump of adrenaline which caused me to suddenly hear Dad's voice saying quite clearly 'Keep it steady. Keep it steady.' I smiled, slowed slightly, raised my head higher, relaxed my shoulders and ran on towards the promenade, towards the very welcome finish line and a very creditable personal best.

I took up running when Dad had finished his. We had never ran together. I would have liked that although I suspect that Dad always really thought that running wasn't for women. When I was growing up I only remember one woman from our neighbourhood who ran. One woman whom lots of people thought quite mad for doing so. She did this on her own, I think, as then there weren't the plethora of groups to enable women to get into running. Probably there was the option of a serious running club but there is a difference between being a club member and a member, as I am, of a local 'jogging' group. Don't ever make the mistake though of calling me a jogger. I jog to warm up, and jog to warm down, in between I RUN. There, that's you warned. When I think back on Mary, the running woman from our estate, I see now that she must have been made of tough stuff. To persist in doing something you like, something that brings you joy and to ignore the constant raised eyebrows or shakes of the head, well, that's true endurance. And she wasn't young. I reckon she must have been in her late forties or fifties when she took up running the streets, canal banks, country roads of my home town. Nowadays it is quite normal to see a woman running. We only think her mad if it is truly blitzing buckets of rain or is icy underfoot. Having said that though I do remember chugging over a snow-laden golf course one Boxing Day with my running mates. Crazy women.

My Dad remains, not so much my inspiration, but as a kind of silent running companion. As my cousin astutely remarked, he would have understood why I run, he does understand why I run, and whenever I take a moment to think on him, he is there with me. Out there in it all. Running, breathing, grinning and running. Whether or not I will ever achieve his remarkable feat of doing his first marathon at the age of 63 remains to be seen. If I am still running by then that will be a feat itself. Meanwhile, I run on.

I came relatively late to the sport. This can actually be seen as a plus in that I started too late in life for my knees to be knackered by now. There just hasn't been the time span for that. I began running 'seriously' when I was nearing my 40th birthday. The word 'seriously' definitely needs scare quotes around it as myself and runners such as Paula Radcliffe are light years apart in experience and will always be thus. My 'seriously' still only amounts to two to three sessions a week. She regularly averages two sessions a day. But then, running is her work, her *raison d'être*. Whereas running for me is neither, fond though I am of it. When I was in my twenties I did a couple of 10ks. This was thanks to a teaching colleague, Betty, who looked at me in the staff room one lunchtime and said 'How about doing a bit of running, Anne? You look like you could do it.' Rather flattered by this I agreed to meet her the next day after the final bell and do a trial session out on the school running track. Betty was quite a bit older than me, probably somewhere in her fifties at the time, and I naively presumed that she couldn't be all that physically fit and would be slow. Eh, no. After half a lap I thought my heart was going to fall out whereas Betty was merrily chatting and loping along. I realised there was more to this lark than I had thought. Anyway, she persisted with me and coached me on to entering and completing the first Glasgow Women's 10k. I was still a pretty rubbish runner. Still hadn't really learned to pace myself. Still felt sick half way round. Still thought it a very painful exercise and subsequently only went for a run in sporadic bursts following a fit of guilt. Betty, by contrast, continued running steadily for many more years, and, despite the later challenges of a brain tumour, walked the Camino De Compostela a number of times before she died. I am now probably the same age as she was when she first introduced me to running. And, when young women turn up at the group I now run with, confident in their youth that they will easily leave us oldies behind, I think of Betty and of an earlier and naive me, and inwardly smile.

After that initial spurt in my twenties I more or less gave it up. At that juncture running hadn't really afforded me any great pleasure and, as it turned out, life was to throw me other physical challenges in the game of childbirth which I had a pretty rubbish run of luck with. One perfect and healthy son was born by an emergency caesarean after a few weeks of hyper-tension and hospitalisation which relegated all books on good childbirth scenarios to laughable myths. This was followed three years later by the confusing emotional roller-coaster of a very late miscarriage of a daughter. Finally, another two years on, and what drew a line over any more attempts to expand our family, was the near-death experience of a ruptured ectopic pregnancy. My body and confidence in my body was, to say the least, very low. However, and although I would have slapped anyone who dared to utter such platitude, time does have a way of healing. Following a wise decision not to try for any more children but to be grateful for our lovely son and the fact that I was alive, I slowly began to feel stronger.

In an attempt to get some measure of suppleness back into my body I joined a yoga class. When I first enquired about this class, I asked the teacher on the phone what kind of class it was and would I be out of kilter in it as I didn't think I was particularly bendy. Joyce laughed and said that the class wasn't one of those lycra-bound ones, with sylph-like women swaying to inner rhythmic music and sitting in perfect lotus positions. Instead, she assured me, it was a class for ordinary women of all shapes and sizes, very low key, very slow lane and which happened in a community resource centre in our town. It sounded ok so I went along. I greatly enjoyed the class, it was fun and although many of the stretches were a bit beyond me, quite a number of them weren't. It seemed to me anyway that perfection wasn't what this class was about. Many of the stretches were greeted with giggles or groans and I certainly wasn't the stiffest in the class. At the end of the class Joyce announced that the next week would be slightly different as a BBC camera crew would be filming us. I thought I hadn't heard right. Why would a BBC crew be interested in this class? Some of the women were pretty good but not that good. What was going on?

It turned out that Joyce's class was forming part of a programme on different forms of faith and, through her other work of Life Coaching and counselling, she had been asked to contribute some of her philosophy. I simply thought that fate was having a laugh. Here's me, first time to yoga class after years of body battering, and asked to form part of a telly programme on healing or some such thing. I hadn't even got any trendy yogic clothes — wouldn't viewers expect us all to be in stylish willowy outfits? — somehow my old bobbled black leggings and sloppy T shirt didn't come up to the expected image. Our budget was a tight one as, since Sam had announced his arrival, I had given up my paid job and had done no work outside of the home for some years. Thoughts of a shopping spree and getting myself some fab gear was out. I decided I would ensure I was right at the back of the hall, away from the cameras which, naturally would be on the teacher herself … wouldn't they? I had forgotten of course that cameras can rove. Watching the programme at home some weeks later, we suddenly got a full screen shot of my red face as I attempted to gracefully push my body up into downward-facing-dog, my backside in its scanky leggings on view to the whole nation. My only hope was that the focus of the programme was on methods of achieving humility and suppression of the ego.

I continued with yoga for some years and even contemplated taking on some kind of teaching certificate but for some reason never did. The ironical thing was that we finally moved out of our tiny modern four-in-block flat and moved to a much larger Victorian one which is our present home. Our house has more than adequate space for yoga practice but, due to the perverseness of human nature, I had rarely spread out my mat in any of the rooms. Life at that point was too full of walking the two large dogs who had made their home with us by then. That tale can be found in another of my books should you be curious.

Some years later I picked up a newspaper one Saturday morning which carried an article whose first line was 'Do you feel like something the sea has washed up?' I sighed and read on. The article was in effect an advert for the Glasgow women's 10k which was once again materialising in May of that year. I was reading this sometime in the early Spring but, even so, the month of May seemed to suddenly loom very close. I asked Colum if he thought I could do it and without lifting his eyes off the sports section of the newspaper said, 'Piece of cake'. Pleased at his confident response but also thinking he was just trying to boost my battered self-confidence, I decided that I could at least try. A few days later while swimming (slowly) up and down at the ladies' hour in our local swimming pool, I mentioned my half-resolve to a friend. She told me that another friend of hers was also going to train for it and that I might like to get in touch with her. That evening I called a woman called Frances and my real running life began.

Our first run together came to pass on a very cool Saturday morning. I drove up to her house feeling quite nervous as we were also meeting up with two other women who had run for quite a while and were a few years younger than us. When I had looked out that morning it seemed very chilly and I had wrapped myself up in thick tracky bottoms, a short-sleeved T-shirt, a long-sleeved T-shirt and a snug fleece top and a waterproof kagoul. Getting out of the car and feeling the cold wind I wondered if I had enough layers on. Some 30 metres along our first road I thought I was going to explode with heat. The sweat was trickling down my back, down my face and I felt terrible. My legs were like jelly and my heart was trying to burst out of my chest. Three-quarters of the way along the road, a road which didn't seem any distance in the car, I had to stop and gasp and gasp. I took off my kagoul and wrapped it round my waist, and then continued on. The two younger and more experienced women had shot ahead and were last seen by us as they steadily climbed up a gradual hill. Glad of each other's company and solidarity of unfitness, Frances and I staggered after them stopping every 50 metres or so to walk and steady our breath. We finally returned to the starting point some fifteen minutes after the first two women. 'The trick,' one of the women said 'is not to stop. Just try going a bit slower instead.' I didn't confess that that was my slowest pace and, if I hadn't stopped I would have collapsed. I just gave a half-hearted grin, said nothing, and gulped some water.

And that was the beginning. Our aim was to run for over seven minutes without stopping. That might be laughable, but to us it seemed almost impossible. I finally broke that barrier when on holiday in Findhorn. On the flat beach one morning I decided to run until I couldn't run anymore and not look at my watch. I did so. When I had given my all, I looked at my watch. Fourteen minutes. Hurrah!! I smugly boasted of this on a postcard to Frances and continued to pound up and down the beach every second day for the rest of the holiday.

Of course, what I hadn't realised in those early weeks, was that the pain or stiffness or sheer 'Why the hell am I doing this?' feeling is just that of a fairly normal warm-up. In his extended essay *What I Talk About When I Talk About Running* (2009), Haruki Murakami tells us of his surprise when interviewing an Olympic runner and asking him if he ever felt he didn't want to train that day. The runner looked at Muakami as if he was an idiot and replied that he felt like that most days. The difference being that he didn't give in to his lethargy — unlike us very lesser mortals. Nowadays, I con myself by beginning many a run by saying to myself 'Right. 20 mins. Just 20 mins today and that'll do. C'mon. You can do that easy-peasy.' And, of course, by the time my watch is registering 20 mins I am a distance from the house, all warmed up, cantering along, thinking other thoughts entirely. In the early days, just being able to run non-stop for over ten minutes seemed a major challenge. However, from the seemingly impossible aim of 14 mins, we progressed to a lot more. We did the Glasgow Women's 10k even though we had only managed to train up to 4 miles. And we ran the whole way. As I came in over the finishing line, feeling highly emotional, there was a line of white-suited young men standing with armfuls of long-stemmed white roses. A smiling lad handed me one. I felt like hugging him but the rational part of my brain told me that being embraced by a sweaty and tear-stained middle-aged woman, probably wasn't what he was looking for. I just thanked him and walked on to collect the finisher's medal. There was a note pinned onto the stem of the rose. It said, *'For Women Who Stop Traffic.'* By the time I met up with Colum I could hardly speak but just kept waving the rose saying 'Oh, *look ... look...!'*

Riding high on our success Frances then suggested that we join up with other women to keep the momentum going. She had heard of a new initiative in our town — a group called 'Jogging Buddies' — started by a woman, Susan, who had once been a Commonwealth runner. Join we did and our running life expanded. Thanks to Jogging Buddies I have met up with some amazing women who have become more than just running companions. They are my friends whom I share the variations of life with. Out there running, meeting up for an occasional coffee or just sharing a long phone call, there isn't much we don't talk about. Other people would pay a lot of money for such therapy that my wonderful running gals provide. And also thanks to Jogging Buddies we were introduced to the incomparable Margo, our running coach for the past twelve years or more. Margo has enthused, motivated, and persuaded us into greater distances, greater challenges. We found ourselves training and doing The Arbroath Smokies, women only, ten-mile race. An event still very fondly remembered for the heavenly home-baking in the sports centre afterwards. And doing this again and again and again. In-between times we did more 10ks around the west of Scotland, the Millport 10 miler (which must be the windiest course ever on record), the Loch Katrine 12k (where we memorably ran around a chair at the half way mark and also drank champagne at the post-run picnic) and finally up to half-marathon stage.

It wasn't all a smooth track. There were a number of events that I entered only to find that my body wasn't up for it. I remember one occasion in particular when, finding myself in hospital, recovering from severe anaemia, I weepily told the phlebotomist that 'I should be out there running the Paisley 10k today'. Looking at my pale face she said 'Really?' Guess she thought my blood count must be very low indeed if I had reached hallucinatory level. On the plus side though, just in case you think I was a total nutter doing distance running while battling with anaemia, my strong heart, good bone density and overall fitness has been a major factor in enabling me to recover well after any illness.

And sometimes running speaks to a part of ourselves that other things just don't. I am completing this chapter in early January. I have just come home from a gallop around the streets. I needed to run, not for the exercise but for the sake of my overfilled mind. The new year was barely born when within the scope of a few days some serious happenings occurred in our extended family. The twenty-five-year-old son of my sister-in-law passed away in his sleep and was found the next day by his flatmate. Neither drugs, drink or depression were the cause but some strange blip of nature. Then, yesterday teatime, a ward nurse had phoned us to say that Colum's brother been admitted to hospital. Another elderly cousin whom we view as an aunt, has cancer of the oesophagus and has been given an estimate of a few months on this earth. And, to cap it all, my old mum was told today that she has cancer of the jawbone. Quite a cocktail of concerns all in all.

My sister came over with our mum after their talk with the consultant. Over lunch we went over the possible options for mum, exchanged thoughts, laughed a bit, drank tea, ate beans on toast, talked of what we could do to make the next few months as pleasant as possible and then they left. I remembered it was also Colum's mum's birthday and that I must phone her. But my head couldn't cope. There seemed to be a tight band behind my eyes and over my forehead. I went upstairs and pulled on my running gear. Time to hit the streets.

'It's sleeting,' said Colum.

'That's ok,' said I.

Out I went. The temp was just above freezing. The light was fading and it was indeed sleeting. The ground was wet but not icy. I zipped my jacket higher up my neck, stuffed one earphone of my iPod into my ears but didn't press my stopwatch. This was not that kind of run. As I began a slow trot along the street warming up my limbs, I thought how wonderfully lucky I was to have running in my life. Running which calms me, clears my thoughts, eases my mind. I returned 45 minutes later, soaking and peaceful, ready to cope. Blessed sport.

Food of the Gods

This chapter isn't beginning the way I planned. I had this lofty notion that I would tell you of the Buddhist teaching — oft quoted by Colum who now says that he can't quite remember where he heard or read it — that the first most enlightened person in the monastery is the Abbot and the second is the Cook. This would then lead me nicely on to a blether about the sacramental and sacred elements of food, how important it is that we all appreciate it as such and how vital it is that our food is produced gently and naturally and wholesomely. Yes, that was the plan. To help me I had to hand *My New Roots* by Sarah Britton which was lent to me by my friend, Amy. Amy had recently treated us to a home-cooked meal which had taken vegetarian, vegan, dairy and gluten-free cooking to a whole new level. Some of Amy's incredible hot and cold dishes, breads, mousses, spreads, cheeses and jam, had apparently been inspired by Sarah Britton's book. It's a very attractive book with colourful and creative photography — and that's just the front and back covers. I accepted the offer of a loan with glee and was looking forward to a decent reading session, a shot at some of the recipes, and a thoughtful appraisal of such. It was also Amy who inadvertently planted the idea that I write about cooking as a form of mindfulness. I had today — a clear day with nothing else scheduled but a road run this evening — to take the plunge. But nobody told the sun.

It is early February, just after Candlemas, and we have had weeks and weeks of rain in all its varieties. So, waking up today to note the lack of water lashing the windows was a surprise. Jenna, refused to come back into the house after her post-breakfast sniff about the garden and Colum, seeing there was no need to insist as I was at home today, had left her there. He then rattled off to his voluntary stint with the jolly Fairtrade folk, and I decided to join Jenna in the garden. There was a straggling mulchly clump of old crocosmia that needed clipping back before the new shoots would make their presence known and this morning felt like the morning to do just that. Armed with pruning gloves, two pairs of socks inside my wellies, two T shirts, old jeans only fit for gardening in, warm fleece, ancient jacket, cosy bunnet, bottle of water to refill the birds' water bowl and an apple for Jenna, I happily clumped down to the garden.

And, oh, what joy to be had. I pruned and gathered and swept and clipped and had a merry old time of it. Pausing every so often to stand and bathe my face in the weak sun that had slowly edged its way into the garden. Weak and yet curiously warm. Such a welcome guest. A wee blue-tit was chirping its heart out as it tummled its wulkies on a branch in one of the lime trees. After an hour and a half I returned to the house for a mug of coffee and sat on the front door step, still wrapped up in my gardening gear, and still loathe to go inside. Jenna had come up with me this time and, tired out from 'helping', was happy to go indoors and find her bed. I left her snoozing and carried on my own for another hour. I was conscious that precious writing time was slipping by but the lure of the outside, the temptations of the light and that sun were too much for my feeble spirit and, rebelling, I gardened on.

The sky began to move back towards its usual grey. The damp began to make its presence known. With a mental pat on the back to myself that I had seized the day, I stored the brush, rake, shovel and secateurs back in the shed, made my way inside, pulled off my mud-crusted wellies and outside layers and put the kettle back on.

It was lunchtime. I judged I needed some food. Having not had time to produce mouth-watering wholefood I opted instead for some ryvita and tuna-mayo with a cup of white tea. That was ok on the 'good food' scale. Well, maybe not the shop-bought high-fat mayo, but so what. When I had become a domestic goddess I would, of course, always have a jar of delicious home-made mayo in the fridge. As it was I had to content myself with the shop stuff. I also wanted something sweet. I ate some Medjool dates that usually suffice in calming down any sugar cravings. They were tasty but … well, I was now tired. I had done my seven-hour stint in the bookshop the day before and had moved a hundredweight of books as well as dealing with the usual array of loiterers … sorry … *customers*. Now, after my enthusiastic gardening session, my body and spirit were nudging me for sweetness. As in chocolate or some delectable cake thing. I opened *My New Roots* and read the introduction and the story of how the author did the paradigm shift of sugar addict to convinced and confident wholefoodie. I sighed and closed the book.

I delayed moving through to my desk by sorting washing. Tidying dry washing to respective rooms, emptying the machine of wet washing, hanging it up and re-filling the machine gave me another half hour or so to ruminate on the concept of 'good food'. And finally, having now no more excuses left, I made myself sit at the computer and pull up a blank page. Despite my earlier anagogic aim of focusing on the divinity of food, I still had a very strong notion either for some squares of dark chocolate or a squidgy slice of Victoria sponge. They would slip down very nicely. Our cupboards however, after a hollow search through them, including all my places for secret stashes, boasted no such delights. Instead I could tickle my taste buds with either a tea biscuit or a fruit bar. I chose the fruit bar as it promised higher sugar content.

There are just some days when sugar or, more accurately, chocolate, is what you want. What your body is telling you to get. I refuse to think that there is anything wrong with that. Specially not if what you are after is dark chocolate without a snifter of sinful cow's milk. At our recent smorgasbord at our friends' home, Amy had made some amazing dark chocolate squares with cacao powder and sprinkled with pumpkin seeds. Unfortunately, I was so full with all else that she had served, I'd had only a nibble. I think I could happily barter my grannie to get a couple of squares of that honeyed stuff today.

Food. A small word but has so many connotations. It's about listening to your body, taking account of its needs, and understanding its cravings. It's about tastes and textures, colours and cultures, memories and moments. It's about identity and passion. It's about blending and mixing. It's about exploring and experimenting. It's about home cooking and cordon-bleu. It's about your mum's great soup or a celeb's signature style. It's about the wider issues of food production, organic versus pesticide, air-freighted versus local, seasonal crops versus imported goods. It is therefore both personal and political.

Food. The dictionary delineates this word as a nutritious substance which is eaten to sustain life and growth. All sounds quite simple. And yet it's complicated. I remember the 80s. The decade when those with a conscience boycotted goods from South Africa in protest about the apartheid regime. These were also the days of 'Campaign Coffee' — an early attempt to highlight the plight of coffee growers in developing countries. What disgusting stuff that was. Ethical, fair, good for the producers and a brave start, marketed in church halls, Oxfam shops and community centres by grassroots workers, but still yuk despite the excellent intentions. It was a measure of just how committed to a fairer world you were if you could stomach more than a half a cup. And then the 90s when we boycotted Nestlé because they aggressively marketed dried milk to nursing mothers in Africa who had no access to clean water. And on it went to today where our buying choices remain hugely important particularly where food is concerned. When I go to the supermarket I only buy bananas that are marked with the Fairtrade Foundation logo. If they are anything else I just do without. Having read an article about children being forced from school to work for huge banana plantations where the workers are also unprotected from hazardous pesticides, I just can't buy anything else than Fair Trade. Other issues connected to large scale producers of bananas are that of low wages, precarious employment and restrictions on the right to organise themselves. And chocolate, that food of the gods, oh crikey Moses, there are issues around that. Lots. The Fairtrade Foundation report that the vast majority of cocoa is produced on small family farms. Growing cocoa trees is a precarious business and, for all their back-breaking efforts, cocoa farmers often only gain a paltry share of the very profitable global cocoa trade and most of them have never tasted chocolate in their lives. It is vital then that the sweet-toothed people of the west buy chocolate from ethical companies such as Divine of which 44% is owned by Ghanian farmer producers. And it tastes darn good.

There are other days though when my principles bite the dust. Like today — the day following my rambling thoughts on the global food and fairtrade issue. A lurking cold had prevented me from doing what

I had planned i.e. meet up with my old mum and have lunch with her. Mum is going into hospital for a major op in the next few days and the last thing she needs is a cold virus. They won't be able to operate if she has one. So, sadly but wisely, I decided not to meet her and focus on getting myself completely well. Some fresh air seemed advisable and, as I also had to pay the local pet shop for a recent order of dog food, I ambled over to a nearby row of shops. The sun has not appeared today but the light is definitely returning and the wee birds are announcing that fact. I hummed the tune to Burns' poem 'The winter it is past, and the summer's come at last / And the small birds, they sing on every tree …' It has a fine melody and imagery. Doesn't matter to me that Burns, as was his want, probably doctored his version from the original Irish song 'The Curragh of Kildare'. It's still very hummable.

As I hummed I was aware that along with my lurking cold I also have a lurking worry associated with mum. She's very elderly and what they plan to do is serious surgery. Necessary, but still serious. Balancing my worry though were the practical things that I could still do for her — like buy some wipes and some face cream for her to take into hospital along with the new jammies and soft shawl I had already got for her. So it was that I found myself in the Co-op perusing the shelves. I got the items for mum easily enough as well as some walnuts, pears, apples and blueberries which are necessities for the classy crumble, as detailed in *My New Roots,* that I plan to make to delight Colum's soul. Then I remembered my chocolate craving of yesterday. Maybe it would be canny to get a wee bar of the stuff in case the chocolate devil appeared again today.

The Co-op usually do a fairly decent line in FairTrade chocolate but today they appeared to have hidden it well out of my sight. There was a queue at the till where only two staff were working and I couldn't see any other staff about. My eye fell on a box of dark chocolate Tunnock's teacakes. I like these. But. Dash it. There is an issue now attached to them. No, it wasn't because they have saturated fat in them, or that they also have cow's milk in them which I try to avoid, but because recently the chaps who own Tunnocks decided to remove the Lion Rampant — the company's symbol since 1890 — from the silver foil encasing the cake and from all packaging. For those of you reading this outside of Scotland that last bit of information might make no sense whatsoever. For those of you inside the nation, it will. Tunnocks is our 'other national biscuit' second only to shortbread or oatcakes. It's sweet and yummy and bad for your teeth and waistline. A perfect biscuit for us. We were proud of this wee biscuit which doubles as a kind of cake. It's squelchy and satisfying. And we were highly amused by the antics of dancers dressed up as Tunnock's tea cakes who cavorted about in the opening ceremony of the Commonwealth Games in Glasgow in full view of a TV audience of millions — the company sales consequently rocketing. Those of us who are protective of our country and would prefer that it think seriously about removing itself from Westminster control as they havenae a clue how we do things here, were seriously dischuffed when Mr Tunnock, 82, who campaigned for a 'No' vote in the 2014 Referendum, announced recently that the biscuit would now be marketed as a 'British' one, not 'Scottish'. Allegedly, to be overtly Scottish is not a good thing. Bang goes all our other national dishes then. Bang goes anything culturally specific to Scotland. What a daft decision. Particularly as following the announcement there were long and loud calls for a boycott all over social media and the word 'Tunnock', as coined on Twitter, now appeared to signify not the biscuit but … um … without wishing to offend, a total lowlife. Well done boys, you may up your sales elsewhere in Britain but in Scotland you are going down. Unless, blast it, for people like me who cave in when feeling low. Who knew something about the issue, hadn't actually researched it properly, and who bought the tempting things because she wanted a wee treat but who now, after reading up on the issue, having eaten and enjoyed the oozy delicacy with a cup of post-shopping tea, feel that any future Tunnock's tea cake will stick in her craw.

Food then comes with issues, which all gets a bit exhausting when all you want to do is whiz round the supermarket and get home to make your dinner. There are, fortunately, other facets to it. Such as friendship, such as nurture, such as sharing, such as love. An appetising casserole from our neighbour Stacy, when I was unwell, was a true gift. My running gals all pitching in to help provide a delectable buffet for a special birthday leaving me free to focus on my guests, was a true gift. A large carton of bruschetta sauce made by my sister-in-law and given simply because we said we loved it, was a true gift. The amazing 'ginger oaties' baked by our friend Liz, because we phoned to say we were nearby and would call in, was a true gift. The community garden-grown potatoes from another friend Sandy, and the numerous bags of garden-grown beans and tubs of raspberries from our neighbour Duncan, were also true gifts. Gifts that don't seek payment other than our appreciation and we give bundles of that.

The philosophy and ethos behind the cooking of food thus flavours its taste. A year or so ago I came across a copy of Sophie Dahl's cookbook *Miss Dahl's Voluptuous Delights* (2009) which made me smile. I thought of our well-thumbed and rather grubby copy of her grandfather, Roald Dahl's fictional food ideas as reconstructed in *Even More Revolting Recipes* (2001). Sam was given this as a Christmas present many years ago. He dived in enthusiastically and experimented with various recipes with various success. His pièce-de-resistance was however his production of 'Wonka's Whipple-Scrumptious Fudgemallow Delight' — a feast, not for the faint-hearted, of ice cream, chocolate, honeycomb, sugar, butter, cream and marshmallows. Adapted, of course to fit Sam's diet by the substitution of cow's milk products for that of soya, and dark chocolate instead of milk and marshmallows with no colouring or additives. He was ten years old when one Christmas Day he whipped up, under the supervision of a hovering adult, this incredible pudding leaving the assembled guests surfeited with its sumptuousness. It has remained his signature dish. Its secret ingredient is in its name. What child or young-at-heart adult can resist its spongy springy mushy title, daring the reader to try it?

This ability to tempt the reader by the use of wonderful words is also a characteristic of Sophie Dahl's cookbooks. Like her grandfather she can write so that the words lift off the page and into the juices of your stomach, your saliva glands and your soul. Food, for Sophie Dahl, is more than just something to fill you up — necessary as that is — but is something that brings enveloping emotions of comfort, serenity, warmth, ease, jubilation or simple happiness. I found Sophie Dahl's book during a time in my life when sleep was eluding me for part of the night. 2am or 3am would find me happed up in my dressing-gown sitting in our kitchen with a camomile tea reading my way through her book.

Making notes about promising sounding recipes, ingredients I needed to find, substitutions I might need to make, I also found nourishment in her memories and musings as I carefully sifted through the pages. In the days that followed my nocturnal reading I experimented with her suggestions. Colum said she had turned his life around as I produced dish after dish with a triumphal cry of 'It's a Sophie Dahl!' When my birthday came around my Mum, at my request, bought me Ms Dahl's next almanac *Season by Season* (2011) and my cousin gave me the DVD, screened in 2010, of the culinary series *The Delicious Miss Dahl* where she demonstrates not just her understanding of cooking but also her easy familiarity with literary influences and the enticement of words. Be warned though. Do not try to read any of her books nor watch the DVD without something tasty to munch on. It would be too denying yourself to the point of cruelty.

Food is a powerful thing. And the withdrawal of food even more powerful. It may interest you to know that the origin of the word *lady* does not have the rather weak, has-to-be-protected, refined, and rather prim association as today's world reads it. On the contrary, the word originates in the Old English *hlǣfdīge* meaning a woman of social standing, usually the wife of the lord of the manor, who was responsible for the provision of bread (*hlaf* in German) to all the extended household. She it was who saw to it that one of the most fundamental human needs — that of food — was made available. And, I think I am correct in saying, that it was also she who decided who wasn't getting a slice. As Woolf advised, 'One cannot think well, love well, sleep well, if one has not dined well.' Making decisions on an empty stomach is always a dodgy thing. Guess that's why, being the astute gender we are, women's gatherings are often graced by cake. After the 2014 Referendum thousands of Scottish women said, 'Right, that was rubbish, it's time we got involved'. We rolled-up our sleeves, got together in groups and pitched into politics. Only, instead of pub-and-a-pint politics, or a tired public hall full of rows of chairs listening to table-thumpers grumping on, we went for cafes where we sit in circles and have tea and cake as we construct active and effective responses to what's wrong in our society and how we can create a kinder one. One of the things we annually collect for is the disgraceful necessity of food banks. In this day and age and in this first world country, that people go hungry is beyond ridiculous. It is more than disgraceful that a C21st government has allowed this to happen when there is more than enough food for all.

So, despite my talk of the blessings of good cook books, special diets and issues around food, at the end of the day I am just thankful that I and my family have enough to eat. The icing on the cake, if you excuse the terrible pun, is that we also have choice. As the famous poem, 'The Selkirk Grace' expresses (the lines attributed to Burns but actually in use long before he put pen to paper, although he reputedly did extemporise it at a dinner given by the Earl of Selkirk):

Some hae meat and canna eat,
And some wad eat that want it;
But we hae meat and we can eat,
And sae the Lord be thankit.

The Dying of the Light ... Not.

Poems by Dylan Thomas run through my mind. 'The Force that through the Green Fuse Drives the Flower' being one. The villanelle, 'Do Not Go Gentle into That Good Night', is also a frequent visitor. My mum, who at the advanced age of 88, has come through a nine-hour operation to remove a tumour from her jaw. My mum, who with the aid of a physio and team of nurses, swung her legs over the side of her bed the next day and walked a few steps, machinery and drips clanking along with her. My mum, who under the instruction of 'Nil by Mouth', longs for a cup of tea, but still smiles and nods when we ask how she is. My mum, who manoeuvres the cumbersome plaster on her arm where they took the bone graft from, to write on her wee whiteboard, with her still clear hand-writing, comments and questions to staff and visitors. My mum, who deftly skims over the ward floor, trailing drains and drip-stand, as I try to keep up with her. My mum, who is apparently a day ahead of usual recovery, amazing the medical staff. In this last age of life but not done yet. Not by a long chalk.

There are two factors at work here. One is her general health. When she was diagnosed with cancer of the jaw, she said to the consultant, 'I feel a bit cheated. I have been a vegetarian for a long long time. Cancer has no place in my body.' So, ok, it's not as simple as that. Cancer has many triggers and many that we do not know of yet. Mum does however have a valid argument. It must surely be true that what you load into your body has an effect on it. More and more we are hearing about the damaging effects of animal fat and all those rubbish chemicals pumped into creatures to fatten them up for our table. I know at least three people, whom having survived a round of cancer, refuse to eat red meat anymore. So perhaps there is much in Mum's viewpoint. The jury, I guess though, is still out on this one.

The other factor surging through Mum's veins is her desire for life. Her desire to 'live deep and suck out the marrow of life' as Thoreau would put it (well, maybe for Mum to suck out the nice feta cheese filling is a more appropriate analogy, but you get my drift). Watching her progress in hospital this week, where she is romping through the expected stages of recovery, I am in awe of her determination and sheer bloody-mindedness that she ain't staying there, that she is recovering and that there is still a lot else she wants to do. And she is totally loving wowing the staff as she romps. Yes, she looks like she and Mike Tyson have slugged it out for twenty-five rounds. Yes, she looks like someone has taken a hatchet to her neck. Yes, her arms and fingers are puffy and swollen and she is most not a sight for sore eyes. But there is something that is making her sit up in bed, attempt to smile, laugh with her eyes, gesture with her bandaged arms, show interest in the doings of us in the outside world, read her books, listen to Gaskell's *North and South* and Austen's *Pride and Prejudice* on her CD player and wait for her body to heal enough so she can get on with her life. I reckon Margaret Hale and Lizzie Bennett were cut from the very same cloth as my Mum.

Determination plays such a part. Mum is refusing, absolutely refusing, to bow down to being either elderly or a cancer patient. We realised that her fighting spirit was up when on the first evening following her long operation, we tip-toed into the High Dependency ward to visit her. She had already by-passed the expected route of staying in Intensive Care for a couple of days. I wonder if she uttered an impatient *Tcha!* to the consultant as he stitched her up making him review her after-care. That first evening Mum had drips and tubes sticking into all parts of her body. It was stomach-churning stuff and the only way I could deal with it was meet it head-on and look at everything and calmly question what it was all for. Mum was distinctly agitated, squirming and attempting to get away from all that was hurting her. The nurse had to tell her a few times that her nose-feed was ok and to try to stop pulling at it. She calmed a little as we held up a laptop screen to show her photos of Sam's recent snow-boarding holiday in France. Mum is like me in that such a holiday holds no attraction for her but she loves her grandson and wanted to see images of his exploits. Then the senior house doctor called by. We asked him questions about Mum while she nodded as best she could and attempted to write on a piece of paper pinned to a clip-board. The effort must have been immense but she persisted and was distressed when we couldn't understand. As we talked with the doctor we realised we knew people in common with him and the round of 'Oh, do you know so-and-so?' began. Mum listened for a bit then began to write on her board and thump it on the sheet. She kept gesturing to a nurse who had entered the room and was dealing with another patient. Mum wrote the word 'Miss!' on her board and indicated in the direction of the nurse.

'Yes, Mum, we're all missing you,' I said.

She shook her head and again pointed at the nurse.

'Um, you want the ... the *miss?* ... to come over?

She hesitated then wrote *Miss me!!* and pointed repeatedly to us then the door. Light dawned.

'Ah, you are worried that the nurse will miss you if we are here?'

She nodded vehemently. She was chucking us out. Injured. Plastered. Cut. Bruised. Still a Mum telling her kids to do as they are told. We left. Promptly.

Prime Importances

It's all getting a bit silly. In the last few days, on top of the continuing situation with Mum where we spend our evenings or afternoons darting in and out of her ward, other life dramas have touched us. One afternoon, as I sat in a quiet corner of the hospital atrium with a peculiar tuna-mayo baked potato in a box that cost some daft amount of money and cursing myself for not bringing lunch with me, my phone buzzed. Colum was in Edinburgh visiting a friend who had just had an operation to remove her eye. His text said that his cousin in Germany, a very fit and active cousin in her early 70s, had gone for a cycle ride that day, had fallen, hit her head and died on the way to hospital. I read it and simultaneously gasped and almost laughed aloud at the random craziness. Later that day my sister contacted me to say my mum's cousin, whom we consider an aunt, had been taken into a Marie Curie hospice for pain relief. Our aunt has inoperable cancer and not many days are left to her. Another for the care and visiting list. The next day we attended the funeral of the dad of my sister-in-law — the same woman who had just buried her twenty-five-year old son and who is in much need of love and support. And yesterday we heard that another of Colum's cousins, a cousin whom he is greatly fond of, has a return of testicular cancer. Lordly Lord. So much going on.

When I get up in the morning I sometimes wait a little before turning on my phone. I know there will be messages and requests all needing responding to. I mentally run through what I need to achieve today. Who needs visiting, who needs a card, a phone call, a something. I claim a half hour of quiet just to order my thoughts while I automatically take Mum's washing off the radiator and put more on, while I iron the items already dried and fold them into a bag to take to her later, while I put the dishes away, wipe the kitchen table, hastily scrawl notes on the kitchen wall chalkboard, feed the dogs, check what food we have for dinner, and all that minutiae that is part of the entry into my day. Today, being Sunday, and today being a morning where Colum has been up before me and has sorted out the dogs, run Sam to work and is now in B&Q selecting a handrail to fit so Mum can have a shower in relative safety when she comes to us post-hospital, I am in a blissful state of padding around the house in my jimmies and an old sloppy joe jumper. There is quiet in my being. I can think. There is much to do later. But that is later. Right at this moment tranquillity is present.

A night or so ago when it felt as if people connected to us were spinning around us in some bizarre frenzied dance, I picked up my copy of *Celtic Daily Prayer*. I had bought this lovely hard-backed volume in the gift shop of our local Abbey. Our Abbey never fails to offer refuge and hush to the over-busy mind. And that's even just from a walk along the ancient stone-hushed cloister to the gift and coffee shop. *Celtic Daily Prayer* is based on the spirituality of the Northumbrian Community — a later development of the original Iona settlement as founded by Columba, as I have already delineated. It is very similar to *The Divine Office,* or *Liturgia Horarum,* which is used by religious communities and individuals in the Catholic church. It offers prayers and readings for the whole year as well as for distinctive occasions. I like the feel of the book in my hand. It is both finely crafted and solid. It is something to hold on to. It offers a reassuring rhythm as it dredges deep into the legacy of the monastic tradition with its awareness of God being in all things. When my tired mind was looking for something to uphold it, I read the advice to go gently through the tumult of these days, to continue to give freely and show compassion. I felt assured that the role life had recently cast me in, was the right one. It was what I was being asked to do. In the doing though I had to take time to be silent, be still and draw strength.

I recognise that there are many ways to reach quietness. For me, reading is one of them. Since Mum went into hospital I haven't given time to reading. It's not really that I have been too busy, but I have been chasing other occupations. I am enjoying shopping for her, choosing nice comfortable clothes for her. Whereas, though, I would have travelled with a book in my bag at all times, I now tend to keep checking my phone for messages, and spend lots of time updating family and friends with news. That is important, but I have spent too much time on this when a half hour at the end of the day would suffice. When I come home from an evening hospital visit I just want to slump in an armchair with some food and watch repeats of *Frasier*. Papers and books remain closed and barely read. When I go to bed my eyes are dropping after only a few minutes of reading. It is, I suppose, all about priorities. I know that a reading session sustains me. I know that it feeds my very essence. I am a writer. Reading informs my writing. I found myself marvelling this week when Colum said he had finished the latest Kazuo Ishiguro novel. He had been as busy as I. Apart from accompanying me to many of the hospital visits, he has also collected and chopped wood, built a new woodshed, uprooted an old apple tree and arranged for it to be taken to a community garden, helped me swop around two rooms in prep for Mum coming to stay with us and also got on with his usual occupations. I, on the other hand, have done barely more reading than what Facebook has to offer. This is not good.

This morning was therefore utter bliss. I left my phone turned off. Got myself some green tea. Went back to bed and read a decent wadge of Jhumpa Lahiri's *In Other Words*. There have been mixed reviews about this latest title from Lahiri — an award and prize-winning author whom I am mightily jealous of. (Yes, I did manage to read a couple of reviews while tidying a forest of newspaper into the rack.) I care not what the reviews say. I like her writing. I like the honest and searching nature of it. I like her short sentences and her acute perception of her struggle to enter and write out of Italian, a new language to her. I empathise with her need to dig deep into her thoughts and to express them as accurately as she can — either in a private diary or for her published work. And after a half hour of reading, pausing, reflecting, reading, I threw back the bedcovers and made my way down to my desk. Forsaking all else I have claimed this precious hour to write. I can now turn on my phone.

Taking Care

Primrose patterend pyjamas
with pink piping
from M & S
keep appearing.
I wash, dry, press, fold and return them to her locker.
'There Mum, those are clean,
they'll do you'.
A day later they wait for me in the
disposable Patient Washing bag
crumpled and sour.

I rarely iron
but now I leave the board up
for clothes that are not mine.
T shirts, nightwear, vests, trousers
most of them new.
'I don't need a thing,' she had said
dismissing shops I wanted to loiter in.
But she did.
Oh, she did.

Separately but together
my sister and I chose
her things.
'You get the slippers,
I'll do the socks and the cardigan.'

We text our findings everyday
après visit
noting the shortages, the necessary needs.

Her resolute Size 16 is gone
as her speechless post-tumour mouth
relearns how to swallow
some of the
slow spoonfuls
of porridge
of soup
of custard
which trickle their wanton path
down her snug shawl and soft scarf
swaddling her scarred throat.

I put two sachets of liquid in each load
with scented conditioner.
One doesn't eradicate that peculiar hospital odour
that gets into every seam
eclipsing any personal essence
causing my son to say
'How come that gear smells so bad?'

Strangely comforting.
Strangely soothing this ironing.
'I don't know … where these clothes …
have come from,' Mum says one day
in a strange staccato voice
erupting from healing trachea
stumbling over severed bone, swollen tissue and tongue.
'They … are all … so nice.'

A Swift Half

It was an unseasonably warm day in late April and the pavements were busy with people who had cast a clout to enjoy the feeling of sun on their wintered skins. I was walking into town having just finished my piano lesson. It had gone well. Not wonderful, but good enough. I am still at the stage of having to mutter 'All Cows Eat Grass' every so often (pianoistas will understand that strange utterance). Any thoughts of amazing my teacher with my dexterity on the ivories never enters my head. My teacher is, fortunately, gifted with the virtue of patience and has never yet rapped me over the knuckles, even though there must be many a time her fingers must twitch to do so. I always experience a small measure of relief though when I leave the lesson. I am not quite over feeling like a wee lass who hasn't done her homework quite right and for whom the marks on the page are still a confusing code.

Back out in the street I was enjoying the light-headedness of knowing that there was a full fortnight before my next lesson — oodles of time, surely, to master 'Englischer Tanz in A' by Carl Ditters von Dittersdorf, which I was still making a total botch of. I also had the afternoon off caring for my mum who was now living with us while she moved towards full healing and a return to her own home. Colum had taken her out for a run in the car giving me permission to skive. Content and free I rambled along into town. Tea was on the agenda. I had earned it and as I had walked to my lesson instead of taking the car, it being such lovely weather, I had definitely earned it. One of the town's cafes has some tables outside and, if lucky, I might get one of those. I could already see myself sitting there with a shapely white china pot of tea and possibly a wee piece of banana loaf to go with it.

One mile later my thoughts had, strangely for me, turned away from tea and were considering a different beverage and a different venue. I remembered as I walked that the town was running its annual beer festival. I'm not a huge beer drinker. A half-pint and, if very reckless, another to follow, are my complete limit. The stuff just doesn't taste nice after that. And it has to be a decent ale, preferably brewed locally, thus ensuring none of your chemical infused dishwater swill and having the virtuous benefits of supporting small local industries and avoiding air-freighting. (See what goes on in my head when I am contemplating buying something? So many issues to wade through no wonder a full weekly food shop is an exhausting business.) Anyway, the shining sun which had been tickling my arms and face was also making me thirsty. A quality beer would slip down nicely I thought. Question is though … dare I do it?

It is the twenty-first century. Women in this country have had the vote for a long time. Women work in all sections of society and hold important positions in all of them. Our First Minister, for goodness sake, is a woman, as are the current leaders of the opposition parties in the Scottish parliament. We have come an incredible way since when it would have been unthinkable for a woman to walk unaccompanied in the streets (posh women that is, the working women just had to get on with it). I am not twenty-one anymore, I have been married for a quarter of a century, am the mum of a grown son, years of experience teaching and working in the literary world. But … am I brave enough to go into the beer festival on my own? That's the question. And one that I am asking myself as I get near the cafe I had planned to have my tea in. I think of my friend, Liz, who is trying to do something that scares her every few weeks so to feel that she is living more fully. Will going to the beer festival, on my own, qualify? I think it will. I have some money in my purse, I know the format — the paying for 'your glass' and programme at the door and keeping it with you as you sample the beers — having been at the festival a few times and I know what beers I like. So that's all fine. Laugh not stronger women, I just happen to have always come with my husband. Well, today is the day I can change that. First I need some more information. I phone Colum.

'Remind me again how much it is to get into the beer festival? And how much will a half-pint be?'

'£6,' he says without hesitation being a veteran of the festival, 'and around £1.50 or so for a half-pint. Good for you. Enjoy.'

I put my phone back in my bag. Square my shoulders. Right. I'm going in.

There are two women at the door. That's a promising sign. They smile as I come in and indicated towards the reception bar where I can get my glass. I pay the £6, get the glass and programme and then, equipped and ready, walk slowly around the hall. Realising the signs are all blurry — and that's without any alcohol in my system — I get out my glasses and put them on. Everything clears. Lots and lots of signs bearing names of beers. None of which I recognise. I remember that last year we had gone upstairs and that last year a nice chap serving at the bar had helped me choose a beer. Upstairs I go. There are people milling about. All men. I trot on undeterred trying though to look unhurried and cool and confident. I find the bar from last year. And am about to ask for some advice from the pleasant looking man serving there when my eye falls on a pump with the sign *Fraoch*. Ah, *Fraoch*. I know this beer. A 'heather ale' and a favourite occasional summer tipple or when we have had a long day decorating or gardening. I decide to play safe. I am being brave just being here. I ask for a half pint and give over my glass. Happy with my choice I then spy the stall of a local cafe — ironically the same one I had thought to have my tea in. They are selling tasty looking panninis and also have cheeseboards. Mindful though of Colum at home making soup and homemade bread, I forgo the food and opt instead for a wee bag of crisps. I don't really want crisps but think that it would be wise to eat something with my beer and it will also be something to do with my hands.

Next thing to do is find a seat and enjoy my beer. There are random groupings in this upper hall. All standing and all men. I go out into the upper landing. More men. I go up to the seated area but all the tables are full — of men. I go back downstairs to the lower hall. There are some women here. Women with men. I see a couple of men standing at the back wall. One man is sitting on a wee camp stool reading the paper the other is contentedly sipping his beer and watching the crowd. I make my way over, casually so not to look keen, and sit down on the floor a little way apart from them. The man on the stool carries on reading his paper. I settle myself down. Bag and jacket on the floor. Open my crisps and sip my beer. It's tasty and just the dab after a warm walk. I look at the programme. Lots of lists of names and descriptions of the beers. There are also adverts for the food festival happening at the weekend. I like the food festival and the carnival atmosphere it conjures up. Last year it was staged well and the area around our local abbey and town hall was filled with stalls and market traders. Some wise-thinking person had also arranged circles of old-fashioned deckchairs and picnic tables on the lawns — where I happily sat savouring a toothsome paella dish made by students following a Hospitality course at the local college.

'Scuse me hen. Sorry to bother you. Any chance you could watch ma stuff while I get a beer?'

It's the camping stool chap.

'Sure thing,' I say.

He goes off and I continue my reading. Five minutes later, he's back. Back with a pint glass of beer.

'Now,' he says, settling down beside me. 'This is an interesting one. My freend over there that served it, says you get the taste on the second or third sip. What d'ye think?'

I am about to demur and say that I don't really want to taste it. I mean, I don't know this chap. I think he has already sipped it. I'm thinking of the hygiene angle. But, oh, what the hell.

'*Mmmm*,' I say after two sips, 'Citrus. And lively. And strangely fizzy.'

'Citrus?' he says. 'Now, that's interesting. See me. See if you were to take an orange oot yer bag and start peeling it. Aifter a minute, mibe two, ma skin wid stairt tae itch. I'm no allergic though. Ma head disnae explode or onything. Jist get an itch.'

'Maybe you need to watch that beer then,' I say.

'Ach, it'll be alright. Ah'll no dee. And it's a wheat-beer. Unusual. Ma pal over there picked it fur me. Ma missus she likes it tae.'

'Oh, is your wife here?' I say.

'Naw. She disnae like it. And she's tryin tae loose a wee bit weight so is aff the beer. She's, whit will ah say ... she's no like me and you ... she's kind of roun. Beer's no the thing fur her.'

Having now had mention of his spouse I feel justified in introducing mine.

'Those wheat beers. My husband has to avoid them. He can't digest wheat.'

'Sat right? That's a shame. But there loads of ithers. Whit is it you're drinking then?'

I give him my glass. Och, well, we're all Jock Tamson's bairns at a local beer festival.

'Fraoch. It's a heather ale. Nice. Light.'

He sips it and returns the glass to me.

'Aye, that's very pleasant. Ma name's Mick by the way.'

'Anne,' I say, shaking his offered hand. And then immediately think I have missed an opportunity. I could have reinvented myself. I could have been a Dolores or Fredericka or something more exotic. But truth will out.

'Ah come here every year. Ah usually take the days off work but this year ah couldnae — staffing an that. So anyway, I got here an hour or so ago. I bring ma wee stool, ma paper and ma wee radio wi earphones and listen tae Radio 2. That's whit ah dae.'

'Sounds very pleasant way to spend an afternoon,' I say.

'Aye, it is. And sometimes ah meet nice folk. There's never trouble here. Aebody's decent.'

A figure of a man looms over us. I recognise Sandy — the husband of a close friend. He looks amused.

'Hallo there. Don't want to interrupt. Just saying hallo.'

I introduce him to my new friend who immediately offers him his citrusy beer. Sandy, with the grace of a gentleman as always, accepts it and offers comment on it. He is a member of CAMRA (Campaign for Real Ale, for the uninitiated) and a volunteer staff member at the festival. He sits down on the floor with us.

I'm beginning to enjoy myself. This is doable. This isn't scary after all. I see Sandy has a Green Party badge on and I comment on that. We have the Holyrood elections soon. Things are hotting up on the campaign trail. The current SNP MSP has already waved and said hallo to Sandy. There's an amicable relationship between the two political parties —

both of them good for each other. In our constituency, we are expecting a landslide to SNP with a second vote hopefully bringing in a Green, all thanks to our voting system of proportional representation.

'I don't do politics at a beer festival,' says Mick. 'Disnae mix.'

'I think it does, perfectly,' I say.

Sandy stands up. He's on duty somewhere in the hall. I tell him my menfolk will be down soon and he goes off, still looking amused.

'Aye, I'll be gettin The Call frae the wife soon,' Mick says.

'I've already been told my dinner will be ready at 5.30 prompt,' I say. 'My husband's making soup.'

'Oh, soup. A've a guid recipe fur soup. Ma wife makes it. Wan can o baked beans, wan can o chopped tomatoes and wan wee Knorr stock cube. Mix it aw up in yer blender. And whammo. It's jist lovely so it is.'

'Sounds like an idea,' I say.

'Aye, lovely. Lovely so it is.'

I begin to gather my gear. Drink the last few drops of my beer. Make my excuses to my new friend.

'Anne, it's a pleasure tae meet ye,' he says.

I put my hand out to shake his, whereupon he takes mine, lifts it up and kisses it.

'See you next year maybe,' I say.

'Aye. I'll be here. In this corner. Ah'll look forward tae that.'

I leave the hall and walk back out into the sunshine. Happy and satisfied. That was worth facing down my demons for. And I've the glass in my bag to prove it.

Think I'll Go for a Ride

The beautiful weather has continued for some weeks. Yesterday I spent the warm afternoon outside under the parasol shading the wooden table near our front door. The sun glinted off the screen of my iPad making my eyes annoyed and my head tight. Yet persist I did, being loathe to give in and retreat to the dark interior of the house. My desk is in a north-east facing room and, after an enthusiastic spurt of sunlight, it cools down to cardigan level. We don't get an abundance of sun and heat in the west of Scotland so it seemed like a mean rejection of the gift given by the gods, to work inside. If it meant I had to squint to read or write, then so be it.

Earlier today I had been at a Pilates class. I love this class. There is a moment when I suddenly become conscious of the music seeping into my senses, music that encourages you to lift your spirit, shake off the stresses accumulated in your bones and reach and stretch and breathe. Pilates though, while excellent for that esoteric part of your body called 'the core', is not aerobic. Used as I am to road-running, which leaves me feeling I've given my all and am content to do little for the rest of the day, Pilates leaves me peaceful but feeling as if I haven't done enough to content my heart area. Today therefore I want to do a bit more than sit in the shade.

As I debated what to do I caught sight of a cyclist swooshing his way along the street. A cyclist wearing a T shirt and shorts, healthy, happy in his skin and I presumed enjoying the rhythm of his bike. Luka Bloom's song 'Think I'll Go for a Ride,' ran through my head. Cycling. Now there's a thought. It had been an age and a day since I had been on my bike. Colum and Sam use their bikes almost every day for transport. I am not so adventurous and usually opt to walk somewhere, or take public transport if not driving. Bikes are great but I find the searching for somewhere to lock it up a bit of a pest and then there's the clothes thing — I don't always have the right gear on to go by bike or indeed want to wear it. I am also not quite brave enough to deal with our roads or drivers who don't understand that cyclists require decent space around them. I'm more of a cycle track kind of lass. A track where cyclists are expected to be; away from diesel fumes and annoyed looks from uninformed drivers. Standing in our kitchen looking out on the street where another cyclist swished along, my body said 'Hey, I'd like to do that, that cycling action thing. That would be good.'

Problem was though, Colum, my trusty shot-gun companion on our cycling forays down the track, armed with puncture repair outfit, a pump, an assortment of spanners and other curious implements for breakdowns, plus the knowledge of how to use them, was already booked up to man a 'keepie-uppie' stall at a local Gala. (I deliberately use the gendered verb here as I have yet to encounter a woman who thinks that staffing such an amusement has anything to do with fun.) So, I would have to go on my own. My own. Right. The words of my friend Irene, who faced with her first tax-return as a self-employed person, and who has so influenced my life for being better and braver since she uttered the words: 'How hard can it be?', came rushing into my mind. 'Not hard', was the obvious answer. Not hard, say in comparison to our young friend, Hannah, who gets up at the ungodly hour of 6am, cycles for a full hour to the elderly care home where she then does a twelve-hour shift, then cycles for another hour home again. And all of that on traffic-complicated roads. That, to me, qualifies as 'hard' and so totally out of my wimpish league. No, something much less challenging was what I was thinking of. Actually a 40-minute cycle on a designated cycle track to one of the lovely parks in the south-side of Glasgow, that also has an architecturally pleasing museum with an equally pleasing cafe, sounded about right.

As I scribble these words — and believe me, my handwriting is a scribble — my bare feet and legs are revelling in the touch of cool grass and my squint-free eyes content with the dappled shade afforded by the large rowan tree stretching out its arms above. I have tea in a strong paper cup — bought at the museum cafe, and a box of olive and potato salad, brought from home. Life, at this precise moment, is just fine. I did it ladies and gentlemen. I did it. Seized the day and got on my bike (after Colum had checked the tires, adjusted the saddle, changed the wonky front light, adjusted the pannier to the correct position and carried the vehicle up to the street for me).

And the ride was lovely. Lovely in all its parts. Colum cycled with me for the first kilometre to check that my bike, not having seen the light of day for some months, was working as it should. Leaving me with a promise to keep his phone on, we parted and I cycled on. A moment later I spied a figure running. A female spare and sinewy figure. The figure in fact of my running coach. She came up level to me as I slowed and stopped. Margo is physically fit to a degree I will never attain, not in my wildest dreams. There isn't time left in my life. By contrast, Margo is determined and focused and rarely spares herself from effort or physical pain. As I hadn't been attending the weekly running group for the last fortnight due to a dodgy hamstring, I was glad that at least I had been found on my bike. Margo's lips were cracked and dry and her skin salty. She had run a fair distance. I offered her my water bottle — cunningly laced with lemon slices — and she accepted gratefully, thus telling me she really had run a distance.

As we blethered about this and that, a bell tinkled and we looked round to see a group of cyclists approaching, a group of cyclists whom we realised were all women as they streamed past us.

'That's good,' said Margo, ever encouraging women in sport.

As we said goodbye and went our separate ways I thought about how the west of Scotland is over castigated as having an appalling health record. I set this belief against the number of cyclists I regularly see using the track which goes past our house. I thought of Margo and my running group. I thought of the batch of women that had just whizzed past. As I trundled the rest of the route to the park I counted no less than 35 cyclists in total and that total didn't include the dog-walkers, the walkers without dogs, and the occasional runner. Furthermore, in the space of time I have sat under this tree, around 50 cyclists of all shapes, ages and speeds have flitted past me. Some of them on the 'People Make

Glasgow' bikes — that excellent scheme whereby for the price of £1 for every 30 minutes used, you can hire a bike from any of the 43 locations dotted around the city, available 24/7, and cycle to your heart's content. I think therefore that we should start ignoring the prophets of doom, with their miserable statistics, and carry on doing what we are doing.

Cycling is such a gift to yourself. Today in this glorious weather it certainly is. At one stage of my journey I pedalled through what I will now rename, in my most Anne of Green Gables fashion, 'Garlic Grove' — a stretch of the track winding through a wooded area beneath which grows a mass of wild garlic, their scent mixing with the cleansed air produced by the trees and causing me to inhale deeply in exultation. There is such freedom in going by bike. No need to worry about where to park, no need to worry if you have enough petrol or deal with frustrating queues of traffic. Nope. Just check your tyres, jump on and off you go.

When I was just a wee bit lassie, growing up in our family home, we had an old bike. A bike without any gears, painted blue with sit-up-and-beg handlebars. I loved this bike. Strange thing is that I don't remember going out in the street on it. Instead I would prop it against the wall underneath the kitchen window and pedal backwards. What imaginary miles I travelled. And was always home in time for dinner. Then there were our holidays in Millport. Millport, the town on the Isle of Cumbrae, destination of many a family holiday, had Mapes, the bike shop where you could hire the machines. This always seemed magical to me. We went into the shop and within a short space of time, wheeled out a bike measured to fit our heights and needs. My dad would get a big bike with a rigid L shaped seat attached behind the saddle. This was for my youngest brother who, in my earliest memories, was a toddler and not near enough ready for his own wheels. It was, I realise in hindsight, not quite what health and safety experts would nowadays have in mind for young children as the safety straps were rather flimsy and helmets hadn't been invented. Fortunately, those experts didn't exist then and we would all pedal off round the island, or a good schlep of it, with nary a care. Years later Colum, with Sam (carefully) strapped into a (proper) child seat behind him, both with strong helmets clamped on their heads, repeated the pattern.

Millport still boasts the very same bike shop, giving delight to young limbs and to older folk who reclaim their youth along with their cycle legs. The young ones skim off round the island, using both sides of the road, racing each other and return in the blink of an eye. The older ones rattle off enthusiastically and return some two hours later, having stopped for tea half way around, exhausted, sore-bummed, but elated. The fact that they won't be able to sit down for a week matters not. They have had fun. Cheap, simple, fun and some much-needed exercise.

To know how to cycle is, I believe, a life-skill. How to maintain one's balance on two wheels and go in a, (more or less) straight line without falling off, is something all children need to learn. Some children though prefer to do it their way. Colum, like many a parent before him, spent a chunk of time helping Sam 'go' a bike without stabilisers. He did all the usual running behind and holding of the saddle, and when Sam got up some speed, employed the time-worn shouts of:

'Right go! Go! Go! Pedal! Pedal! Pedal! … Keep going! Keep going! … Whoops! … It's ok … It's ok … Up you get … Oh dear, let's get a plaster for that. Want to try again? … No?'

Sam thought this riding without stabilisers lark sucked. It was my mum who hit on the perfect motivational training plan. One afternoon, doing a stint of Sam-watch while Colum and I did something else, she said to Sam if he could ride, unassisted, up and down her garden path on the red bike kept in her shed for wee legs, by the time we got home, he would get a Twix. Sam had it nailed within an hour. Sometimes it takes a granny to find the right way.

Cycling, you will jalouse from what I say here, is a good thing. Good for the environment, good for health, good for sheer zest of living. Just good in itself. I am not alone in this judgment. As Arthur Conan Doyle advised in the 'Cycling Notes' column published in *The Scientific American* in 1896:

When the spirits are low, when the day appears dark, when work becomes monotonous, when hope hardly seems worth having, just mount a bicycle and go out for a spin down the road, without thought on anything but the ride you are taking.

Ikebana

'Scandal is afoot,' she said, her eyes twinkling.

'Oh, excellent. Tell me about it,' I replied.

Waxen and weak from a hungry tumour gradually eating her throat, my aunt smiled slowly and reached out towards the little glass bottle that I had brought her. Three sprigs of cherry blossom, picked earlier in my garden from the little tree that we planted there last year, poked their pretty heads out of the neck. There weren't many sprigs on the tree, it being only two feet tall, but there were enough for what I needed and I had taken three. The taking of them meant that those delicate stems were lost to the tree but I felt the tree would not mind and would gladly give them. I had photocopied A E Housman's poem, 'Loveliest of Trees', scissored close to the stanzas, glued the paper rectangle carefully onto a piece of black card, outlined the shape in silver pen, punched a hole in the top left corner, pulled some velvety silver ribbon through it and tied the card around the clear glass bottle that once held a sample of the best malt but where the half-opened cherry blossom now tasted straight water.

My cousin had contacted me the evening before. 'Mum is very low now and we are spending the last few days with her.' He didn't say to come. He didn't ask that. I wanted to though. So, go I did.

What do you take someone who is dying? Someone who has no need of anything much but love. Thus, expecting her to be close to the end by the time I got to her, I thought perhaps some poetry might be useful. When my dad was in a similar state I had sung to him — a bit shakily, but sung nevertheless. Favourite lines remain with us all our lives. They are personal. They are powerful. They offer sustenance and reassurance. I had no idea what my aunt's favourite poems might be but I suspected the oft quoted best loved ones would be in there. Those perhaps cited by her schoolteacher father. Flicking through the small poetry book that resides in my bag these days I came across Housman's poem. It speaks of fragile beauty that is transient, passing, arriving out of nowhere, gracing our vision for a brief period then casting its florescence at our feet and vanishing. It was, I thought, just the poem for my aunt.

When Colum and I got to her room in the hospice, life had asserted itself. We found her sitting up in the big chair, very pale, very thin, very weak, but very much there. Her daughter-in-law had driven up from the coast earlier and was perched by the window. They had been quietly chatting but broke off to welcome us. I kissed my aunt's tissue-like cheek and gave her my simple offering.

'How lovely,' she whispered, fingering the small bottle, and peering at the attached card.

We took off our coats, fussed about with chairs, made cursory remarks about the weather and settled ourselves. I had not spoken with my cousin's wife since their wedding. Two wee girls, that always made me think of Mairi Hedderwick's tales, were now part of their story and there were things to ask about. My aunt followed our conversation, nodding and occasionally adding her own faltering comment. We paused whenever she did, conscious that whatever she had to say was precious, time-limited. At one point she coughed and then tried to lift the plastic cup — lidded with a feeding spout — up to her mouth. The effort was too much so I moved myself onto the bed next to her and helped her lever the cup into her dry mouth. Weeks of helping my own post-op mum to do things made the gesture automatic. When she'd had some sips of water, or whatever liquid it was in the cup, she said faintly but distinctly:

'Scandal is afoot'.

'Oh excellent. Tell me about it,' I replied, relishing her vocabulary.

Reaching for the glass bottle with the blossom sprigs, she ran her fingers down its contours and continued.

'There was a young man. He said he wanted to take me for a turn around the garden. He was doing a PhD … in … in poetry … or something,' she said, her eyes on the lines on the card. 'He said he would come for me. We had a date. A date. Then he came yesterday to say he couldn't take me. We couldn't have our walk.'

The three of us in the room looked at each other. Was this true? Was this a morphine-shaped narrative? I remembered how it was with my dad, when what he has seen on the telly or in the paper or repeated to him became fused into one seamless text that made utterly no sense to us. Would young men be wandering around the hospice taking very sick residents for walks? Had my ikebana of pretty twigs prompted a fantasy, a dream? Or indeed a real memory? When teaching poetry I often ask students what it is they 'see' in their minds when they read a word or particular phrase. All of us have a huge mass of accumulated baggage, distinctive to us, with which we unpack a word or string of words. Our culture, upbringing, life experience all kick into play every time our eyes and mind alight on marks on a page. Those clever bod literary theorists name it our 'interpretive community' — see Mr Stanley Fish's essay 'Interpreting the Variorum' (1976) should you be curious. My aunt was in her early-eighties. Her Gaelic-speaking childhood home of Arisaig in the West Highlands of Scotland, her move to the huge city of Glasgow for nursing training, her marriage to a linguist, the coming of her beloved boys, the loss of her husband and the long walk of widowhood where she was the constancy for her sons, a brief second relationship, the expansion of her family with her sons' marriages and the coming of grandchildren with all their unique characters and spirits, the houses she lived in, the gardens she created, the birdlife she watched, the books she read, the poetry and music that delighted her, and the trillion Proustian experiences she garnered throughout her life, were still somewhere in her mind. Who are we — us smug people who expect to be on this earth for a while yet — to say that when she looked at Housman's poem or at a small bottle containing cherry blossoms that there is not a story, a memory, attached to them that is as valid, as meaningful, as any other interpretation? And her room did open out onto a flower-bedded balcony where it is possible to walk. And hospices do attract all types of researchers.

'But he came yesterday,' continued my aunt. 'He came to say that we couldn't have our walk. We couldn't.'

We all nodded but said nothing. The obvious reason for the cancellation of the apparent walk needed no utterance. I was just about to swing off onto another subject, where real or imaginary walks did not figure, when my aunt spoke again.

'He said we couldn't have our walk because ... because ... the cherry trees were not in bloom.'

The lightness and purity of Bashō's haiku printed in a Penguin paperback on my study shelf; a cotton print of a Geisha girl given to us by our friend Masahumi which I have always meant to frame but which is still in a drawer of our Welsh dresser; a miniature model of a house with a strangely designed roof-top also given by him to us; jasmine tea in tiny porcelain bowls owned by my sister; animations of perfect snow-topped volcanic mountains in bold sunshine by Miyazaki — his films introduced to me by Sam; the photography of Toshitaka Morita on the cookery book stand in our kitchen sent to us by Masahumi's mother; *From Kyoto to Carbeth: Poems and Plants from the Hills* by Gerry Loose and Takuya Fuji — an expensive booklet I impulsively bought after going around their enchanting exhibition in the university gallery on my way to a teaching day; Puccini's *Madame Butterfly* and the sadness of the song 'One Fine Day You'll Find Me' on the BBC wireless programme *Friday Night Is Music Night* that played each week in my childhood living room while Mum wrote letters on Basildon Bond notepaper at the table. All of this gallimaufry billowed like a blossom cloud into my mind.

For a few seconds none of us said anything, arrested and entranced as we were by our own respective pictures. Then we laughed and I said 'What a perfect reason to cancel something. How could you argue with that?' Then, turning to Colum, said 'Next time you don't want to do something, just tell me we can't because the cherry trees are not in bloom and I will accept it. It is the loveliest of reasons.'

*

My aunt died some three weeks after this visit. Dying just as the sun began to seriously warm the earth one May afternoon. My cherry tree was in full bloom and Aunt Cathie's soul was out walking with a heavenly date.

The Sleeper

They are there but I am here. Here in another world that I never knew
was there, or rather, here. I did glimpse it once before — from over there.
There from my seat looking over to here. Here where I am now. Here
where I am in it. In it. Then I had seen small lamps gently illuminating
the curtained windows which framed the heads and shoulders. The
heads and shoulders of seated people. Seats different from mine because
the lights didn't silhouette the faces side-on but more like cardboard cut-
outs. They did not look over at me but I looked at them. Those people
across the platform from me and my space. My space that time was full of
hard seats, tired people, the smell of chips and swallowed alcohol. Here
there are tired people too but the smell of alcohol is muted, understated,
and there are no chips. Over there I had a paper cup with tea in it. Here I
also have tea but it is served in a curved handle silver pot on a tray with a
white ceramic cup and saucer, two milk sachets, two sugar sachets and a
square of sweet tablet on a doilly-covered tray. I also asked for an oat bar.
That came with the tea. And a few moments later my requested dram
— a Balvennie — also appeared. Here is elegance. There, there is, and
was, perfunctoriness. Appropriate and useful, oh yes. Sufficient enough
to our need, yes, but sometimes in life something more is what we desire.
Something like this. Like here. Here where I am — on the Sleeper to
London with a first-class ticket.

I did not know that I was to be here when I woke this morning. Or when
I, with extended family, met at a small church near the Campsie Fells to
pray for the soul of our Aunt Cathie. I still did not know when we laid her
bones to rest in a graveyard where a piper played and where, shivering,
for the wind cut cold, we passed around a quaich full of Balvennie (you

will now see the connection to my later choice), or when we thankfully gathered for hot drinks, sandwiches, blethers, news and promises to 'keep in touch' at a hotel. And there was still not knowing as me and my husband drove the miles home. But when my mobile phone rang and the convent number came up, it began. It began then even though I didn't know it. They said another aunt, my Aunt Clemmy, was very very ill and that they wanted the family to know. I thanked them, said I would indeed let others know and ended the call. We continued to drive but we talked. We turned into a garden centre. Switched off the engine and talked some more. My throat was sore and my eyes were full of tears.

'Do you want to go down?' asks Colum.

'Yes.'

But how? But when? were the questions.

'The Sleeper,' said Colum.

So, here I am. My suitcase on wheels is stored in my cabin where there is a bed with white cotton sheets and plump duvet. Where there is a wee sink with a complimentary Arran Aromatics selection. Where there are different lights — an overhead one and a berth one. Where there is a card with advice on *How to get a Good Night's Sleep*. Where there is a steward who is in charge of looking after us who ticked my name off on his clipboard list, checked that smoked salmon, scrambled egg and fresh orange juice was the correct order for my breakfast, who showed me to my cabin, showed me how the sink top flipped up and how the door locked, who wished me a pleasant journey and told me where the saloon was.

The day had been long. The temperature, despite it being May, was not comforting. The funeral had been fitting, had been grace-filled, had been that curious mix of sadness and joy that a gathering of a clan for such an occasion can conjure. My throat was still sore. Not from emotion this time but because my freshly-washed and slightly damp hair had made my skull prey to the keen wind that had whipped around the kirkyard and now a cold was deciding whether or not to take hold. I had to stymie that. Hence the Balvennie in my glass next to my tea tray. A good enough reason should I require a reason. Or perhaps it is simply just a cheerful and comforting companion as we chunter over the bridge spanning the Clyde, running through the Friday night city, and begin our 500-mile dive south.

I alternate my tea-sipping with the whisky and the oat-bar-munching. And I look around. Strangers thrown together. Individuals, couples, and one family. The family, a mum, dad and young lad of around ten years, are respectively occupied drinking hot beverages, reading the paper, and doing something on an iPad. The son has a hot chocolate. I know this because the mum asks him if he has 'Finished your chocolate yet?'. She has noted how his head has dropped onto his father's shoulder. The son says that he is waiting for it to cool. I wonder if this is his first trip on The Sleeper too. The mum and dad don't look interested enough for it to be their first trip. The mum checks her watch, sees that it is now past midnight and decides that they should go to their cabin. I remember how the steward assured me that the connecting door from my cabin to the next was firmly locked and now realised why it might be left open. There are only two drop-down beds in each cabin, a family would have need of another. The family opposite me gather their gear, lever themselves off the couch — yes, couch — and disappear. My eyes dart, surreptitiously, around the classy carriage some more, alighting on and plucking detail. I am like the young boy not wanting to go to bed yet and miss all of this.

There is a table further up the saloon with three people sitting round it. Two men and a woman. The woman is laughing at some story one of the men is telling her. Need she laugh quite so loud or so extensively? Is she laughing because it really *is* a hilarious account of something or is she just doing that female thing — you know that thing where women look extremely interested in what men say just because they think they should? As Woolf comments in *A Room of One's Own*:

Women have served all these centuries as looking-glasses possessing the magic and delicious power of reflecting the figure of man at twice its natural size.

So, even if the story is a witty one, I wish she would be a bit less delighted with it, her laugh is impacting on my temples. The apparently enthralling story ends and she laughs for a full minute more then stops and talks. Ah, I see, she has just met these men on the train. She is out to flatter, to make herself agreeable, or even fascinating. I look at the men. I wouldn't say they were worth the bother. And it's far too late at night for the energy required.

'This is why I *loooooove* travelling!' exclaims the woman. 'You meet such *amaaaazing* people.'

I look again. The men don't strike me as amazing. Hen, you are coming over as desperate. Gie it up and go tae your bed, is my advice.

My attention is diverted by another woman who has been earnestly scrolling her phone using the available power socket, neatly tucked into the tray rests, next to her couch. Now she is speaking to the saloon steward. She asks for 'The cheeseboard'. There's a cheeseboard? So, is there other food? I only saw biscuits and sandwiches listed on my wee card. She must have done this before. I wonder at her choice of cheese though. I bet the *How to get a Good Night's Sleep* card back in my cabin doesn't advocate the eating of cheese around half-past midnight. Rather her than me. I do admire her coolness and aplomb though. Not fazed remotely by anything. Or at least not letting it show. Not like me, sitting here watching everything, wondering how it all works, scribbling furiously in my notebook.

Does anyone else think this saloon is like something from a low-budget *Poirot*? We are lacking the tasselled curtains, eminent gentlemen in linen-suits, red-lipsticked women in silk dresses waving opera-length cigarette holders or white-gloved penguin-suited waiters, but there are definite similarities. Such as the feeling of ease. The expectancy of comfort and of courteous service. The presence of a germ of excess. This is how it seems to me anyway. To me as a first-timer. Perhaps it wears off if you do this too often. Perhaps the excitement wains. But for me, someone who has never been here, here in this selective carriage, I am savouring the moments. Hurtling south, hurtling away from my usual haunts, hurtling towards my precious old aunt who may or may not be there when I get there sometime tomorrow morning. Hurtling as quickly as this night train can carry me. Doing my best. Paying what it costs. Appreciating the ride.

Aunt Clemmy

She has always been there. Slightly off-stage yet figuring significantly in the narrative of our family story. A small slim person whom I first remember as being clad in white from head to foot but with curiously tanned arms and the same very slender wrists as mine. One of her friends, known by the delightful name of 'Angels', once took hold of my arm and said, 'D'ye know Corona has such a thin wrist that you can put your thumb and first finger right round it? … Oh, you're exactly the same! Is it a family thing?' As far as I am aware only Aunt Clemmy, me and cousin Emma have such wrists — wee but mighty. Curious that. But it is not just of Aunt Clemmy's wrist that I want to write. Where, though, to start with all the rest of it? That's the perplexing question.

Perhaps it is best to follow the excellent advice of the King in Carroll's *Alice in Wonderland* (1865), who said to the worried White Rabbit: 'Begin at the beginning and go on till you come to the end: then stop.' A proper biographer would possibly start way back at Aunt Clemmy's own beginning, but I am ill-equipped and unequal to the onerous task of detailing her full life — even if such a feat were ever possible. Instead I shall start at that bit in my memory which is standing in front of the picture of the Sacred Heart in our living room long ago. It is a chilly Winter morning and the four of us are lined up, boots on, coats buttoned, hats pulled down, bags in hand, ready to go to school. Mum is going through the Morning Offering prayer with us. I can't remember how the opening of this goes — I wonder if any of my siblings do? — but I remember the lines 'all the works, joys and sufferings of this day', because to me 'works' just meant 'school', 'joys' meant getting to do painting or making stuff and 'sufferings' meant trying to cope with the obscure maths questions in the loathsome Beta Book which always got tangled up in my mind and made me panic. Anyway, it was somewhere after that line that we then said: 'And please keep Aunt Clemmy safe in Africa', or was it 'And please keep Aunt Clemmy, in Africa, safe'? The syntax was kind of important for meaning when I now think about it. So, way at the beginning, she was already in our everyday routine. Not physically present but there all the same.

Our mental picture of her was enlarged when we saw photos or slide projections of Aunt Clemmy standing by the side of a large Land Rover about to cross a swollen river. This also taught me the highly useful knowledge that land-rovers are the vehicle you want in such situations as they had a strange pipe that wound up from something called 'the exhaust', right up the side of the van to the roof. Because of this clever pipe the water couldn't get into the engine. I also learned that it might take a few days for the river to subside enough, even for this great and useful vehicle to get over to the other side, and there was often nothing to do but wait. Then there were photos of Aunt Clemmy standing beside a man who was sitting on the ground and he had no legs but strange stumps. He had something called 'leprosy' and we felt really sorry for him. And there were photos of her weighing a plump black baby while a queue of women, also holding babies, waited for their turn, and others on the veranda of a 'bush hospital' which had mats with people lying on them. It was all very very different from what we were used to. Notably the whirring sound. It took me until my teens to realise that that sound wasn't particular to the remote mission in Kasaba, Zambia, but was the sound of the fan on the projector. I just thought Africa must be a kind of annoyingly noisy continent.

So, we continued to ask the Sacred Heart that Aunt Clemmy would be kept safe and we continued to see an occasional photo of our aunt doing extreme things like making bricks for the new hospital building and travelling by a laden and fragile canoe — all the while totally clad in long white garments. I have no idea how these photos arrived. In the 1960s, technology such as we enjoy in today's twenty-first century world, was unthought of. Mail to the mission arrived only once a fortnight after being collected from a village seventeen miles away and mail often didn't arrive at all. Incredibly, these photos, or undeveloped spools of photos, got to us in our council house in the west of Scotland, and informed my childhood.

Then, one Summer, we went to visit Aunt Clemmy because she had apparently, after almost sixteen years in Zambia, 'come home' to the motherhouse of the Franciscan Sisters of the Divine Motherhood, in Godalming, Surrey. We all went. All the way from our home in Scotland right down to my Uncle Frank's house in Stanford-le-Hope, Essex. We got the train which took forever and a day to get there and must have driven Mum and Dad to the limits of endurance. Our Uncle's house and particularly his garden, were however worth the tedious hours. He lived in something called 'a bungalow' and joy of joys, in his overgrown jumbly back garden, sat his old defunct car which we could play in. JEV was the epitome of our childish delights. Its old leather seats were hot under the summer sun and we would squeal when we sat on them. We took turns 'driving' and honking the horn, working the stiff pedals, 'picking up' passengers, going on rescue and important explorations, winding up and down the windows, adjusting the wing mirrors, or riding 'up top' on JEV's roof. All without him budging an inch. The other wonderful thing about being with Uncle Frank, apart from his fantastic old car and the walking distance to a great sweet shop in Corringham, was the miraculous fact that he had a real car. A proper car that 'went' on the roads. Ah me, those were the days before all that Health and Safety seatbelt regulation stuff. My uncle, my mum, my dad and the four of us kids all got in his five-seater car and tootled off to Old Leigh, to Southend-on-Sea, to Chalkwell and other great locations and then, one afternoon, to see Aunt Clemmy in her convent.

It was strange to see her in real life. She had always been a name, a flat unmoving image in a photo or colourful slide. Now here she was — a wee figure in a crisp white nun's outfit that only showed her tanned face and arms from the elbows. Even her shoes were white. I don't remember her sitting down with us. Maybe she did. I do remember the tea coming in on trays that other smiling and white clad people carried. Lovely tea and sandwiches and cake. The room, or 'the parlour' as my mum called it, was the most polished room I had been in in my life. And the oldest. The windows had criss-crosses over them. Uncle Frank said that was something called 'led'. And the couches were all flowery but a bit hard to sit on. And the other white-clad people called our Aunty Clemmy 'Sister Corona' or just 'Corona', and they smiled and imitated our Scottish voices calling her by her family name.

After our tea we went to see the chapel. I can still hear the click-clack sound of my feet in their summer sandals walking over the parquet flooring as we went along. The chapel was big and airy. As no-one was there my aunt took us right up to behind the altar so we could see the big picture painted on the wall. There were figures of saints in this picture. I knew they were saints because I had a book at home called *Famous Saints* with pictures of them all. I liked the ladies the best as they had lovely dresses, especially one with the name of Elizabeth. My sister looked up at one of the figures on the wall and said 'Aunt Clemmy, they've spelled my name wrong. It's not 'C L A R A' it should be 'C L A R E'. I looked along but couldn't see anyone with my name at all, but I liked the lady with the dog jumping up at her. My Dad said she could be St Margaret of Scotland and it was good she was there. (Only recently have I done the research and discovered she is actually St Margaret of Cortona, a farmer's daughter from Tuscany and a reputed beauty who had a bit of a checkered life until a Damascian experience returned her to a purer way of being. Reportedly though she had to be restrained from penitential extravagances. Sounds like an obvious No. 4 on the Sufi mystic Enneagram personality-type programme. A character in other words who must have done much to spice up any community. The mosaic she is depicted on, was executed in Venice, shipped to England accompanied by Venetian craftsmen who hung it in 1959. An exquisite example of quality devotional art.)

We then went for a walk round the grounds and over to the farm that belonged to the congregation. I wondered how the nuns who worked there managed to keep their lovely long dresses and veils clean, but when we got there we saw that they had discarded their usual sandals or flat shoes for wellies and had long blue overalls over their kilted-up white robes 'So that we looked like balloons,' Aunt Clemmy reminisced many years later. Not quite as ethereal as their usual garb but good choice all the same.

Aunt Clemmy then said we could go to 'Vespers' if we wanted which turned out to mean lots of prayers in the chapel. I remember sitting very quiet near the back of the chapel and watching the nuns stream in. I should say here for the pedantic of you that yes, I know that it is only correct to call religious sisters 'nuns' when they are part of an 'enclosed' order. The Franciscan Missionaries of the Divine Motherhood were not and still are not an enclosed order thus, by rights, I should call them 'sisters' but that gets confusing for lay people or for those unfamiliar with Catholic terminology. So please excuse any slippage of term. Anyhow, the nuns walking composedly into the chapel, all had a light blue veil over their usual white one and it fluttered as they walked past us. I wondered how it didn't fall off but then saw that they pinned it on. Some sisters were better at this than others but they all looked just beautiful to me. Just like the saints in my book at home.

The next time I saw Aunt Clemmy she was in our house. It was 1972 and summer. There was great excitement before she came and my dad freshly papered and painted the boys' room and mum bought and hung new pretty curtains in it because Aunt Clemmy was to sleep there while she was visiting us. I have no recollection of where the boys slept. Probably on the pull-out in the living room. Then she appeared, still in her long white clothes but she had a white cardigan over them for the evening and a funny wee white close-fitting cloth cap to wear at night with her long nightdress and dressing gown if she needed to go to the bathroom. I thought she must be really hot in all that gear but Mum said that Aunt Clemmy was used to Africa where it was far warmer, so our weather must actually seem quite cool to her. Thinking of it she was probably more weather-appropriately dressed than I was with my yucky crimplene and nylon saturated dresses and skirts. I was ten years old and plump. I wore my favourite jumper constantly in the belief that it covered the puppy fat around my waist. I heard Aunt Clemmy commenting to Mum that I seemed to wear it every day no matter the temperature. Comfortable and affordable young teen fashion hadn't quite reached our town yet and I just had to sweat it out in my scratchy clothes. It was funny though hearing a nun commenting on clothes. I suspect the walkers in Glen Nevis that summer were also rather surprised to see a white-habited Franciscan nun easily trotting up the path and smiling at them as she passed. A kenspeckle sight that probably figured in many a story over a post-walk pint.

Aunt Clemmy's clothes continued to impact on my senses a few years later. I was somewhere in my mid to late teens, had long lost the unsightly bulge around my waist and much happier in my skin. I was also, reportedly, the same size as Aunt Clemmy. Congregations of Religious Sisters were in the process of updating their daily costume. The long dresses and veils — or 'habit' as is the correct term — were based on medieval dress and deemed out-of-step with the modern world. Vatican II had made the habit optional and many religious congregations had already adapted their dress to be more in line with the world around. My dad's tailoring skills were called upon. He was, as I have said, really a man's tailor but somehow it came to pass that he was making up three modernised habits for Aunt Clemmy. These were dresses that aped the old robes in that they had a false tabard but could now be either in white or in the traditional brown of the Franciscan and were still very tailored. The main difference was that they stopped at the knee, were not joined by another piece of material to a head veil but had a simple mandarin collar. I had to spend a number of evenings being pinned into one of these developing garbs while Dad harrumphed and sighed over the complicated mathematics behind their construction. Have to say that I didn't really like the material he made them in. It was like suit material and kind of slidy. I thought the strong cotton of Aunt Clem's old habit far nicer. Still, times change and the original decision to clothe themselves in 'simple dress of the day' meant that the medieval-style dress was not now in accordance with the charism of active religious orders.

The adoption of a new style of dress must have been quite a decision and quite a change for all concerned. A friend of mine, who had spent ten years of her life being a Carmelite nun, told me that on the day she left the convent, she couldn't describe what it felt like to take off her long black and brown clothes that she had worn every day for a decade and put on a brushed cotton blue blouse and denim jeans. It probably was a similar shift for Aunt Clem but just not as extreme. I remember lots of discussion going on about the change of dress for religious sisters — Mum had to keep explaining to anyone dropping by the house why Dad was making these new costumes. Even today, some thirty years on, I find that I still have to explain to the confused why modern-day sisters don't wear what everyone thinks they wear. While visiting my aunt towards the end of her life, she said she wondered 'if they had gone too far' in their adoption of modern day dress. On the flip side of this she also said that continuously covering your head, day in day out, played havoc with your hair and scalp. The same arguments range over the wearing of the head veil for muslim women. And it seems to be that those with the strongest opinion are those who have no cause to wear the garments in question. It is certainly true today that the young religious sisters, native to Africa or Asia, say that it is safer for them to wear the obvious dress of the religious for sheer protection. It is also true that the founders of most religious congregations desired that their followers should go about their ministries among the people in as simple a manner as possible. If we stretch this one a little further we could say that all that married women wear to declare their dedication to one singular relationship, is a simple wedding ring. This is normally enough to state them as off-limits to any other. If religious sisters and nuns view themselves as married to Christ and his gospel, then a simple ring or cross should also suffice. We are judged, are we not, more by our actions and conduct than by variations in our dress? This subject though is erring near a thesis so let me stop and return to Aunt C.

The next thing we heard about my aunt was that she had given up nursing and midwifery and looking after people with leprosy — her back having taken all the heavy lifting that it could — and was now busy with some form of teaching. This took her to various points in the globe where the FMDMs had established missions — Gibraltar; the Franciscan College in Amman, Jordan, where she reported that despite the troubles, tensions and unrest of the Middle East, she lived happily and safely and was accorded much courtesy; and then to work with traumatised refugee children in London. She would often read to the children and she spoke of her delight when, one day, a little boy from Ethiopia, told her that he had dreamt he was helping Mole to whitewash his house. Only a few weeks earlier this same little lad could only speak of guns, tanks and soldiers. The healing touch of Grahame's Edwardian tale, *The Wind in The Willows* (1908), had worked its magic.

Finally, after many years of ministry, Aunt Clemmy was called home to Ladywell where she took up the managerial and pastoral post of

Reverend Mother for six years. Back in England however, Aunt Clem was to cause occasional confusion. Not many people expected to see the actor Joan Hickson, (aka Miss Marple) walking about as a FMDM. For indeed the similarity was striking. Not just the physical features but the fact that both women — fictional and real — had a mind 'like a meat-cleaver' as Superintendent Slack in the BBC adaption in 1992 of Agatha Christie's *The Mirror Cracked from Side to Side*, so eloquently puts it. And it has always been thus. Little got past Aunt Clemmy. When an unsuspecting workman was sent for to deal with the problem of insects swarming in an area of the convent, he innocently asked Aunt Clemmy, if she 'had a problem with flies?' She looked at him with those clear blue twinkling eyes of hers and rejoined, 'Oh no, lad, there are no flies on me.' Quite so.

And it was this same clear-sightedness and ability to shift through the extraneous, that enabled her to do her greatest ministry for her congregation — that of write up their history. After arduous days of sifting, ordering and selecting archive material, checking, questioning and investigating gaps and silences, chasing details, documents and permissions, her first volume, *Our FMDM Story Begins* was completed and bound in 1998. This was followed by *Our FMDM Story Continues* in 2006. Then, in 2010, at the age of 81, Aunt Clemmy produced *Our FMDM Story — Another Step.* These three volumes, spanning the congregation's early beginnings in the mid C19th to the opening of Ladywell in 1956, currently sit in the small museum style ante-room, near the chapel in Ladywell, thus providing narrative to the other photographs and artefacts collected there. Another volume or two, will need to be penned by another, to bring the history up to date. Aunt Clemmy's volumes, being conscientious documentation of what is a remarkable social history, are what future historians will refer to and thank her for.

Apart from her research writing, Aunt Clemmy was also a poet. In 1981, *Borne on the Wind*, a collection of her poems was published by T. Shand Publications. Some years later, in 2007, the year of her Golden Jubilee marking fifty years as an FMDM, I had the privilege of helping bring this collection back into print under the slightly revised title, *Carried on The Wind*, ironically under the imprint of Covenanter's Press. In the introduction to the 2007 edition, Aunt Clemmy writes:

Sometimes, whilst in Kasaba going about my duties as nurse, midwife and general factotum, I would find thoughts running through my mind. These reflective thoughts would link themselves together in couplets or simple stray lines. I loved these thoughts and found comfort in them. One day, whilst in one of the villages vaccinating children against smallpox, one after the other after the other after the other in a never-ending line of tired mothers struggling to hold crying children, we sat down to take a short break as we had been at it for hours. The mothers sat too and the children quietened down, now that we, their tormentors, had stopped attacking them. Except for the heat and the flies, all was more or less calm. It was whilst sitting there and thinking my own thoughts, that I decided that later I would write down the reflections which had, for some time, been playing quietly somewhere deep inside my mind. It was thus that these poems came to be written.

The poet will out and this is surely an illustration of Wordsworth's oft-cited belief in his preface to *Lyrical Ballads* (1798), that poetry 'takes it origin from emotion recollected in tranquillity'.

Only in recent years did I begin to see Aunt Clemmy as a real person. People forget that nuns are still women with all the feelings, emotions and desires that all women have. It is no surprise to me that Aunt Clemmy chose to read *The Wind in The Willows* to those little refugee children in London. I actually have her own copy of this much-loved story which she gave to me some years ago. Inside the front cover is the inscription: '*To Darling Clemmy, With my fondest love, your Howard. 1952.*' Howard, who asked his sweet-heart to marry him and who was refused because she was determined to follow the attraction of a different love. Following that different love was no simple task. When I was in my mid-twenties, Aunt Clemmy told me of a very troubled period in Zambia when their mission and the sisters themselves were in real danger. Many years later she wrote of this time in their in-house magazine, *FMDM Voice*, (Oct 1996):

In the years leading up to Zambian independence politics threatened to dominate and overwhelm the [Kasaba] mission. Warring factions tried to stop us treating members of rival parties. People with all kinds of hideous injuries came to us and we often wondered when our turn would come for we, in the eyes of the local politicians, represented the British Government and therefore were legitimate targets. Some of the lepers' huts were burnt down, stealing reached a crippling level, our windows were broken, trees were being put across the road, our landcover was stoned, sometimes with us inside it, staff were threatened. It was hard to know who one's friends were for fear does strange things to people's loyalties. During these times lack of communication was the sorest trial. Rumours sprouted from every tree — we heard that all the expatriates had fled the towns; such and such a party were torching all the missions; Sisters in other missions were being systematically raped; if we did not get out we would be caught.

The sisters remained in Kasaba — despite incredible temptation to leave. For my aunt temptation also came in a particular form. A priest friend also serving there urged her to let him take her away from it all. Afraid for her life she came close to accepting his offer. 'But then, I looked down and I saw my ring, the ring we are given when we take our vows, and I remembered I had already given a vow and I said no to him.' I have no idea if she ever regretted her decision. I suspect not, but there must have been times she must have wondered. And there must have been other times she questioned her chosen way of life. But she, for whatever reasoning, continued to choose it. In my preface to the 2007 edition of her poetry, I concluded with the words that in her poetry 'I hear the voice of a single soul who is singing her credo of all that has mattered to her [...] it is a beautiful lyric and a testament to a life lived deeply and lived well.' I still stand by my words.

Aunt Clemmy left us after a long long walk with cancer. Never actually physically strong, despite her heroic years in Africa, Aunt Clem proved that what you do in life often comes down to a matter of inner will. In the last few years every time I visited I wondered if it would be the last time I would see her. And all but one of these times she proved me wrong. Living for the last few years of her life in 'La Verna', the specifically designed extension for sisters needing nursing care, she was looked after with delicate and considerate compassion. She had her own room with her own things around her, her own photographs, her own books. Bede's *Ecclesiastical History of the English People* (c. AD 731) was one of the tomes she was re-reading when I visited one time. The life of the mind, while her body decayed, was still of high importance and interest to her. On days she was able she attended the daily community mass in the main chapel and would join her sisters for morning or evening prayer. In later days communion was brought to where she lay in bed. Her ministry now that of prayer for all those dear to her and prayer for the comfort and healing of the wider world. And, finally, prayer that she be released soon from her tired body. Her clothes, ever smart, ever simple, ever neat, ever few, were replaced by fleecy pyjamas — pyjamas which had a cheeky penguin and which matched the pretty pink of her bedsheets last time I saw her.

On my penultimate visit to her I sat with friends of my aunt in their community dining-room. 'Ah, you've come to see Corona,' they said. 'She's very sick but she's still Corona.'

I knew exactly what they meant. She had made me giggle at her mischievous recount of a recent visit she had from a priest:

'When you near the end of your life, it can be a bit frightening. I asked to see our priest. He came in and I told him how I was feeling. He said "Right, let's do a bit of prayer together and we'll tell the Devil to bugger off." I told the story to your mum the other day but I had to leave out the 'bugger' word as she wouldn't have approved.'

I was restless one evening during that same visit, and wondered if it was too late to go back and sit with Aunt Clem. It was around 8pm and sensible people might have warned me against it. I am, however, not always sensible. I went back to her room. Her light was on and so I stole in.

She was awake and happy to see me. I had taken some nice body lotion as a present and some posh Turkish Delight. I could see now that she would need help making use of either gift but there was one other gift that I could give.

'Would you like me to read to you?' I asked.

'Oh, yes, please,' she replied. 'There is a book on the table. *The Snow Goose*. It's one of my favourites. Read that please.'

It's one of those books that I thought I had read. Always thought I knew the story. I didn't. It was of no matter though. What mattered is that that is what she wanted. It is perhaps no surprise that this little book is one of her final reading choices. Set in the marshlands of Essex, the county of Aunt Clemmy's birth, before it was tawdry and industrialised, Gallico has captured the timelessness of beauty, of love, of loyalty and of dedication — qualities, experiences that triumph over despair and evil and come from human beings when in their highest form. Published in 1941, it commemorates Dunkirk, an event Aunt Clemmy would have heard of from her safe refuge in Arisaig and Fort William, in the West Highlands, where she and my mother lived with their aunts for the majority of the war years while their older siblings, father and mother remained and endured the bombings of London and the threat to the south-east coastline. Thus, for my aunt, *The Snow Goose* qualifies on a number of levels as a favourite story.

I was aware though that it was really important to read well. When someone is in pain the last thing they need is to hear someone stumbling over words that are precious to you. I had to plunge in, enter the words and imagery, so that my reading would give relief, would catch her thoughts and direct them to another instance, another scene, another time, and so be temporarily soothed. When you read properly the words begin to soften, to move, to shape themselves into a melody or composition that the writer has heard in their own head. Punctuation, correctly observed, picks out the intended pulse and vibrations that can lie dormant if the eye has just skimmed over and rushed on.

I read for perhaps fifteen minutes or so. A nurse quietly slipped in the room as I came near the end of a paragraph. She sat quietly near the door and waited until I paused.

'That's so lovely,' she whispered.

At this, Aunt Clem, opened her eyes and said 'One of our sisters can also read like that.'

'Will I stop now?' I asked.

'Just read to the end of the sentence,' she replied.

I did so. Kissed her goodnight and went off, contented, wondering if my reading was my gift to her or her gift to me.

Back in my room I dug out my notebook from my bag and began to write this chapter. Writing allowed me to release the memories of Aunt Clem that had been circulating and clamouring for attention in my mind. There was one thing I needed though before I could use my words.

The next morning I told her that I would like to write about her, write about her from my perspective, but that I needed her permission to do so.

'Yes, of course,' she replied, 'that will be fine.'

'And what name will I use?' I asked. 'Would you prefer I used a pseudonym?'

'Oh, no,' she said. 'Why would I not be me?'

My final visit to her was in the month of May, having hurtled over 500 miles south during the night on what had felt like a hurricane-buffeted train which had afforded a very unnatural sleep, and I was very tired. My aunt had been doing her own difficult travelling since I had last seen her, travelling which paled mine into insignificance. Her face was deathly pale and skeletal thin. Her wasted body like that of a dying bird. She was unable to move her arms over the bedsheets to greet me or to turn herself in any direction. She was, nonetheless, my amazing aunt with remnants of her old vivacity. The sister in charge lent over her, saying:

'Corona, it's your niece all the way from Scotland. She's come to see you on your birthday. Corona, it's your niece Anne. Anne from Scotland. Corona ...'

'I know who she is,' said a weak but decisive voice. 'I've known her all her life.'

As Shakespeare's Juliet questioned: 'What's in a name?' — in the case of my Aunt Clemmy, Clementina Agnes Ahrens, Sr Mary Corona, there was much.

A Persian Poet, a Literary Lady and Me

The Green Man came on, the traffic stopped and we stepped out into the road. Me, Lily and Omar Khayyám. Poetry ricocheted off the scruffy tenement walls, the boarded-up shops and the littered gutters like a superhero come to lift us from our miserable state. The traverse to the waiting pavement was a line to be followed, a measure of iambic length, changing the ugly prosaic tarmac surface into a pathway of delight.

'*The Moving Finger writes; and, having writ,*' began Lily.

'*Moves on: nor all thy Piety nor Wit,*' I rejoined.

'*Shall lure it back to cancel half a Line,*' continued Lily.

'*Nor all thy Tears wash out a Word of it,*' we proclaimed together as we reach the quatrain and road's end.

What poured glory was in that moment. What majesty. Me, with an eighty-nine-year old lady and a twelfth century Persian poet, triumphant on a Tuesday afternoon. Did the drivers of the waiting cars feel it? Did they wonder at the strange rush at their senses? Question the way their minds suddenly moved sideways to philosophical thoughts? Know why the two women walking arm-in-arm seemed to straighten up with each step, grow glorious, and appear to shine? Perhaps not, but they were the unfortunate ones. Not us though. Not me and Lily who were lifted up by words, by imagery, by sheer beauty of expression capable for centuries of removing the most ordinary of actions, the most humdrum moments, to something higher, something lasting, something eternal.

It had begun in an ordinary way. I looked up from where I was ordering the music boxes — which so often get into a transgressive state — to see a petite elderly lady struggling to open the heavy bookshop door. I yanked the door open for her and she trotted in. I asked her if she needed any help and she said she was looking for a book to give to her grand-daughter who was interested in studying veterinary science. She followed me round to the Pets shelves where I thought there may be something of use. While she looked there I also checked the Health section where we also store the more serious medical books. Nothing resulted there so I went back to Pets. On the topmost shelf was a hefty tome of encyclopaedic layout. I showed it to the lady who pronounced it perfect for her grand-daughter's needs. She followed me to the counter to pay for it. The owner of the bookshop was in residence there and he recognised her as a customer who was also fond of collecting editions of *The Rubáiyát of Omar Khayyám* and he had kept aside a particularly nice hardbacked one for her. Hearing this I skooted to Poetry and found another four paperback copies of the same text. Should you be a scholar of the poet you may wish to know that they were all the final version by the Victorian poet and writer Edward Fitzgerald, apparently questionable in its accurate translation but which has nonetheless stood the test of time and remained popular since it was posthumously published. I laid these out on the counter for her to look through. She announced she would take the lot, 'to give out to people' and would also take the large book on animals.

I studied her frail figure. The animal book was large and heavy. She looked as if a strong breath might blow her over. The owner of the bookshop commented that he hadn't seen her for a while. She replied that was due to her having had to be in hospital to have a carpal tunnel seen to. As she spoke she lifted her left hand up to show us.

'It's not right yet,' she said.

No, it wasn't right yet, her hand curled into a tight twist. I looked at her book choices lying on the counter.

'Do you live nearby?'

'Oh, yes, just over the road, above the Subzero cafe.'

'Above the cafe? So, you must have stairs to climb?'

'Yes, but I can just bump up. It's only two flights.'

'Kelvin,' I said, 'Do you mind if I go with this lady and carry her books for her?'

'That's fine,' says he.

'Oh, no,' says the lady. 'I can manage. I'll go slowly.'

Now, as you will appreciate, I am well up to speed these days with the needs of elderly people. The thought of letting this lady leave the shop, attempting to carry five books, and get to her home in one piece without a trip to the local A&E, wasn't washing with me.

I gathered up the books and said 'I could do with some air. I'll come home with you.'

Without further protest she accepted my offer and paid for her purchases. She then paused to relate an exemplary story of how people should never judge by appearances, and how elderly women have their purpose in society. She told us of how some months previously she had noted a restaurant opening up nearby her flat.

'They had called it after my favourite poet but had spelt his name wrong. I went in and said to the young lad there that day that it was wrong and to tell his boss. I went back in the next day and he said he had told his boss but the boss had said "How would someone like her know how to spell it?" I went home and returned with a copy of *The Rubáiyát* and told the lad to give it to his boss. Next day I looked out my window and there were two men up ladders taking down the sign.'

'Yey!' said Kelvin.

'Power to the People,' said I.

Smiling, she comes with me to the door which I pull open and, once over the doorstep, automatically stick out my arm.

'Cleek on,' I say employing the Mill girl term. She does so without a murmur.

And so we move to the traffic lights. Waiting for the lights to turn I ask her how she knows the poetry of Omar Khayyám so well. She tells me she learned it in school. I tell her how in the shelves built around the fireplace in my childhood home, my Dad kept a copy of *The Rubáiyát* which he would read from every so often and which my Mum quoted, or rather shouted, down the phone to some jobsworth council employee when they had mistakenly sent us a rent arrears notice and refused to acknowledge their mistake. I doubt there have been many obstinate rent clerks that have had the words 'Sultan after Sultan with his Pomp / Abode his destined Hour, and went his way,' hurled at them. Lily giggles. I then ask her what her favourite lines are just as the Green Man comes on. Without momentary hesitation, she begins: '*The Moving Finger writes …*'

Poetry of antiquity. Ever ancient, ever new.

In the eye of the storm

The newspaper columns, the television channels, the radio airwaves, the social media postings are all full of it. The daftness that has come upon us. Come upon the UK as a consequence of a vote to exit the European Union. Panic and speculation abounds. Politicians and public figures all have something to say, actually lots to say. The pound has plummeted and the Prime Minister has resigned. South of the border the two major parties — Labour and Conservative — are in complete disarray. My country of Scotland fairs better. Our inexorable First Minister, her set-lipped small shape standing firm, holds us all together as she sets about securing what needs to be secured, sorting what needs to be sorted. Remaining calm, refusing to be bullied or rushed. A still point in a churning sea of uncharted water.

Yes, we have her. We have options and we have hope that our wishes will not be ignored, cannot be ignored. We wait to see what she will do for us. We believe in her. Yet the gales against her steering are strong, determined to blow her off course and us along with her. Once adrift on unmapped deeps we will be easy prey for cruel species.

Perhaps. Possibly. Those words are hinges. Connecting one state to an unknown other. That's the thing. It is unknown. Despite the ocean of rhetoric pouring forth from every source of verbiage, we do not know what will happen or indeed how it is to happen. We do not know.

This morning therefore I went about my usual business. Our First Minister had said it was business as usual and that the Scottish government still had a country to run. And I had my own tasks to do. Tasks a little random in some way, but then my life is not a regular neat one. The life of a writer, at least of a woman writer keeping afloat all that she has to keep afloat, cannot be neat or precisely timed even if it is a Monday morning. The kitchen bin still needs emptying, remnants of last night's dishes still need washing, the dogs' water bowls still need refreshing, their tummies filled and their bladders and bowels evacuated. On top of that I have a package to post to a friend in London, tickets for a concert to purchase, an appointment with a solicitor to secure and oh yeh, that thing called Writing to do. As I walked around our town doing the first three things on that list I noticed how normal it all was. People still queued quietly in the Post Office, people still drove their cars, paused to chat on the pathways and pavements, our local train still ran to schedule, shops still opened and the cafe I went into still stocked soya milk. The only unexpected thing was that the university library where I had planned a focused writing session was in the clutches of enthusiastic men with hard hats and drills. The upper floors were, apparently, still operating as usual. As I also seemed to be carrying around a headache, perhaps the result of the sultry weather we had been experiencing, and the men in their hard hats and drills had also caused the library cafe to shut, I opted to take myself homewards. There are some days when you have to go with the flow but without tea and something sweet to accompany it, I knew that creative flow just wasn't going to happen.

Trying not to feel frustrated I began the walk home. Half way there I passed a pub which I remembered was happy to sell tea and coffee any time of day. Walking around the side of it I found that the large wooden tables outside were devoid of any other customers or men with hard hats and drills. My feet turned me towards the pub door. Inside the bar-tender barely batted an eyelid when I asked for Earl Grey tea, 'for outside, but in a proper cup please'. The note on the door connecting the inside to the outside area advised that only plastic glasses would be issued for outside drinks. I hoped this wasn't the case for quiet middle-aged women with the modest request of tea and a bit of carrot cake.

'Of course,' replied the bar-tender.

Happily ensconced outside, under a large awning which I realised was useful in keeping off the very slight drizzle that had decided to make its appearance, I pulled out a book from my bag. Like the majority of the modern-day population I often resort to checking my phone when there is a lull in proceedings. It's easy, it's handy, and it satisfies the need to know what's going on. This morning though I didn't want to know what was going on. I knew what was going on. Craziness. In a few hours it would still be crazy. People would still be panicking or at least posting on Facebook that they were panicking. Politicians and other folk would still be proclaiming whose fault it was that there was panicking.

What was required for the moment was a good solid reliable book. Indeed a book of poetry. A book of poetry I had picked up in the bookshop and taken home and then proceeded to carry around with me for almost a week without opening. *A Choice of Emily Dickinson's Verse, Selected with an Introduction by Ted Hughes* (Faber and Faber, 1970). Now, please do not tut at me, but Emily Dickinson is one of those writers whom I have known of for a long time, but I actually know diddly-squat about. Her or her writing. There are the lines from one of her poems that have, curiously, stuck in my mind: 'I shall forget the drop of anguish / that scalds me now, that scalds me now'. The usage and impact of the word 'scald' is superbly done and is probably why it has hung around in my psyche. That however is about as far as my knowledge of her vast oeuvre goes. This Faber edition of her poetry was my opportunity to get acquainted with her.

The fact that Ted Hughes had written an intro amused me. Some years ago, I was listening to some academic laud Ted Hughes — for what reason I was listening to the lecture totally escapes me, but listening I was. The speaker said something like 'I mean, he had so much to put up with. Both his wife and the woman he had an affair with, committed suicide.' I wondered if only I could see the funny side to his statement but, out of politeness, repressed a derisive laugh and contented myself with a raised eyebrow. Now, holding Hughes' edition in my hand, I wondered if I did him a disservice. I opened the book.

Hughes' words were the perfect words for the moment. He wrote of how Emily Dickinson produced her poetry against a backdrop of uncertainty. How, when she was writing, America, through the ravages of Civil War and the conflicting ideologies which challenged all previous certainties, was being made and unmade. Amidst all of this Emily Dickinson withdrew to concentrate on 'that Campaign inscrutable / Of the Interior'. Finding all that she needed in the privacy of her own home to allow her to read, to think, and to write of it all.

I laid down the book and sipped my tea, raising my eyes to watch the dance of the trees rustling over the high wall of the cycle track a few feet from where I sat. I thought of how peace can still be found in the most confusing of times if we but stop and reach for it. Not exactly an original thought granted, but one that I needed reminding of. And one that many before me had arrived at. Including the previous owner of the edition of Dickinson's poetry I had now claimed. I know this because a large leaf and a small piece of paper fell out of the pages. A delicate veined leaf pressed flat. On the small square of paper were written the words 'Emily D, p. 51'. I turned to page 51 and found pencil marking around the verses:

It is an honorable thought,
And makes one lift one's hat,
As one met sudden gentlefolk
Upon a daily street,

That we've immortal place,
Though pyramids decay,
And kingdoms, like the orchard,
Flit russetly away.

Some critics judge Dickinson's decision for seclusion as a rejection of the tumult of the world, a disengagement from real life. Others are more generous and take into account the gendered norms of the 19th century, where women were not expected nor encouraged to take part in public life and thus Dickinson was simply conforming with that principle. Many also accept that in her control over her seclusion, in her rigour and defence of it, came her independence. Refusing to be drawn from her home and refusing to attend church — even though the rhythms of the hymnbook and the vocabulary of Christianity run through her vast output of poems — Dickinson challenged what was expected of her and therefore carved out her days in the shape she preferred. A wide circle of epistolary correspondents kept her informed of what was happening elsewhere in the world and that was sufficient for her. A true contemplative, she preferred solitude and quiet so as to explore the full intensity of her unflinching thoughts. To find in the compass of her home's boundary, space to investigate and address the deeper concerns of the world, was her ultimate life task.

Would that we had a cohort of contemplatives advising our politicians at the moment. We can only hope the Dalai Lama will magically appear in the debating chambers of Holyrood, Westminster, Brussels and Strasbourg and that peace and right thinking will prevail. We can only hope.

On Beauty

Guitar music is falling on our ears like mist. It rolls over the hum of the car engine and the silent people within. There are no words but there need to be none as my memory is supplying them.

Tantum ergo Sacramentum
Veneremur cernui:
Et antiquum documentum
Novo cedat ritui:
Praestet fides supplementum
Sensuum defectui.

Tantum Ergo, the final two stanzas of Thomas Acquinas' *Pange Lingua Gloriosi Corporis Mysterium*, is forever affixed in my memory with the Carmelite Convent in my childhood town and Benediction. It is 5.15pm and the air is filled with smoking incense issuing from a swung thurible. Two nuns, one bent almost double with age, clothed in their long habits, are in the front rows, on opposite sides of the aisle, like benevolent sentries. Their black leather shoes squeak as they slowly stand up, sit or kneel. The chapel is a low ceilinged hexagonal room, surprisingly modern. There is a large floor-to-ceiling french window on the lefthand wall. The window is veiled with white voile curtains. Behind this I can see shapes moving and shuffling, the occasional cough, nose blow, sniff. They are the Enclosed. They are the ones who don't come out — unlike what I know to call the Externs. The ones who deal with us out in The World. Sitting in our usual bench halfway up the small chapel, I would wonder if the nuns behind the curtain were as curious about us as we were about them. I would wonder if the curtain was like a two-way mirror and they could see us quite clearly but we couldn't see them. I would wonder if they noticed when someone had their hair cut or was wearing a new jacket or if someone had fallen asleep or if someone was a new attendee. Maybe they had more lofty thoughts.

Genitori, Genitoque
Laus et iubilatio
Salus, honor, virtus quoque
Sit et benedictio:
Procedenti ab utroque
Compar sit laudatio.
Amen.

The skilfully plucked melody to Aquinas' hymn, with all its serenity and sublimity, ends. I come back to the present. To the country road that we are driving along. It is Saturday afternoon and we are taking my mum back to her home. She has been with us for a few days while my sister is away on holiday. Mum doesn't now need the constant post-operative care she did need. Instead she is back in her own home, happily pottering about on local buses, having coffee with her friends, going to Mass, doing bits of shopping, engaging in her usual life again. There does need to be a family member within shouting distance though, as, despite her strong spirit, she is a very elderly person with medical needs, so as a family we still aim for a light supervision while respecting her independence.

We have enjoyed having Mum around but we are all quiet on this journey. We are all still struggling with the news that a cousin, whom we are all very close to, has been diagnosed with an aggressive cancer. What was thought to be an annoying arthritic hip eventually pointed the way to a far more worrying condition. My cousin is only in her early sixties. Is slim. Had recently been enjoying an almost daily swim. Is tall and graceful. The news she was told yesterday still takes our breath away. Is still stunning us to the extent that it seems surreal. We haven't words to meet our dazed minds. But the purity of Acquinas' thirteenth century composition — developed from a sixth century Latin hymn and thus adding reassurance by its antiquity — has done something to supplant the void. It subtly reminds that there has always been a well of peace within our consciousness, a well able to speak to our alarmed selves, drawing as it does from a deeper source. Medical science only goes so far. Only has so much power. There are other energies informing us. And there is still beauty in the world.

In his *Summa Theologica*, Acquinas teaches that there are three primary constituents of beauty: *Integritas, Consonantia,* and *Claritas.* The very sound of the words are elegant and pleasurable, immediately issuing poise, balance, steadfastness. The interpretation of each word adds further quality. As I understand it, *Integritas* signifies completeness and perfection where nothing essential is lacking and nothing extraneous is present — thus something is perfect just as it is, self-contained, in its own right. *Consonantia* signifies the result and sum of parts in right ratio. The third element, *Claritas,* is the hardest to pin down. It appears to be the presence of something which reveals its ontological reality — the properties and relations between — where the physical and spiritual combine and shine out. It's all deep stuff and one that can easily give one a headache. James Joyce, in his *Portrait of An Artist as a Young Man* (1916), provides us with a more accessible interpretation. Reconciling his own Catholic formation with the Modernist sense of the aesthetic, Joyce has his character, Stephen Dedalus, explain Acquinas' teaching to his friend Lynch, by means of a butcher-boy's basket. Giving a tripartite reading of a simple basket, Stephen reduces Acquinas' belief to the more accessible explanation of *integritas, consonantia* and *claritas* as being, respectively, *wholeness, harmony* and *radiance.* I muse on this and wonder if I could further reduce the components to 'What, How and Wow!' but the very words feel too blunt to be associated with beauty and far removed from Acquinas' decorous Latin.

My cousin, who is ill, is a creator and appreciator of beauty. Surely there is no more greater function, greater contribution to the world, than that. As an extension of that she receives energy from witnessing love in action, love around her and being loved. The body need not be perfect to do that. As I write this it is now some weeks on from her diagnosis. Her body is weakened as the cancer has apparently spread to other parts of her body. She is facing a major operation and possible other invasive treatment. Her smile is still bright though and her spirit is strong because love has risen and surrounded her. Love calls us all to act from our higher selves, our selfless selves. Sitting with her a few days ago, holding her thin hand, we agreed that there was nothing more important than love. Love sustains and will see us all through as we, each in turn, leave our material body. As Rumi expressed it:

Your physical attributes, like your body, are merely borrowed. Do not set your heart on them, for they are transient and only last for an hour. Your spirit by contrast is eternal: your body is on this earth, like a lamp, but its light comes from that everlasting Source above.

*

And light has come. Overturning our expectations, driving through the darkness with a clear steady intensity, light and hope and joy have reasserted themselves. Following an intensive bone scan, a consultant deduced that the pain in my cousin's hip was caused not from cancer but from tuberculosis, and although hospital treatment will be required, she is not the terminally ill person that she, they and the rest of us, had thought. Call it what you will — prayer, positive energy, karma, life force — has come through and is glowing strongly.

The essence of the hymn *Tantum Ergo* urges us to believe in the greatness of mystery. *Mystery* from Anglo-French *misterie*, Old French *mistere*, Latin *mysterium*, Greek *mustērion*. That which we cannot know fully. That which remains unexplainable. That which is impossible to understand.

Grunkern, Gerste und Sago

Three white ceramic pots sit on my kitchen window sill.

Three white ceramic pots given to me, Anne — from the Hebrew, Hannah, meaning *grace or favour* — by my mother-in-law, Dorothy — from Greek, meaning *gift of God*. Dorothy got them from her mother, Gertraud — from the Teutonic, meaning *strong spear*, who received them from her mother Rosa — from Latin, meaning the botanical Rose genus — when her daughter, Mignon — from French, meaning *dainty* or *delicate* — had no more need for them.

Three white ceramic pots are on a window sill in Scotland — from the Latin, *Scoti*. I brought them from my mother-in-law's house in England — from the Old English, *Angles*. Dorothy got them from her mother who was living in Ireland (Eire) — from the Gaelic goddess, Ériu. Gertraud got them from Rosa who was living in Germany (Deutschland) — from the Old High German *diutisc*.

Three white ceramic pots have words on them. One has *Grünkern* — meaning *green kernel*. One has *Gerste* — meaning *barley*. One has *Sago* — meaning inedible starchy stuff that becomes a poor excuse for a pudding. I like the sound of the words and I like the meanings. When my mother-in-law translated *Grünkern* with it's assertive umlaut — *um*, about, *laut*, sound — as 'green kernel which comes from *dinkel*, or spelt,' we clapped our hands. We eat a lot of spelt in our household. It was meant to come to us. We understood it. It could have a home with us. My brother-in-law, William — from Old German, *Wilhelm* and Old Norse *Vilhjálmr* — who was sitting at the kitchen table in my mother-in-law's house, told us the meaning of *Gerste*. It is strange what the mind retains. There cannot be much or any call for the word in his day-to-day life but remnants of

German lessons taken as a younger man have lingered. Similarly, when I was in Paris fairly recently, decades after learning French volcabulary from a tatty old text book in my secondary school, the words *parapluie* (umbrella) and *pamplemousse* (grapefruit) popped into my head just when I needed them. When I ask my mother-in-law about the meaning of *Sago*, thinking that perhaps it might have a different one than I expect, both William and I instinctively screw up our mouths in disgust at her confirmation that it is the gluey glop, as revolting as semolina, that frequently presented itself as a school dinner pudding. Then we laugh at each other's expression as we image the slippery sago and instinctively stick out our tongues, while my mother-in-law says, 'Oh, but it's lovely with jam…!'

In the *Grünkern* pot I have planted parsley. *Parsley* — from the Old English *petersilie* (identical to the contemporary German word for parsley) and the Old French *peresil*. If the parsley grows sufficiently thick I will use it in salads. If the plant is unhappy I will plant it in an outside pot and perhaps a passing swallowtail butterfly will note it as a possible home for its larvae which will become black and green striped yellow dotted caterpillars which will then become a cloud of butterflies. Bees and other nectar-feeding insects may also visit the flowers. And goldfinches might feed on its seeds. All of that would be a good thing. I wonder if I am being selfish by leaving the parsley plant on my windowsill where the butterflies, bees and goldfinches cannot get to it.

In the *Gerste* pot I have planted chives — from the French *cive*, from the Latin, *cepa* (onion). One tablespoon of chopped chives contains 1 calorie and 0 grams of fat, 0 grams protein and 0 grams of carbohydrate while providing 3% of the daily value of both vitamins A and C and K, folate, choline, calcium, magnesium, phosphorus and potassium. If I leave them to grow and resist snipping them so to gain all that dietary goodness, I will still benefit from their joyous purple flower that apparently repels insects.

In the *Sago* pot I have planted oregano. Oregano — from the Italian, *origano,* and medieval Latin, *oreganum.* Some gardeners refer to it as *wild marjoram.* Anything that has the word *wild* prefixed to it adds piquancy. It is also a genus of the mint family. I wonder if they view it as the black sheep — if that is not straining the metaphor. The oregano was already in flower when I planted it, so far it has not produced more flowers. Perhaps it is yearning for its native mediterranean home. Perhaps it is still upset from being squashed into a too small plastic supermarket container labelled 'Summer Salad Growing Variety' which insulted its dignity and refused its individuality. I will give it some more time and, if it does not show signs of recovery, will release it into the less tamed environment of the garden.

Three white ceramic pots have travelled a long way. When they were new and standing pristine and perfect on a shop shelf or market stall in Frankfurt, Germany, they were bought and carried home by Mignon, daughter of Rosa, in her basket, bag or perhaps delivered by a sweating delivery boy. Mignon was married first to a music teacher. His name was Hermann — from the Teutonic, meaning *army man*. This music teacher then had a dalliance with another woman with whom he had a child. At this time a man called Adolf Hitler — a name not worthy of its origin from Old High German, meaning *noble wolf* — wanted Germans to produce little Germans, Hermann left Mignon and went with the other woman. Mignon then married a better man — Lazlo, from the Slavic *Vladislav* — who was a baron from Hungary and a violinist. Mignon liked her musical men.

Mignon had a sister, Gertraud, who had married an Irishman. Her husband was a soldier with the British army based in England. He was then sent to Egypt. Gertraud was left in the army house in England with their two children and an unborn child. It was lonely for her so she took her children to visit her mother in Hindenburg. Her father, Franz — from the Latin, *franciscus* meaning *Frenchman* — died shortly after they arrived. Then the man, Hitler, made a lot of trouble and a world war broke out. Gertraud stayed with her parents in Germany until it was not safe to do so. People said she and her children were British and thus were the enemy. They went to Tüntschendorf, lower Silesia, which is now part of Poland, where they lived in a chateau owned by a friend of their Uncle Fritz — from the German, *Friedrich* meaning *peaceful ruler*. But even people with names of peace have to do difficult things when war happens. Uncle Fritz was a lawyer and he was told his business, and thus his family, would suffer if he did not join the SS — the Schutzstaffel, German for *Protective Echelon*. He did not want to do this but he had to. Rumour had it that he helped people when no-one was looking. War changes everything even for peaceful people.

Then the Russians started to move and the safe chateau was not safe anymore. They had to leave and do this as quietly as possible. On the pretext of visiting their Aunt Marianne — from the French, *Marie* and Hebrew, *Miryām* — who lived on the Czech border, Gertrud and her three children began what was to be a very long journey. Dorothy, who was nine years old, was told to leave her favourite doll, Christa — from the Greek *Christos,* (Χϱίστος), meaning *anointed* or *chosen one*, behind in the chateau so it would look as if the family were coming back. They did not come back and instead made a long long trek across Europe from their aunt's house, to Bavaria and to Frankfurt where they stayed in a house that had once belonged to a Jewish family. Eventually their soldier father arranged for an army lorry to take them to a small hotel in Belgium near his barracks. Sometime later they went on to France by train, to England by ship and finally to Cork, Ireland, to her husband's family.

Gertrud waited for four years until the world had settled itself then, once again, with her three children, visited her mother, Rosa, who now lived in Frankfurt. This time there was no war, no suspicions, no secret leavings, no frightening cold and hungry journeys. They stayed in Frankfurt for six weeks. Uncle Fritz could now do what he wanted and, as well as being a lawyer, he liked the more attractive business of importing French lace from Calais. To amuse his nephew and nieces he let them come to his workplace where they helped make up books of samples of the pretty weblike material and label them for his customers — *Chantilly … Guipure … Aleçon …*

Like all good things, the holiday ended and Gertrud and her three children returned to Cork. One day, six years later, a huge container arrived from Germany. Mignon, Gertraud's sister, had died. Their mother, Rosa, had sent many of Mignon's possessions to Gertraud. Gertraud's husband had proved to be an unreliable sort and Gertraud had very little money. The container with its wonderful bounty of furniture, cutlery, curtains and crockery — including three white ceramic pots —

brought joy to Gertraud. What was inside the container was useful and meant much to Gertraud but the outside shell proved to be the best part. Gertraud had it taken to Fennels Bay in County Cork and, for a small annual rent, sited it there. She had two windows and a door cut into its side. Then put two sofas, a lounger, a sink, a cooker, and cupboards — made out of orange-boxes — inside. She called it 'The Lift' and it became a unique holiday home. Many people, including the Cork German circle, came to sit outside on deckchairs to drink tea, eat scones and jam, sing, laugh, and enjoy the silliness of it all. In 1963 when Gertraud died, the land was sold to a man who wanted to build a house on it. Because the land already had a building on it the law decreed that he must build his own house around the existing building. He did so and so the layers of accumulated laughter and fun compressed into the walls of The Lift infused this man's new home.

Before the ending of The Lift, Gertraud's two youngest children — Peter, from the Greek meaning *rock* and Brenda, from Old Nordic meaning *sword* or *torch* — grew up and decided to go and live in their mother's country of Germany. Dorothy, the eldest, didn't do this but had instead already met and fallen in love with a tall and handsome Cork man. This man, Edmond — from Old English meaning *prosperity* and *protector*, had to go to Essex, England, for work. Dorothy followed him there. Her husband-to-be was Roman Catholic so Dorothy decided to also become so. Gertraud couldn't come to the wedding as it cost too much to travel to England. Having a mother's heart though, Gertraud sent her daughter a big hamper full of linen and crockery to help start her married life with. In this hamper were three white ceramic pots with the words *Grunkern, Gerste* and *Sago* painted on them in bold gothic script.

Dorothy and Edmond had four children. The second was a son, named Colum — from the Latin and Irish meaning *dove*. The family had moved to the north of England when Edmond had been told he must do this for work. Colum was six years old when they moved on a wet wet day. They got there before the removal van, the removal van carrying all their possessions — including three white ceramic pots. So, the family sat on the floor in the new empty house and ate fish and chips. The new house was bigger than the Essex one and there was a communal field at the back where Colum played endless games of football with his new friends and was happy.

The school years came and went and Colum applied to a university in London. He was accepted and did a degree in Nuclear Engineering. He also got engaged and eventually unengaged to a pretty Parisian girl who played the piano, but that is a story for someone else to tell. After university he got a job with a computing firm who sent him all around the world installing banking systems. It was a good life until he got bored, homesick and noticed an empty feeling travelling with him. He decided to leave the life of business and high finance and trained as a teacher of Mathematics and began helping at a centre in London where homeless people could come in for soup, a hot drink, a chat and a game of chess. He began to feel less empty. Helping people made him happy again. He wondered what it would be like to do this all the time. He decided to free himself of his flat in London, his car, his camera, his collector's train set, his bed, his stereo and his bank account. When he had done so he joined the Society of Jesus and began the long training to become a Jesuit priest. The Jesuit novitiate was another happy time and he swam along with it all, studying, laughing, praying, trekking across Spain in the footsteps of Ignatius of Loyola, visiting the dying in a local hospice, playing the guitar at the local parish church, wood carving on a thirty-day silent retreat, teaching Mathematics to street children in Johannesburg, seeing Mandela in the stadium in Soweto, playing football with the local lads, and rejoicing in the constant opportunity for the deepening of life. One day, back in England, their novice master said all the novices were to go on a residential course on Communication. The venue was Loyola Hall, Merseyside. Other novices from other religious orders would also be going. Waiting at the toaster one morning in the large dining room of the retreat centre, a young woman who was a novice with another congregation, came up and said to him in her Scottish voice, 'So, you must be Colum …'

We were married a few months later and made our home in the west of Scotland. A son, Samuel — from the Hebrew meaning *called by God* — was born to us one year later. A beautiful son who is now a grown man. Sam's grandad, Edmond, has passed away, but his grandmother,

Dorothy, still lives in the same town in the north of England. Sitting around her table one early summer evening, our bodies and souls satisfied with the lovely food she had provided, we got to talking about her past and how she had come to be where she was. Dorothy went into her kitchen, and returned carrying three white ceramic pots. 'Would you like these?' she asked. 'Let me tell you their story ...'

Three white ceramic pots sit quietly on my window sill. Redolent with their history, peaceful in their present, tranquil about their future. I am not fooled by them though. These pots are glazed with a determined wandering spirit. I wonder where they will go next and to whom?

Mallaig

There are some words, some names, that catch the mind and send it spinning into an orbit of memory. 'Mallaig' does this for me. When our friend, Polly, ladling out tasty home-made soup in her kitchen in Perthshire, said she had just returned from there as she was organising the first ever Mallaig Book Festival — with the excellent title *A Write Highland Hoolie* — my mind immediately went stravaiging.

Mallaig. Seven letters signifying much.

To begin with, it is the first home of my grannie — Catherine McLellan — one of ten children, who grew up in Croiteachann (pronounced Cotchecan) a croft sitting above what was then a small settlement. I always liked the sound of the name of the croft. I liked how it clicked at the back of your mouth, came forward, then clicked again. Like the light, but definite first steps, of a Scottishe. *Heel, toe, heel, toe, tum te tum te tum.* I liked the esoteric nature of it too. A word from another language, unEnglish, remote, different.

And I always knew our family had a connection with the town because of the way we said the name. When Glasgow people, or family from England, said it, they laid the emphasis on the second syllable. Mal*laig*. It made the word all pointy and sharp. My mum and dad always said it differently by placing the importance on the first syllable and dismissing the second. *Maaa*lig. Drawing the sound out like a soft bleat of a sheep. So I said it like that too. And I still do.

Only recently did I research what the name actually means. Strange how I had never done so. Perhaps my own meanings for the location sufficed. However, should you be curious, the modern-day name apparently derives, (according to the Mallaig Heritage Centre and those chaps should have it correct, one would jalouse), from the Gaelic *Mol* or *Mal* meaning 'shingly' and the Old Norse *vik* meaning 'bay'. Interesting. Interesting too that the website of Gaelic Place Names in Scotland, or Ainmean-Àite na h-Alba, says that the meaning is obscure and David Dorward in his *Scotland's Place Names* (Mercat Press, 1995), contends that it means 'seagull bay'. If my memory serves me rightly though either of 'shingly' or 'seagull' bay suffices. No obscurity is evident for, when I go to the part of my mind labelled 'Mallaig', I hear seagulls and lots of them.

I am standing on the pier. There are only one or two boats moored around and my mum, Teresa, is saying how sad it is that the fishing industry has died. My baby son is sleeping in his buggy, parasol shading his sturdy wee limbs already healthily browned by the sun which has been with us all week. I have sandals on my feet and a hat on my head covering my (then) brunette hair. Mum is indicating towards the hillside above the town. Telling me where she thinks Croiteachann was positioned and that she thought it meant 'Hector's Croft'. Telling me again the story of her great-grannie, known as 'Kate Mhór', born Catherine MacLeod in the remote Glenaladale off Loch Sheil, accessible only by boat or foot, whose daughter agreed to an arranged marriage with a Mallaig man, Donald McLellan. And how, once the young couple had finally settled in Mallaig, or Mallaig Bheag (little Mallaig) as it was then (and still is although the road sign has been Anglicised to 'Mallaigvaig'), had a large family of ten children. Then the story of their daughter, Clementina, —a forebear of my Aunt Clemmy — who became gravely ill and had to be taken by boat to a hospital in Glasgow, and how, as her mother couldn't leave the other children, had to go without her. Then how one morning a blackbird alighted on a sack of oatmeal and my great-grannie knew her daughter had died. Stories. Family stories of things uncanny yet things accepted as true. Just as my cousin Cathie MacDonald, a cradle Roman Catholic but, being from the 'Rough Bounds' of the West Highlands — an area where the old faiths were never extinguished by the Protestant Reformation — once told me of 'a green lady' who appeared to her grannie in the dairy area of the Croiteachann one day and asked for milk. Without murmur or fright, her grannie went to get some, believing this was 'God testing her kindness', but on return found the green lady had gone. A story, I learned during my doctorate research, that was illustrative of documented fairy belief in the Highlands. Stories. Stories that are the warp and weft of family narrative.

And near the pier are side streets, one of which is where Great Aunt Maggie Jane lived in the Railway Buildings with her husband and family, downstairs from her brother-in-law and his family. Great Aunt Maggie Jane who, well into her nineties, appeared without any announcement or previous warning on the doorstep of our house in Kirkintilloch one evening. Come to visit us and attend a funeral we didn't know she knew of. Great Aunt Maggie Jane, originally from Eyemouth in the north-east of Scotland who 'followed the fish' and came to Mallaig to work in the herring industry. Great Aunt Maggie Jane whose nephew, Donny, was the station master at Rannoch where Mum would hang out the train window to chat to him on early trips with us up to visit Great-Aunt Annie in Fort William, or Great-Aunt Mary in Arisaig and cousin Molly in Morar whose husband died at sea while out round the points in his small boat. The women continuing to exist, to tell the stories, to connect up the family just as my sister, Clare, is the keeper of our family tree, shoring up spaces, correcting false information, adding new additions. Ready for when someone asks.

Later, on that same holiday, we go to the Cemetery in Morar where my great-grannie is buried. Mum, me and my son on my lap, sit next to the grave. The generation missing is Mum's mum, my grannie Catherine, who left the highlands to train as a nurse in Glasgow, met an English soldier through a friend and he came to meet her when on embarkation leave during the First World War. Walked with him around Glasgow's Botanical Gardens, thought him a good enough fellow and when he later asked her to come down to London, did so and married him. She lived the rest of her life in Essex, England where they did not speak Gaelic and where they were threatened by bombs and invasion during the Second World War. So her two youngest children — my mum and her sister, (my Aunt Clemmy) — were sent to the safe refuge of her Highland home. Mum spent the majority of the war years in Fort William with her Aunt Annie where she joined the guides and learned how to identify and tease out sphagnum moss for soldier's wounds, but her wee sister lived with their Aunt Angie (Angusina) in Arisaig, wife of Simon-the-

Master, where their grannie now lived and whose only question to the wee girls from Essex would be a halting: *How ... isss ...your... mither? ... ah, Katie m'eudail...'* And who would also rattle her walking stick at the two rascals, Clemmy and her cousin, Iain, who had deliberately crawled under their grannie's bed to giggle and annoy her. *'Come ... ocht! Come ... ocht!'* the old woman would cry.

On the Sunday, we go to the Roman Catholic church in Morar — in its picturesque setting on the shores of Loch Morar. The existing church and presbytery of *St Cumin and Our Lady of Perpetual Succour* was built in 1889 but, previous to this, a slated chapel had been established in Bracorina in 1836. Before this there was a church at Inverbeg, further along Loch Morar built c.1780 — the ruins of which are still standing. The land the Inverbeg church was built on was apparently that of our family's croft. My mum told me of how the bishop of the time had asked her ancestor for the land and in return gave him two crofts in North Morar or Mallaig Bheag.

Pieces of our family's story. A story that is important, as like all families, it makes us who we are. As Alistair MacLeod knew in the shaping of his novel *No Great Mischief* (1999) it's not so important if the stories are historically and factually accurate but more that they are told and told again thus sustaining and weaving a continuing story that can be passed on to future generations. And stories identify us — as my sister discovered some years ago on a boat trip up Loch Sheil. She had got chatting with the boatsman and a friend of his and was attempting to explain our family's connection to the area. As they were passing Glenaladale she happened to mention the story of our great great grannie, Kate Mhòr, who died in the glen from sunstroke. One of the men laughed and said 'Och, I've got ye now. I was just reciting that tale to someone else the other day. Ah, so that's who you're descended from ...'

There are many other family stories of course but that which is conjured up by the word 'Mallaig' comes with such a clutch of association and memory. I last stood on Mallaig's pier twenty-four years ago. My baby son is now a strong young man, delighting in climbing Scotland's peaks, a gentle Lowlander with a Celtic soul. My mum is now the venerable age of 90, one of the last few people who remember the large family from Mallaig Bheag and who married who, who did what and who went where. She returned to her Essex home towards the end of the war as her mother wanted her daughters home. The close connection to the west highlands remained though and it was in a house ceilidh in her aunt's home in Arisaig that she met my dad, a Glasgweigan, enjoying a walking holiday in the area after his years as a POW in Poland. She met her love in Arisaig 'where the rhododendrons grow' as the song goes. Met, and a year or so later, married him and settled in Glasgow and finally Kirkintilloch where I grew up. Growing up knowing Mum's family story and her link to the west highlands despite her English voice. She was and still is a storyteller of family history.

Writers exist to tell stories. Perhaps it is time I revisited Mallaig, re-establish the connection, update it a little and add another chapter. The first and forthcoming Book festival seemed an opportune beginning.

*

Walking up from the station, Merril, a very pleasant woman we had met on the train and who had grown up in Mallaig, said 'I miss the seagulls. It was always the first sound.'

Engulfed by the exhilaration of the train ride — such a ride! — and happed up in memories, I hadn't noticed the lack of seagull sound. I brought my attention back to the present moment. It was true. No screeching cries, no clouds of flapping white, no swift darting shapes. It was almost 6pm, the fish and chip shop on the station platform smelt wonderful. My mouth could taste the steaming salty packages. Perhaps the seagulls had gone home for their tea. Maybe that was the thing. Herring is what they would have. Herring. But the herring had gone. Gone with the fishermen and the army of workers who depended on them for a living, the kipper girls, the gutters, in crews of three, working from early morning till late evening. Gone with the boats, the baskets, the barrels and boxes full of sliding fish. Gone with the coopers who fitted the lids and iron hoops. Gone with the smoke, the guts, the bree and the fish houses on the Point. Gone with the sweat, the blood and the laughter.

Should I feel sad? Possibly. As a Scot, lamenting for the past comes easily. But I am not from here, from this west highland town, the former home of the seagulls and my grandmother. It is not my place to feel sad. Again, as a Scot, I am good at knowing what is my place and what isn't. The past and present and future of this port are not for me to assess. I can only listen and observe. And the cry of the gull is forever fixed in that part of my mind marked 'Mallaig' anyway.

What then has replaced the fish and the seagull? Cafes. Cafes have come. Nice cafes reflecting a modern contemporary Highlands where tourism in-fills the lacuna left by the demise of the fishing industry. If there were cafes in Mallaig when I came here as a child or teenager, I don't remember them. We would either have had our tea in Great Aunt Mary's chilly flat above the library in Arisaig where the fire was a parsimonious one and we instinctively knew that best behaviour and no noise were expected, or perhaps with Great Aunt Maggie-Jane in Mallaig. I don't remember the truth of it. Having our tea in a cafe did not happen. Of that I am certain. And staying in a hotel the like of which I am trundling my feet and case towards, did not happen either. Hotels were for the well-off visitor, a bracket we did not belong to. There was no need at all anyway as in all probability we were 'just down for the day' from Fort William where we were staying with our Great Aunt Annie.

It wasn't until I was a young mother that we took a house out on 'the Rhu Road' in Arisaig. The Rhu Road that was thick with midges that July. So thick that I fretted about the vulnerable skin of our infant son and asked Colum to literally run with him, from the cottage to the pub, any evening we were going there. Run as fast as the wheels of the pram would turn, to outwit those evil beasts, that would attack my son. Our son, who sat up, toothlessly grinning, holding with his wee chubby hands to the sides of his wonderful chariot, strapped in, safe, netting draped over him, delighting in the charge. When our train passed through Arising of today, I nudged Colum, saying, 'Remember that? Remember the Rhu Road and the midges and Sam...?'

The train pulls in at Morar. I can see the hotel once owned by a Macleod cousin. Then as we move out of the village I see Kinsadel. Home to the MacDonald family, friends of my own sister. Friends who gave her a little collie pup to carry home on the long train journey to Glasgow. A little collie pup she named Ruillean Dhu — *dark rascal*. Kinsadel who took her with them while they delivered the post. Kinsadel who took her to collect whelks (mussels) around the points at low tide or go looking for the shiftless cows when they strayed down to the shore. Kinsadel who always had tea, kindness, warmth and humour for the visitor. I hadn't seen Kinsadel since the new road, the A830, had come. There it was though, still sitting in its corner overlooking the sands. Reassuring in its survival.

In her intelligent and sensitive book *Love of Country: A Hebridean Journey* (2016), Madeleine Bunting, a London-based journalist and writer, notes Neil Gunn's description of 'the hidden landscape' which lies below the geographical. A landscape only known by those who have a deeper connection. As Madeleine explains, this hidden territory rests on a relationship that cannot be detected by the incomer concerned only with the topography of the area. I read Madeleine's book some months after the book festival, and now realise that I'd had a firsthand experience of what she means. As our train, slowly snaking its way across the Glenfinnan Viaduct on its way down from Fort William to Mallaig (we always said 'down' even though it is actually more 'up') brought exclamations from passengers who were gazing at the heaven-touched scene of Loch Sheil in all its autumnal glory, I had moved to the opposite window to see better. A couple of people sitting close by said in English accents, 'Lovely, isn't it? We moved up here last year so see it a lot.' I replied, 'That's nice'. What I wanted to say was: 'I am seeing it though as the loch that takes you to where my ancestors are buried, in the rough graveyard on the Green Isle. I am seeing it as a wee lass then teenager then young mum on holiday in the area visiting relatives, one of whom was the resident priest of St Mary and St Finnan Catholic Church, Glenfinnan. Glenfinnan where the monument to the Jacobite supporters was built and raised by others in my family's history. I am seeing it as my grannie's grand-daughter, come back to the area of her first home. That is how I am seeing it.'

So here I am, walking up the short brae to the hotel where the book festival is to be. A book festival. Here, in Mallaig. Cafes and books. Are they the new shoals? Will they provide and care for the people here and attract the incomer as the fish did? Trundling my suitcase and memories

I wonder how this new Mallaig will be. And I wonder if my grannie, my grannie long dead, knows I have come.

She may or may have not known but word went out anyway. Word went out that 'a Croiteachann McLellan' had come and was asking if any of her relatives were about. So it was that on the second evening of the festival three people came to find me. Billy, son of Sandy, is today the local postman — and if anyone knows anyone, surely it is the postman. His niece Jacqui and her cousin Margo all came to the hotel to have a drink with me. McDonalds and McLellans all. Relatives all. It mattered not that we were strangers to each other. We shared a name and a lineage. That was sufficient for them. They knew of others living in Mallaig who were related to me but I had to be on the morning train home. I was content for the moment though. It was enough to have met them and begun the process of reconnection. I will be back with more time in my pocket and a copy of our family tree. It will all keep for now. Blood ties are durable things. I felt my grannie nod in approval.

Foremothers

Have you ever just discovered a writer and that writer's excellent writing, only to find out that he/she is no longer with us? That sense of the heart moving sideways and the deep sigh that it emits? This happened shortly after I had come across the writing of Carol Shields. Idly perusing a 'discard' table in our local library, I had picked up her *Collected Stories*. I had no idea who the writer was or what her work was like. My mind whirring with the pre-holiday list I wanted to achieve that day, I opened the book. At that point in my life I wasn't really a short-story reader. I tended to find the format frustrating and truncated but there was something about the physical feel of this collection in my hand that I liked. Weighty and attractive. I read the first few lines of 'Segue' and I was in. This was good writing. I bought the book for the ridiculous sum of 50p and took it with me on our camping holiday.

I read Carol Shields' stylish and intelligent stories in my sleeping bag as the cool air wafted my senses, I read it in the whole food café, I read it in sheltered nooks in the sand dunes on the breezy beach, I read it slumped in a deck-chair my shawl tucked around my legs. Then I finished it. Bereft, I wandered into a nearby second-hand bookshop and to my joy discovered her novel *Unless*, published in 2002, shortlisted for both the Man Booker prize and the Orange Prize for Fiction. If you haven't read this, then put my book down and go and do so. Or rather, no, don't do that. You won't return to me if you do. Ah, if anyone understands the power of words, the slippage and the resilience of them, then Carol Shields does. If anyone understands that writing about ordinary people, usually women, dealing with ordinary problems and situations, is both interesting and appealing to many of us, Carol Shields does. Or did.

Having completed our holiday, gone home, tracked down more of her writing I then began the bare bones of what was to become a critical (but highly positive) essay for a Canadian journal. Then I found out that she had died. Died, age 68, some years before I had picked up her collection of short stories waiting for me on the discard table in the library. So, there would be no more writing. It was end-stopped. Complete. Finite. I felt as if a door had banged shut. True she had managed to produce an impressive corpus of novels, plays, poetry, short stories and a small amount of non-fiction, but there would be no more. Or so I thought. In the writing of this chapter I thought it wise to check my facts and discovered, to my joy of joys, that a posthumous title has made it to the light of publishing day. *Startle and Illuminate: Carol Shields on Writing* (2016). A volume drawn from her essays, notes, comments and letters and edited by her daughter and grandson. A collection which now sits at my elbow on my desk, like a wise tutor, generously sharing collated percipience, encouraging me to reach for better words.

There is another woman writer whom I must speak of. Her writing isn't as famous as that of Carol Shields. I have never seen any of her titles in high street bookshops nor in the random boxes that come into the bookshop. But I live in hope. Fortune again provided me with one of her books in yet another library 'discount' shelf just after I had left academia and was feeling a tad lost and a tad skint. *Without Reservations: The Travels of an Independent Woman* by Alice Steinbach lightened my load. This book is the one you need if you find yourself unwell and unable to travel abroad to the holiday you had so been looking forward to. It is the book you need if you can't afford to travel. It is the book to read if you never intend to physically travel. Forget slugging it out in 'rustic' hostels with a bunch of other sweaty travellers, forget low-budget travel or being stoical and uncomplaining when everything goes wrong. Alice travels as I would love to travel but probably won't. Actually, definitely won't. Retiring from her career as a Pulziter prize-winning journalist, and suffering from empty-nest syndrome, Alice decides to be bold and brave and to travel to locations she has always wanted to go. And she does so in style. Real style. Not glitzy-glam, but with poise, taste and quietude, entering each city, each country with keen eyes and a courteous perceptive attitude and pen. I will never go to Paris and enrol in a cordon-bleu cookery course, I will never shop in Milan or learn ballroom dancing in Oxford or hang about with Sloane Rangers in London (do they still exist?). In truth, I don't want to do any of those things, nevertheless it is just great to follow Alice around and share in all she encounters. She tells the detail and I like that. Cold objectivity and distancing isn't of interest to me. That's easy. That's safe. Chuck yourself in, why don't you? Happily, *Without Reservations* is cut from braver stuff, outlining how Alice relates to everything she comes across, refusing a mundane charting of how many miles or museums she has packed in that day.

We are, despite our best efforts, but mortal. Alice Steinbach died aged 78 in 2012. Another fact that I just caught up on very recently. Having just lent her travel book to a friend, an unwell friend who couldn't go on the holiday she had planned, I did a quick search to see if there were any new titles and discovered that Alice Steinbach had passed away at a comparatively young age. I wished it were not so, for another of her titles *Miss Dennis School of Writing* (1996), an intimate personal collection of essays, remembrances and columns, encouraged me in the structure of this book. I had thoughts of contacting her and thanking her. Now I wouldn't be able to do so. That potential for a writerly conversation would never come to fruition now. I also wanted to thank her for writing as she did. I so loved her style that I abandoned my pathetic attempts to write fiction and realised that my voice had its home in the life-writing field. Perhaps it sounds strange that I feel sad that I can't tell her that. I never knew the woman — but I, possibly like many of her readers, felt that she was just across the table from me, sharing a pot of tea and her thoughts on what constituted a well-written piece of writing.

A writer, I have come late to, is a woman sadly better known for whom she was married to. Zelda Sayre Fitzgerald has been cast as the archetypal 'flapper'. Beautiful, glamourous and flighty Southern Belle, one half of a 'golden couple', what else she was has been overlooked, down-played or simply ignored. I add myself to the generations who have so misread her. Her famous husband, whose titles still sell, whose titles are still found on school and university reading lists, who is known for his exposé and, arguably, his coining of the name 'The Jazz Age', has left little elbow space for the talent of his wife. When a box of proof copies came into the bookshop my hand plucked out an arresting cover and title — *Z: A Novel of Zelda Fitzgerald* by Therese Anne Fowler, (2013). It was an attractive cover depicting a large letter Z, cut out to reveal a head and shoulders profile of a woman wearing a fetching cloche hat and signature beads of Roaring Twenties high fashion. I have discussed Scott Fitzgerald's *Great Gatsby* with numerous young people seeking to pass their Higher English examination, I have read various critiques of it, watched film versions, each time marvelling at the use of sumptuous patterning, detailed description and sharp, almost elegiac, social observation. I have delighted in the subtleties of his *Tender is the Night,* enjoyed Dennis Potter's 1986 BBC mini-series of the novel and have dipped in and out of other of Fitzgerald's acclaimed titles. Materialism and hypocrisy are always skillfully interweaved with sensitive accounts of personal tragedy and his stories are rightly lauded and recognized as quality literature. Critics tell us that Fitzgerald drew greatly on his own life and his relationship with his wife to inform his work but, what they don't tend to linger on or spill much ink over, is how Zelda faired being married to a famous writer. In the enchanting film *Midnight in Paris* (directed by Woody Allen, 2010) which I judge one of the best antidotes to the irksomeness of life, Zelda is portrayed as an unstable and empty-headed socialite whom her husband has to manage and protect and who holds him back from his true calling. I thought this fair enough if I thought of it at all. Then I read *Z* by Therese Anne Fowler and now wonder how fair this representation was. Did you, for example, know that Zelda was an accomplished ballet dancer and greatly desired to become a professional? Did you know she was also an appreciator of art and also painted seriously? Did you know that she was also a writer and that her numerous newspaper articles, short stories, a play and her novel, *Save Me the Waltz,* (1932), were published — but some of them under her famous husband's name? I didn't know any of that. I do now. How true Fowler's own representation of Zelda is, is hard to ascertain, but it was the impetus for making me take a longer look at this creative woman who has been overshadowed by her husband's success. As Woolf notes in *A Room of One's Own*:

When, however, one reads of a witch being ducked, of a woman possessed by devils, of a wise woman selling herbs, or even of a very remarkable man who had a mother, then I think we are on the track of a lost novelist, a suppressed poet, of some mute and inglorious Jane Austen, some Emily Brontë who dashed her brains out on the moor or mopped and mowed about the highways crazed with torture that her gift had put her to.

Neither Carol Shields, nor Alice Steinbach, nor Zelda Sayre nor many of the other women writers I have cited in this book, will be mentioned in the same breath as Shakespeare, Wordsworth or indeed F Scott Fitzgerald. And I don't care. I like their writing just the same and am unapologetic in stating so. There comes a time in life when you have to own up to who you are and what you like to read. What interests you. What speaks to you. I happen to enjoy reading the thoughts of other women about the lives they live. Their honest thoughts — as far as any writing can be honest. It is not universal writing. It's not representative of the whole of the human race. It still has something to say nonetheless.

John Donne told us in the seventeenth century that 'no man is an island' and, (overlooking his exclusive gendered language), he was correct. We are all interconnected, to a variable degree, by each other. That happens in the literary world too. Isolated achievement is almost impossible. Roland Barthes argued that every text is a woven fabric of quotations drawn from many sources. Sometimes we spot the presence of another text lying just below the surface, sometimes we don't. The fact of the matter is that writers are indebted to other writers. When the gatekeepers of the literary canon seek to detach one writer from the rest, and elevate them, claiming that 'S/He is unique' or, even the sweepingly subjective, 'S/He is the best', it denies a writer's natural connectivity. As Elaine Showalter in her ground-breaking *A Literature of Their Own* (1977) argues, the focusing and elevation of a very few women of letters — Jane Austen, the Brontës, George Eliot, and Virginia Woolf, (guilty, guilty, *mea culpa, mea culpa*) — overshadows and eclipses other lesser known writers. It's up to us then to speak up and say who we actually enjoy reading, not just who we think we should say we enjoy.

The ocean's roar

The seagulls have come inland. They must sense a storm. Their cry arrests my attention as I walk into a room at home and hear their piercing screech darting through the open window. A wind billows out the curtain and my mind goes elsewhere …

I am on a shoreline. Fresh fresh air surrounds my senses like a strong physical character. It settles salty on my skin, tangles my hair, wipes my eyes, wafts my cheekbones, ushering and urging me along as I stride breathing in, breathing out, glorying in the moment, feeling alive.

I am in an unknown yet familiar house, by the sea. I fling wide the windows and let the tangy air flood in and swirl around the rooms. Cleaning, exfoliating, honing. A house from where I walk by the sea. Walk every day possible. Where I scud along the shore, in every season, skimming the thermals thrown up by the waves. Where I hear the cry of the gulls every day without it yanking my thoughts to a coastline miles away. Where, instead of imagining, I am already there.

My imaginings do not however include a peopled promenade with carnivals, kiss-me-quick hats, ice-cream sellers and noise, noise, noise. That all has its function — yes, it is fun — but not for me. No, my seafront is where you feel the gusting weather; hear the slap of the waves; follow the swoop of the gulls as they dare each other to ride higher, turn faster and swifter; where I rejoice in the wind as I wrap a scarf closer around my neck, zip up my jacket and plunge on.

The shoreline of Findhorn beach is such a place. When the tide is out and the flat flat beach is revealed, I have found heaven running on it. Running until I am far from the village and the campsite, running until my legs say 'Turn! Turn!'. Running rhythmically, steadily, feeling as if laughing angels are blowing my body along. Running. Breathing. Running. Elation filling my veins. I also twirl on this beach. When first we come. When first we return to the beach after months of town dwelling. I stretch out my arms and in a personal greeting to the beach, to the wide wide sky, to the clouds, to the stones, to the sand, to the curious seals, I twirl. Sea … dunes … village … sea … dunes … village … all swim and fuse past my eyes till, breathless and dizzy, I come to a stop and lower my arms laughing. As Henrietta Musgrove remarks in Austen's *Persuasion*: '*Oh yes! I am quite convinced that, with very few exceptions, the sea-air always does good'*.

Yet, I cannot stop my mind from reminding me that the sea is not a joy for all people. I think of people who have packed themselves and their loved ones in vulnerable dinghies and faced the strength of the sea as they attempt to reach a safe shore. I think of those whose inadequate vessels and fearful hearts were but a plaything of the sea. I think of those who survived the cruel cruel turnings of the currents but whose wife, husband, child, sister, brother, mother, father, friend, did not and who now weep by the sea hating it. I think of young men, out there in fragile fishing boats, their barely just begun lives precariously balancing between life and death, their families waiting at home, anguish in their sinews. I think of the people who risk their own lives to rescue those entwined by the sea. And I know that I am lucky. Lucky to be free to see the sea as a blessing, as a balm to my soul, lucky because I do not need to place all my trust in it but simply walk or run or twirl along its perimeters, happy in my relationship with it, letting it be it and me be me.

And words uttered and shared when walking by the sea are borne from a different resonance, a different energy. I think of my friend, Siobhan, saying not many days after she and her family had moved to their new home in a west-of-Scotland coastal town, 'Don't laugh, but I want to write.' My friend, Siobhan, who went on to do just that, crafting words out of the ether, drawing vigour from daily walks with her black Labrador who happily investigated clumps of seaweed and promising rock pools or chased sticks by the water's edge while sun, snow and clouds jostled the eye line as they illuminated and backlit the Sleeping Warrior's dark shape on Arran's peaks just across the firth. Watching

Siobhan follow and work on her dream of being a writer, attending evening classes, then following a more demanding academic course, being published and then reading from her work to attentive audiences, I thought on how dreams voiced on the sea's wind seem to have a way of coming true. As Longfellow has it in his sonnet 'The Sound of the Sea':

The sea awoke at midnight from its sleep,
And round the pebbly beaches far and wide
I heard the first wave of the rising tide
Rush onward with uninterrupted sweep;
A voice out of the silence of the deep,
A sound mysteriously multiplied
As of a cataract from the mountain's side,
Or roar of winds upon a wooded steep.
So comes to us at times, from the unknown
And inaccessible solitudes of being,
The rushing of the sea-tides of the soul;
And inspirations, that we deem our own,
Are some divine of foreshadowing and foreseeing
Of things beyond our reason or control.

Mrs Sanjeev

'It's good how they do it,' she says. One neighbour to another.

'Aye, better than the twenty minutes at the Crem,' replies the other.

I want to counter this, to say that my formation in Roman Catholic faith structures and liturgical rubric — with its fusion of smells and bells — means that my experience is different than the women standing next to me. I go to say, 'Oh, but we do the full bhoona,' but don't because my choice of wording strikes me as rather ironical. It is also not the moment to be competing in a discussion of who gives the best send-off. I am also mentally arrested by my neighbour's use of the word 'they' and the fact that one of them is calling the main participant 'the old lady'.

'Mrs Sanjeev,' I say. 'Mrs Sanjeev.'

The neighbours hover uncertainly. It is nice that they have paused in what they were doing or intending to do. One crossing over the road to speak to me. Another stopping and getting out of her car to join us. They are not sure what else to do. What is expected of them. Other neighbours have already 'been in' and taken cards, flowers, low voices, kind words and condolences, but the two women beside me at the moment don't have the same history of relationship.

'You can go in and pay your respects, if you like,' I assure them. 'The family said anyone is welcome.'

They still look doubtful.

'I'll go when all this is over,' says one, gesturing towards the waiting hearse.

The shiny car, with its smart-capped driver, has its engine off. It had driven slowly and carefully up the street a little earlier bringing the body of a precious person back to her home. A few minutes before it was expected I had left two lanterns, both glowing with a lit tea light, at each side of the Sanjeev gate, to welcome the soul of Mrs Sanjeev and assure her grieving family that the community of our street cared. As I had straightened up from placing the lanterns on the ground, an older man, whom I didn't recognize, emerged from the house. I gestured to the lanterns and he in return gave me a smile of understanding that wordlessly crossed cultures.

The format now is that there is opportunity for family and friends to gather to pay their final respects and offer prayers around the open coffin — an opportunity which will last at least an hour. Colum has already gone in. I'm not going as I have a streaming cold and would just splutter and cough where spluttering and coughing is not needed. I do understand the neighbours' hesitancy to join in. I would be exactly the same if I wasn't me. Wasn't me in that Mrs Sanjeev wasn't just 'the old lady' to me, but was Mrs Sanjeev.

Mrs Sanjeev. A brave lady who came to this country as a young bride not long after the partition of India which claimed the life of her brother. A lady who brought up her family in a very different country — with an often cold and wet climate where they spoke strange languages and had no interest in learning hers. A lady who lived frugally and thriftily, giving away any excess. A lady who could swing an axe with precision to stock the open fires in her home and who could cook delectable dishes from memory and instinct. A lady who made the effort to speak to and greet everyone in the street. A lady who hugged my old mum when she came out of hospital, two elderly women from very different backgrounds who shared an understanding of what it was to be vulnerable and ill. A lady whom a piper in full Highland dress — playing the tunes 'Amazing Grace' and 'The Dark Island' — processed ahead of as relatives, wearing traditional Indian mourning dress, carried her coffin to the waiting hearse. A lady who brought cultures together without really meaning to.

We came to this street seventeen years ago. Mrs Sanjeev and her husband and family were already here. Had been for quite a few years. I met Mr Sanjeev when, a frontrunner in the early Christmas card deliveries, he was dutifully going around the street popping white envelopes into letterboxes. I met his wife when she called over the fence one day. 'Missy, Missy …? One minute. One minute … Come … Come …' I stood on a chair and peered over. Mrs Sanjeev held out two brown paper bags. Brown paper bags with a warm alluring aroma emitting from them. I took the bags and peered inside. Samosas. Two bags of what looked like freshly cooked samosas. Mrs Sanjeev gestured to me then to our neighbours' windows. 'You give please. You give.' How lovely. I thanked her and backed this up with bows and smiles, my Punjabi being non-existent.

Our over-the-fence relationship thus began. Colum endeared himself to her by raving about her cooking and wangling a chapati-making session in her kitchen, when she henceforth dubbed him 'a good Indian boy' much to his delight. She took to naming me 'Missy Colum.' I could have protested that I had a name of my own but it seemed unimportant and a little churlish considering she was communicating with me in my language and I had not a word of hers. It took a few years for me to evolve to 'Anne'. I have a very short name which actually makes it difficult for people of other tongues to learn it. If my name had another syllable they could catch on quicker. As it is I usually have to repeat the single-syllable sound a few times until it registers as they initially think I am just saying 'I am …' and then are waiting for the name. Such are the trials of life.

Not only samosas came over the fence. Sam's very first basketball hoop arrived that way too and was promptly re-hung on the back wall of our building — thus fuelling his continued-to-this-day love of the sport. A large floor-standing lamp lit our living room for many years, a stainless-steel colander is still in use in our kitchen as well as a large wok. Outside butterfly lights used to decorate their half of the building when a son married, also found their way to us and still cast their merry glow in our hallway. My mum benefited from various pairs of slippers, socks, cardigans — either all slightly the wrong size for Mrs Sanjeev or just something that she felt she had enough of. And I doubt I could count the mangos, cartons of fruit juice, tins of pears and peaches, or apples carried up from her son's garden that found their way to us. Giving. Always giving. One of her sons, home from his long day in his dry-cleaning business would often look over the dividing fence to see us sitting out enjoying the evening air and munching an offering from his mum.

'Hey, you lot,' he would banter, 'you've eaten my dinner!'

'And very tasty it was too,' Colum would counter, 'shame you missed it.'

In return for Mrs Sanjeev's generosity we told the family to pin our phone number on her fridge. 'For emergencies and that,' we said. Mr Sanjeev had passed on and Mrs Sanjeev would often have stretches of time alone in the house during the day. She never did call us for any emergency but only for us to come round to collect something she wanted us to have that was too difficult for her to hoist over the fence. Other times she just wanted me to unpick the confusing admin-speak in a letter from some authority or other, or wanted the correct information as to which day she should put out which wheelie-bin — blue, brown or black. Sometimes I would stop and have a cup of strong tea with her. Sometimes I didn't. Very occasionally I would take her some flowers, for no particular reason other than that I knew she liked pretty things — as the roses in her front garden attested to. One morning I overheard someone from Scottish Gas attempting to ask her about the quality of service she was receiving. He used far too many needless words and I knew that Mrs Sanjeev would be getting worried. I popped my head over the fence saying:

'Hallo there. If you tell me what you want I can tell Mrs Sanjeev.'

He promptly did so. I then turned to Mrs Sanjeev and asked her, 'Gas, Gas ... ok?' and imitated the lighting of a match to a flame and the glow it makes.

I watched her face and saw in Mrs Sanjeev's eyes that she had understood. She was now smiling and nodding her head.

'Och,' said the gas chap, 'I thought you were going to translate.'

'I did,' I retorted. 'The answer is that her gas service is fine. That's what you wanted to know wasn't it? You can tick the box now.'

'Suppose so,' he muttered and stomped off.

There were countless other small happenings, small communications, that made up our relationship with Mrs Sanjeev and her family. One of the more comical ones concerned a dead cat — a story which Mrs Sanjeev was never party to nor aware of. It began one dismal winter morning just after 7am, when Colum's mobile phone rang.

'Yes, I'm up. What? What now? Now?' I heard him say.

'What is it?' I asked

'Kamal, wants me to go over. Says not to chap the door but he'll watch for me.'

'Is Mrs Sanjeev ok?'

'Don't know. He says to come round quietly. Won't be long.'

Fifteen minutes later he returned just as I was wondering if I needed to phone for an ambulance. Apparently not. No human was ill. There was, however, a dead cat in the basement of the Sanjeev's house. Kamal had shown it to Colum.

'Do you know if it belongs to anyone in the street?' he had asked.

'No idea,' said Colum 'We can do some research if you want.'

'Well, can you do it without telling them that it is dead or that the body is here?' said Kamal.

'Eh … why?'

'Because I don't want anyone thinking we've clonked their cat on the head.'

'So, I've to ask people if they are missing a cat but not say why I am asking?'

'Yeh, that'll be good.'

'And don't you think they'll wonder why I'm asking?'

'Nope. I mean you are the Indiana Jones of the street. You and animals just go together.'

'Right.'

Myself and Sam were also commissioned to casually ask any cat-owning neighbour if they had seen their cat, 'Em … alive … recently … that is.' There were a few raised eyebrows and a few frantic scurryings and loud callings, but after some hours — cats do tend to only drop by their homes when they feel like it — everyone confirmed that their respective moggies were all accounted for. Looked like the deceased cat next door was an unnamed stray. This simplified things a little.

Returning home from his work Kamal phoned Colum again and asked if he could come and help him bury the unclaimed and unnamed cat.

'But, can you come when it's dark?' he said in a deliberately hushed tone. 'Mum still doesn't know. It'll freak her out if she finds out. She'll think it's some kind of evil omen. Phone me when you're on your way round.'

Thus, sometime after 10pm, carrying an old sheet, a spade and sporting a head-torch, Colum tootled back round to the Sanjeev basement. Kamal was waiting for him and together they lifted the inert cat onto the old sheet and trogged, as silently as possible, out into the night and down the garden path. I was watching from our back window and thinking to myself that if Mrs Sanjeev happened to be looking out, the sight of two moving figures carrying a lumpy bundle through the dark garden might not be the best thing for her heart or nerves. Thankfully, no screaming was heard and the men reached the back fence uninterrupted.

Allegedly, the gallant two with their inert load squeezed through a gap in the fence onto the rough ground above the railway line, dug a deep enough hole, heaved in the stiff body, covered it, then stood up.

'Em ... do you think we should say something?' asked Kamal.

'What ... like a prayer?'

'Yeh, well, it was a living creature.'

This was certainly true. Both the Christian and Hindu codes of ethics concur with this sentiment and sentiment — even though the jury is still out, in Christine doctrine, if animals have a soul or not. Colum would argue they most definitely have and he was moved by Kamal's sincerity. Being unsure though of the poor cat's religious persuasion, they decided it would be best just to have a minute silence. A minute silence was duly accorded then the duo squeezed back through the gap in the fence and up the dusky garden. It was still silent next door. I heard no screaming. The basement was empty. The cat had been buried and buried decently. Mrs Sanjeev slept on undisturbed.

Years later, sitting on the white sheet that covered the living room of the bereaved Sanjeev home in mourning for their mum, drinking tea and eating the delicious home-made chapati and dahl offered to all guests who had come to say their sympathies to the family, I asked Kamal if he had ever told his mum of the dead cat. I could see his mind dredging up the memory and an amused smile lifted the corners of his mouth.

'No, I did not,' he said, 'And don't you go telling anyone about that.'

Would I ever.

Although it is November, I'm writing this chapter outside our house at the small wooden table next to the shared fence between us and the

Sanjeev home. It is the best position to write these words. The house next door is silent. None of the family are there at the moment. I have rarely sat here without being aware of Mrs Sanjeev moving around over the fence or hearing her voice issuing out of the kitchen window, talking on the phone to her daughters in the US, or outside laughing with her sons and grandchildren. Or, when she thought I might be around, calling over: 'Missy Anne, you ok? Everybody ok? Your mum ok? Sam ok? Colum ok? Me ok. Sometimes good. Sometimes bad. Thank you. Thank you.' Short interchanges. Short communications. Meeting me more than halfway. I hear her voice clearly in my mind. Her spirit is not far away.

The postman comes and gives me two letters and a folded piece of paper. One is a reminder for an annual eye-examination, one is the slim catalogue from Persephone Books and one is from Scottish Water advising us that there will be interrupted service due to 'essential maintenance' between the hours of 9am — 5pm in two days time. I automatically turn to the fence to call Mrs Sanjeev to explain to her she must fill some saucepans and her kettle before the water is turned off. And then ... I remember.

K2, s1, K1, psso, knit to end

Knitting has often been given a less than laudable status in literary depictions. In the nineteenth century, Dickens fashioned his character, Madame Defarge, in his *Tale of Two Cities*, as a powerful bitter knitter. Charlotte Bronte, in *Jane Eyre* makes a passionate plea that women should not be restricted to only 'making puddings and knitting stockings'. Margaret Oliphant provides a slightly different spin on the craft in her novel, *Kirsteen* (1890). Upset at her brother's leaving for service in India, and more upset by the leaving of his friend Ronald — her newly betrothed secret sweetheart — Kirsteen feels stifled in the house. She cleverly uses the designated sphere of female chores to provide her with a workable reason for absenting herself:

> Kirsteen [...] suddenly remembered something she had to get at the 'merchant's', which was a full mile off — worsted for the mother's knitting and needles for herself, who was always, to the reprobation of the elder members of the family, losing her needles. She was glad to represent to herself that this errand was a necessity, for a house without needles how can that be?

In twentieth-century literature knitting is again viewed as a fairly worthless activity. Norman MacCaig personifies female pigeons in his poem 'Wild Oats' as douce and purse-beaked characters, judgemental of a glamorous newcomer, while they resolutely knit. The narrator in Janice Galloway's memoir novel *This Is Not About Me* (2008) tells us of her aggressive and abusive older sister, Cora, who was also an accomplished, creative and skilful knitter. J K Rowling, has the fey but loving Mrs

Weasley knit outsize and ugly jumpers for her offspring, and their friend Harry, each Christmas. Garments of fun and indulgent comment from all the receivers. Even Jane Marple, that sharp-eyed, hatchet-minded detective by Agatha Christie, disarms her suspects and opponents by taking her knitting wherever she goes. Miss Marples' quietly flying needles — equating 'harmless' in the minds of those who observe her — together with her white fluffy hair and old lady fussiness, disarms suspects and allows her access to the underlying premises for all those murders in sleepy St Mary Mead. Knitting, *qua* knitting, according to many writers, is something for the slightly dull, dutiful, daft or downright evil. It is unhip, boring and belongs to the unfashionable world of overt domesticity.

It is rare that a writer expresses one of the main impetuses for knitting — i.e. that the very process is an end in itself. There are few fictional characters who emulate this. I can only think of two — this is now your opportunity to flood me with others of your ken. There is Fr Tim of Jan Karon's novel *At Home in Mitford* (1994). Set in a small pretty town in North Carolina it depicts the myriad minutiae of Fr Tim's parishioners and townspeople. He is a faithful pastor but an increasingly tired and lonely one who dreams of, one day, sitting by his fire in the company of a wife. A wife who would be knitting, because to him, the regularity and repetitiousness of it soothed the soul. Ah, Fr Tim, despite the rather sugary-sweet nature of your author's books, how right you are. It does precisely that. There is contemplation to be found in the craft and the task itself. It stills the mind and steadies the senses. For those of us who find it hard to relax and feel guilty if not achieving, knitting offers a result and end product even though we are hardly moving. Margaret Drabble's character Candida Wilton, the subjective narrator of *The Seven Sisters* (2002), divorced because of her adulterous husband who somehow has been curiously positioned as the blameless party, finds herself alone in London where she slowly, very slowly, begins to rebuild her life. I won't tell you the rest of her path as you should read it for yourself and judge Candida — a rather slippery narrator — for yourself. The relevant point is that way towards the end of the novel we are told that Candida has been 'seduced' by the artful hanks of hand-dyed Finnish wools and has taken up knitting — which she has discovered preferable to playing Solitaire. Why she was in Finland is again something you will discover if you read the novel, but I find it refreshing in its overturn of assumptions, to find the practice of knitting used as a symbol of new freedom from a previously frigid life.

Candida also discovers the usefulness of knitting in certain social situations. Nowadays, when I am visiting someone for any length of time, I take some knitting with me. When you sit and knit you send out a signal to your host that they need not worry about entertaining you. You are creating your own entertainment but are still available to chat if they wish. 'It's nice watching someone knit,' said my brother-in-law to me during a visit to his mum. 'It makes me feel calm.' Unfortunately, this benefit wasn't appreciated by the police officer on duty at the door of our local law court. Having been called as a witness to a recent break-in on our street, and presuming a long wait would be entailed, I took along my knitting.

'Do you have any sharp objects in your bag?' enquired the officer.

'Just my knitting needles,' I innocently declared.

'*Ouf!* We'll need to take those off you,' the amused officer returned.

'Why? Miss Marple always knitted through every case she was involved in.'

'Aye, maybe she did. I'll take them from you anyway. I could do a few rows for you if you like.'

'Touch it and your dead,' I said, handing over my bag.

It should also be said that skilful knitting — the type that is beyond my very basic efforts — is surely an outward sign of inward intelligence. When my Aunt Clemmy was first diagnosed with a brain tumour I, with my mum, trundled down to visit her. Believing that I may be sitting at the bedside of a very unwell old lady I had packed some knitting. I hadn't knitted for years but something prompted me to pick out a pattern for a beanie hat, buy some plain grey wool from an 'Odds n Ends' box in a local charity shop, and stuff it all in my bag. Before I left for the train I had to do an internet search to remind myself how to cast on. So, we're talking basic knitting. Effective, but basic. Still, it would do to fill an hour or so if my aunt was breathing her last. I should have reminded myself about the character of my aunt, who, despite her diagnosis was up and about, slower and reliant on a stick, but up and about she nevertheless was. One evening she came over to the guest house of her convent where Mum and I were staying. Seeing me take out my knitting as we were all settling down to a DVD, she trotted off to get hers. When she returned she pulled out of a proper knitting bag what looked like a version of the Bayeux Tapestry. I looked at my pathetically easy pattern and questioned which of us had the brain tumour.

Knitting can also be a furious affair. Another aunt of mine who took up knitting for me and my siblings when our mum's shoulder froze and prevented her from doing so, could knit and gossip at the same time. The more juicy the gossip, the faster she knitted. Tense tight stitches stretched to breaking point grew on the needles — culminating in taut feeling jumpers and cardigans. Even as a child I felt that there was something not quite right with the things my aunt sent up. The kindness behind the action was certain but, strangely, what was being talked about while the rows increased, was somehow imbued in the wool. Just as a garden reflects the gardener, so a piece of knitting tells us something about the knitter. Not just how skilful they are, or how creative, or how aware of weave and style and colour they are, but also what frame of mind they were in when they were knitting. My aunt had a hard life and very little luxury. The wool she used, by necessity, was the cheapest. Widowed young, she had her own family to care for and her days were, like her stitches, wound too tightly with no slack.

My memory balances this rather negative memory with other more positive cameos. There is for example, the photograph my sister-in-law, Maria, showed me quite recently of her two-year-old grand-daughter wearing a dainty lilac pinafore Maria had knitted for her. Knitted with love and thoughtfulness down to the row of cotton flowers stitched along the rim of the bodice. A pretty garment for a pretty and precious girl. This all bears out what the owner of a shop in Crieff, Perthshire, said to me. We were visiting family in the town, but had deliberately arrived early to allow ourselves a bit of a stroll about the high street and check out what it had to offer. Colum parked himself and an interesting book in a snug coffee shop while I did a swift skim around the shops. Returning some half hour later I spotted an arty looking establishment just across the road from the coffee shop that advertised itself as a fibre and yarn emporium. We really should have been making our way to our cousin's house but the look of the shop was too compelling. Apart from being a delight to the eye and a quality stockist of materials for felting, knitting, spinning and hand dyeing, I left the shop with something more than any of that. Having been seduced by a large A4 size book on knitting which offered a very useful section decoding and demonstrating a range of knitting instructions which continually challenge me, I chatted a bit more with the person behind the counter. She may or may not have been the owner but whoever she was she understood that knitting isn't always about the churning out of garments.

I was currently knitting a shawl for my sister-in-law whose son had died without rhyme nor reason those months ago, leaving her heartbroken and sore. Wondering what I could do to in any way to ease her pain, I remembered the 'grief shawl' in the artist's installation in Lindisfarne and the artist's written invite to pick it up and wrap it around oneself, if you had the need. Inspired by this I was halfway through just such a shawl. Mine wasn't soft and enveloping like the Lindisfarne example though. Mine was made from a course type of 100% Icelandic wool. Instead of a lacy open-weave pattern, I had one of intertwining cable, reminiscent of a Celtic pattern. My sister-in-law, Bridget, is part of a large Irish-origin family and I somehow felt that my choices of yarn and pattern were right for her. I told the shopkeeper of how I had begun it. Begun it again and again and again because I couldn't get the wool to sit easily on the needles. Colum joked that it was indeed a grief shawl as I had to rip it back so many times. Then, my son's girlfriend at the time, watching me wrestle with it one evening, suggested that I use bigger needles than the pattern detailed. A few days later I bought some. A size larger, quite a few centimetres longer and … wooden. The shawl settled down and grew and grew quite happily. The shopkeeper nodded and said 'Yes, the manner and method of knitting have to reflect who or what you intend it for.' The small steel needles I had been working with just weren't compatible with the nature of the shawl. It wanted something more natural, more yielding and warmer to touch. Bridget had more than a fair share of sharpness and anything intended for her needed to be of a kinder quality. Thus, I realise, knitting can be a contemplative, indeed a prayerful act. Focused on the recipient, mindful of where they are in life, mindful of their tastes, interests and needs, a piece of hand-knitting can be more than just the outcome of a hobby.

This is precisely the premise that another establishment — *The Wool Haven* situated in the southside of Glasgow — has as its foundation stone. Owned by the lovely Frances, who took a leap in the dark to leave her IT job and take the lease on a vacant shop unit, *The Wool Haven* is a lesson to us all about what can happen when you listen to the whisperings of your soul. When you visit the shop the atmosphere of warmth is tangible. The very balls of wool splashing colour, vibrancy and texture seem to chuckle and dance in expectation of being picked for some creative enterprise. Handcrafted wooden 'yarn bowls' in varying sizes lure the hand to stroke them, while jars and jars of pretty buttons stand ready to add piquancy and complement to any piece of knitting. Central to all is the wooden table surrounded by cushioned seating, inviting customers to sit and peruse pattern books, ask advice, deliberate over complexity of stitch, share stories of embryonic, growing and completed knitting projects and perhaps have a cup of tea. Explanations of the who, the why, the where and the when surrounding a choice of pattern, are spoken of. Frances thus gathers up the weave of her customers' days. Drawing ends together. Connecting people. Doing far more than just selling them wool. I went there with my sister-in-law, curious to see the shop. I was also entertaining the hope of buying some nice yarn for a jumper I had promised to knit. An addicted knitter actually hardly needs an excuse to look at wool, but we use them all the same in the hope that the altruism will cover the covetousness. The shop worked its magic. Having not knitted for years, and although only a self-confessed 'plain and purl' knitter, the balls of enticing wool and subtle shades were too much for Bridget's feminine fingers. We left the shop an hour and a half later, both carrying bags of wool, dusky reds in Bridget's, forest greens in mine. A pattern for a snuggly snood in hers, a pattern for a vintage-style cardigan in mine. Both of us happy. I texted her later that afternoon. She replied. I texted back. She replied again and ended '*Mst gt bck to knitting, no time to chat.*' Ah, the process is at work. May it bring healing.

The Strip at the Cenotaph

'Twas a measure of the extremity of his feeling that Sam had lowered his fork — fully loaded with crisp baked potato, hot beans, tuna mayo and random salad leaves — which had been on an express route to his mouth, and stared at his father.

'I don't think that's your best idea, Dad.'

It was a dinner time in the Scriven household. The three of us were sitting round the kitchen table enjoying being there with each other and with the simple, yet highly satisfying, nosh. Sam had been working long hours at his beloved climbing academy in Glasgow and we hadn't eaten together as a family for a number of days. There were things to catch up on, news to impart, plans to share. Things move on apace quickly as there are many strands to the weave of our respective interests and employments. I was already au fait with one of Colum's plans. Sam had just been told of it.

'What do you think Mum?'

'Um, well, it's a really innovative idea and it could raise a lot of much needed cash and highlight a really important issue, but I have to admit it worries me.'

'What worries you exactly?' asked Colum.

'Eh, the possibility of you getting arrested.'

'Exactly,' agreed Sam.

'I'm not going to get arrested. That's not going to happen. It's for charity!'

'And have you ran this past the Police?' persisted Sam.

'Not yet. Don't know if I will. I'm not doing anything illegal.'

'Not doing anything illegal. Like taking your clothes off in public? Not illegal?' continued our son.

'Oh c'mon, lighten up. It won't be the full Monty. No one will object. It'll be funny. Where's your sense of humour?'

'I really think you need to think about this properly, Dad. And you definitely need to check it out with the Police. Definitely.'

A silence descended on our repast. Both men stabbed at their dinners with moody forks. On one level it was comical. Our mid-twenties son grilling and putting the brakes on a scheme of his dad's. A dad who had spent years upon years advising and guiding a son, always interested in all his exploits and dreams, supporting them, persuading against or finding an acceptable alternative when a plan seemed impractical or downright daft. The tables, it seemed, had turned.

Why my menfolk had reached this impasse on their respective understandings of what constituted harmless fun and what constituted risky tomfoolery, perhaps needs some explanation now that your curiosity is roused. Our local fairtrade charitable organisation and shop was in deep financial schtook. To keep going it needed to raise a lot of money. As a member of the management committee as well as a voluntary IT and shop staff worker, Colum was well aware of the state of play. It wasn't just that our town would be the poorer if the shop had to close and our local schools lose a quality educational resource and source of Sale-and-Return stalls, but a number of producer projects in the developing world that totally depended on their quality crafts and foodstuffs being sold through the shop and its on-line outlet, would grind to a halt with devastating consequences for the suppliers. Something had to be done. That was a given. And it needed to be something different. Something that would attract attention.

One of the results of a collective and creative evening with loyal supporters of the charity was Colum's inspired idea of 'The Ironed Man Event'. The nuts and bolts of this — a fitting metaphor perhaps — was that Colum, along with two crazy chums, were collecting sponsorship for their intention to dress as 'Blues Buddies' and, while dancing to Aretha Franklin's 'Respect' (sung by the excellent local gospel choir), would remove layers of their clothing and iron them as they did so. Colum had grafted his idea from the Extreme Ironing sport — where people trek up mountains carrying ironing boards and, at the summit, remove every stitch they have on and have photographs taken of them 'ironing' their clothing. There are no crowds at the top of a mountain however. Colum thought a shift in location was required. Also, let it quickly be said, in his event, the participants would remove everything down to their especially purchased fairtrade undies. The point of the fairtrade undies — apart from protecting the sensibilities of sensitive onlookers — was to draw attention to the truly shocking issue of exploitative practices in slave-labour type conditions in clothing factories that supply UK high street shops. An inspired and unique idea you must agree. As the event was to be staged at our town cross, in broad daylight, on a Saturday afternoon, it was thought that if this didn't catch the eye of the public then little else would.

My man is an affable type. Calm and mostly undaunted by the vicissitudes of life. Respectful indeed of both people, animals — particularly dogs — and our planet. Unwilling to upset or cause offence. Keen to do the right and good thing. Help others as much as he can. A good all-rounder you might say. But … there lurks an untethered streak in his otherwise sensible head where also runs a strong stubborn vein. I have come to know this camouflaged combination rather well over the years. I should have been warned when, in the first few days of us meeting, he performed in a spoof take-off of Cilla Black's highly popular 1980s TV show *Blind Date.* Nothing too startling in that you may say, but if I add into the mix that at this time Colum was in a Jesuit novitiate, you may get my drift. Other examples of the existence of his fondness for fun was when he shaved his hair completely off the day before my sister's wedding, causing my mum to comment in Captain Mainwaring diction, 'Stupid boy'. He did this again some years later not just for a laugh, but to raise money for a Habitat for Humanity house-build in India which our eighteen-year old Sam was involved in. Shaved his long pony-tailed hair off in the full glare of a packed atrium at the council offices — his place of work — amid much glee and heckling. History has thus proved that silliness is highly attractive to my otherwise steady life partner. If there is also a dollop of exhibitionism in it, that's all to the good.

Thus he found himself in the drab front reception of our local Police office facing a rather non-impressed-and-having-none-of-it, Community Police officer.

'You're doing *what, where?*' asked an eye-glaring member of the constabulary.

And they continued to glare as Colum patiently outlined his event plans, told her of the background to the gig, the creditable reasons for the gig, the support from the local council, his awareness of decency etc etc. The upshot to the interview — which left Colum wondering what must be meted out to an actual criminal suspect if that was just 'a chat' — was that she didn't actually say he couldn't do the event but neither did she say it was a wonderful and inspiring effort by an upstanding citizen either.

The stumbling block, as far as the Inspector was concerned, was 25 feet high. Dominating the town cross is a huge bronze sculpture, 'The Spirit of the Crusades', which depicts four WW1 soldiers from the western front, accompanied by a medieval knight – modelled by Alice Meredith Williams atop a pedestal designed by Robert Lorimer. It was unveiled in 1924 and commemorates the Paisley men who had lost their lives in the war. Now, if I had been the one speaking to our worried Community Police officer I wouldn't have used the word 'Cenotaph'. I am far more sleekit of mind than Colum. He has a level of honesty that once caused his boss to purchase and pass him a huge gob-stopper, with instructions to use it in sensitive meetings, when there is detail best left unsaid. No, I would have instinctively stuck to a less loaded usage of 'the Town Cross' where the Cenotaph along with other statues to remarkable men, a flower stall, a regular farmer's market, sellers of mobile phone companies or suppliers of gas or electricity, a host of skateboarders, political party persuaders, a Big Issue vendor and random buskers, are also to be found. 'Cenotaph' comes pre-packaged with images of ceremony, wreath-laying, rigid respectability and, above all, absolutely no laughter. The proposal that three men dressed up as Blues Brothers, would be dancing and removing their garments while ironing ... well, you can see the issue. It took a bit of effort on Colum's part therefore to persuade her of the actual applaudable ethics of the event, that he really wasn't a nutter but a resident of many years standing who just wanted to raise money for an excellent cause.

The Saturday in question dawned. Sponsor sheets filled, dance steps choreographed, choir rehearsed, irons and ironing boards and collection buckets at the ready, sound system people and guitarist and compere all hooked up, black suits, white shirts, trilby hats, sunglasses and serious expressions donned, the Ironed Man event was ready to go.

'But you can't dance on any of the red tiles,' said one of the police officers on duty.

'Why not?' asked Colum and his Blues Buddies, Graeme and Craig.

'Because it could be construed as being disrespectful to war vets. You are in front of the Cenotaph. And the Cenotaph extends to the red slabs all around it. You'll have to move out into the grey slabs.'

At this juncture I was, fortunately, not in earshot. Colum appraised me of this persnickety dictate when I arrived a few minutes later. Already quite wound up, having heard of the unhelpful and abrasive attitude of the Community Police officer, and knowing the incredible effort my man had put in to co-ordinate the event almost single-handedly, I was in fight mode. Let anyone dare try to mess up this event. Let them try. When pushed to it, I am quick with words, they issue out of my mouth like an old testament flood, and hell mend those in receipt of them. I was perhaps also the only one who was thinking that if the ironing boards now had to be a good ten yards away from where the choir was standing at the Cenotaph, then it would be difficult for Colum, Graeme and Craig to co-ordinate with them. I thought of the hours they had put in diligently rehearsing in our dining room, with the choir in the church hall and, that very morning, in the fairtrade warehouse. Actually, Graeme and Craig might be fine. Colum was a slightly other matter. He has what Sam and I have dubbed 'Corporal Jones timing' i.e. he is a half beat behind everyone else. It's normally a source of high amusement to us but, on this occasion, here in public after so much effort has been put in to get everything as slick as can be, the stipulation that the ironing boards have to be where they have to be, makes my blood boil.

'I mean, right enough, you don't want semi-nudity at the Cenotaph.'

I spun round. A photographer, at least I judged as much from the outsize camera in his hands, was standing with some on-lookers. I strode over. This narrative needs correcting right now before it does serious damage. Wording is everything.

'I completely disagree. What these men are doing is an incredibly brave thing. They are risking derision in the public eye because they are raising money for a charity. A charity which helps starving weans in developing countries (NB: in my experience, moving into the reductive demotic works when you need to get a point over, in a short space of time, to local townspeople). They are also drawing our attention to the plight of thousands of sweatshop workers who are paid around 26p a day so that we can get cheap bottom-end clothing. They're standing up for decency and human rights. Show me a war vet who would disagree with that?'

'Eh, right enough hen, if you put it like that. Aye, it's a brave thing as ye say.'

Graeme, one of the Blues Buddies, has overheard me. 'Anne, can you go over and say all of that again to the Police? Maybe they'll let us dance on the red slabs.'

'Sure thing. They're not red anyway. They're pink.'

I am truly on my highest of horses now. My rhetoric is marble-cast ready for combat with anyone. It was one of those things that other wives will understand — i.e. we are allowed to criticise and question the motives of our men anytime we choose, but let anyone else ...

Fortunately, the gods outmanoeuvred me. Before I had the chance to verbally batter the two policemen who had now positioned themselves away from the performers, Colum stopped me.

'It's ok,' he said. 'It's ok. We can work round the stipulations. It's ok.'

I could see he was fine with it. Truly fine. Unruffled. So be it. I shelved my script and went to stand by some friends. They had heard all the daftness about the red / pink slabs.

'Hey, Anne, let's cause a diversion. Let's go and strip off down a side street. That'll keep the Police busy. Then the boys can put the boards where they want them. I've always fancied getting arrested for a good cause.'

I giggled. Felt my shoulders relax. Put the smile back on my face. Our pals had turned out. It was all going to be fine.

It wasn't fine though. It was brilliant. It was hilarious. It was a spectacle our town had never seen before nor are likely to do so again. The choir, with their vocally amazing choir mistress, Emilie, sang their hip-swinging best. The MC, a friend who had dressed himself as the Rev

Cleophus James, asked the crowd in his adopted southern state accent, if 'they had seen the Light?' and later wondered if 'ah might have seen some Moon there too!' The crowd roared and cheered and wolf-whistled when the men took their shirts off and burst into unconfined laughter when trousers came off but hats, sunglasses, socks and boxers (fairtrade, don't you know) stayed on. The quality of ironing was … what will I say? … unique. The quality of entertainment and unorthodox fundraising, quite ingenious.

One of my best memories of the day, was surprisingly not seeing my man strip down to his undies in the middle of our town in front of a Saturday afternoon crowd, but of watching Craig, now decently clad again, running after the two departing police officers offering them both a fairly traded rose.

Buckets filled with pennies and pounds. Smiles put on all faces. Blues Buddies, you done good.

A different leaning

In 2013, *Lean In: Women, Work and The Will to Lead,* was published. The author was Sheryl Sandberg, Chief Operating Officer of Facebook. It was a persuasive argument for female empowerment particularly for those seeking equality in the boardroom. *Lean In* underscored where women were being poorly treated and its aim was to encourage women to seek higher office so to influence effective change for good. It was a book that was quoted, referenced and alluded to. It was a book which trended. Re-issued in 2014 under the title *Lean-In for Graduates,* it now included new chapters by leading business experts. Both books topped the best-seller lists, nationally and internationally. The title 'Lean In' became a catch-phrase.

I am reminded of Sheryl Sandberg's book while sitting around a large oval table in a pleasant atrium area of an old Victorian mill, which was converted into a business centre around 2001. My friend, Liz, is saying 'You see? You see? Look at us. Leaning in. There's something about that.' The major difference is that we are not intent nor focused on a spreadsheet, sales report or some other money-related document, but instead are looking at a folder containing numerous swatches of cloth which have distinctive designs embroidered on them. The designs vary in expression but are contained within a same uniform shape. A shape once deeply attached to a thriving business and industry which put our town firmly on the world map. The designs we are leaning in to see better are those of the distinctive Paisley Pattern.

In other hands, in other minds, with other targets, the swatches of cloth with their intricate tear-drop or palm frond shapes, might be the focus of a very different kind of discussion. Indeed, the specially-drawn up team of people who have been grafted together by Renfrewshire Council to put together a water-tight bid for Paisley as the UK City of Culture 2021, are utilising and promoting the ancient design in clever and innovative ways. The group I am meeting with, the women I am leaning-in or as the Scots has it, coorieing-in with, are the Paisley Thread Mill Museum Stitching Group who are working together to contribute to *The Tapestry of Renfrewshire*.

This tapestry is the latest endeavour to capture Scotland's story stitch by stitch. *The Great Tapestry of Scotland*, launched in the Scottish Parliament in 2013 and then exhibited around Scotland, including Paisley, comprising of 163 panels, 1 metre high and 143 metres in length, involving over 1,000 stitchers, was quickly followed by *The Scottish Diaspora Tapestry* in 2014. Both tapestries were a feast for the eyes and intellect. Intricate and conscientious craftwork combined with historical research and accuracy. I would however be failing as a scholar if I did not cite an interesting curiosity told me by my friend, Peter, ever a reliable and erudite source: "The Bayeux Tapestry and the Great Tapestry of Scotland aren't tapestries. They're embroideries. Tapestries are made on a loom, embroideries are stitched ... they're misnomers." Illustrating the point that the documentation of history is always subject to limited human understanding, or quirkiness, and is always open to revision.

Misnomer it may be, but when *The Great Tapestry* (or *Great Embroidery*?) was situated in The Domestic Finishing Mill, (now known simply as 'The Anchor Mill') in Paisley, I visited it three times. Colum went at least twice more. There was just so much to soak in that saturation point was reached when only halfway around the panels. *The Renfrewshire Tapestry*, launched in Paisley Abbey in February 2016 with an ambitious completion date of the end of 2017, promises to be just such another feast of detailed stitching, storyboarding and celebrating the rich culture and history of the area.

In a cleverly coined leaflet 'A Call to Yarns', the Renfrewshire project asks for donations of Coats or Anchor embroidery thread which have never been used. When I arrive at the atrium two women are sorting two large piles of thread, exclaiming: 'Oh, this is very old. This is lovely! And look at this one! That's a Clark's for sure.' There is history, it seems, in the very labels containing the threads but it takes an experienced eye to recognise their lineage. By deliberately using 'authentic threads' in the sewing of the trademark Paisley Pattern, the Renfrewshire Tapestry stitchers are bringing together the two dominant strands in Paisley's textile history — that of the cottage shawl industry and that of the thread mills. The two industries are inclined to get fused or muddled-up, but each have their respective story.

The distinctive Paisley motif — the teardrop, tadpole, pine, palm frond or arabesque pattern as it has been variously described — originated in Chaldea, Babylon and from there spread to Kashmir, India, where from the 11th century onwards shawls incorporating the motif began to be woven. Samples of the Kashmir shawls were brought to Britain, early 18th century, by travellers and traders. These Kashmir shawls were very popular but were expensive and only the wealthy could afford them. Paisley weavers proved themselves skilled at the imitation of the Kashmir designs and also by their clever method of sub-division of labour (where small sections of a shawl were made by different weavers then pieced together), quicker production was possible. Up until the 1820s weaving was a cottage based industry, but the introduction of the Jacquard Loom was the catalyst for much greater production and this in turn effected a move to the factory. Paisley soon outstripped its other British competitors and by 1850 there were over 7,000 weavers working in the town. The popularity of the Paisley pattern shawl was furthered by the ascension to the throne of Queen Victoria who was fond of a particular shawl design. Shawls also became usual bridal presents and formed part of a trousseau. Most moderately wealthy women would own at least two shawls of the Kashmir pattern. Working class women favoured the much plainer, large checked shawls — known as Scotch Plaid. The industry began to decline with the introduction of the crinoline in the 1870s. With such attention to detail now focused on the back of her costume, ladies disliked how a shawl obscured it. Thus the Paisley shawl, sadly, slowly fell out of fashion.

The famous Anchor and Coats thread produced in the town has its own story and it is apt that the tapestry group meets twice a week in a mill building that once was very much part of that story. The specifics of when the cotton thread industry began in Paisley, and by whom, are a little obscure. It is agreed however that the Clark and Coats families were fundamental players – building mills at Seedhill and Ferguslie respectively in the early nineteenth century. The two firms amalgamated in 1896. It is interesting to note that, previous to the rise of Coats and Clark, there was already in existence a linen thread industry in Renfrewshire and historians position its initiation to the enterprising and creative vision of a woman.

In *Paisley Thread Industry and the Men Who Created and Developed It* (1907) – the overt patriarchy of the title rather amusing – Matthew Blair documents how it was none other than Christine Shaw, she of the infamous witchcraft trial of 1697, an appalling miscarriage of justice which need not be rehearsed here, who was responsible for the origins of the linen thread industry in Renfrewshire. More relevant to the discussion here is the detailing of how Christine Shaw married the Rev John Miller, minister of Kilmaurs in 1718, and when widowed some three years later, moved to Johnstone where, as Blair details:

Mrs Miller [née Shaw] excelled in the production of fine linen yarn, such as was used in Paisley for making lawns, but up till this time it had never been twisted into thread suitable for the sewing or embroidering needle.'

Christine Shaw then managed to obtain a twisting mill from Holland which was able to run twelve bobbins simultaneously and enabled the production of a fine linen thread. As William A Metcalfe outlines in his *A History of Paisley 600 — 1908*, published in 1909:

Samples of her industry were shown to Lady Blantyre, who took a parcel with her to Bath, then a chief fashionable resort in England. At Bath, her thread was greatly admired and readily bought by some lace manufacturers.

One wonders if Jane Austen's family, who moved to Bath in 1801, were familiar with what became known as 'Bargarran Thread'.

In Renfrewshire, competitors soon appeared and the thread industry blossomed. By 1787, as Matthew Blair notes:

There were not less than one hundred and twenty machines at work in twining thread in Paisley [...] the Bargarran thread was linen, a fibre well adapted to sewing thread because of its strength. Its defects were that it was uneven and rough, and could not be spun to a very fine count. Cotton, which possessed better spinning properties, but less strength, became its powerful, and ultimately, successful competitor.

Intrinsic to the changeover to cotton thread was the political interdict from Napoleon in 1806, decreeing that trade with Britain was to cease. As the supply of silk dried up, Patrick Clark was spurred on to perfect a cotton heddle yarn which had the smoothness of silk. With the invention of the sewing machine mid nineteenth century, demand for cotton sewing thread grew to a new height. When the US government laid a discriminatory tax on imports, Paisley thread manufacturers opened mills in America – Kerr and Clark at Newark in 1864 and Coats at Pawtucket in 1868. By the time the Coats and Clark families joined forces in 1896 they had seen off other competitors and had the complete monopoly of the cotton sewing thread trade in Paisley.

Habit dies hard however and, as Evelyn Hood notes in her *Mill Memories* (2003), that despite the amalgamation, both companies retained their distinctive trademarks — Coats the symbol of the chain and Clark the symbol of the anchor. Paisley people have always referred to the two great mill complexes as 'Clarks' and 'Coats'. At the height of its power, J & P Coats Ltd, the assumed name of the amalgamated company, employed around 10,000 workers in Paisley and had subsidiaries in fifteen overseas countries. Three quarters of this vast work force was female. It could be argued then that the common expression that 'Paisley was the mills, and the mills were Paisley' should be modified to 'Paisley was the mill girls, the mill girls were Paisley'.

The Paisley Thread Mill Museum Stitching Group meet in Mile End Mill. This mill, along with an impressive listing of other remarkable buildings of the area, is listed in the recently published 850 paged Pevsner Architectural Guide, *Lanarkshire and Renfrewshire* (eds. Close, Gifford and Walker, 2016). It is perhaps worth noting that this volume, the 68th Pevsner and the fifteenth and final volume in *The Buildings of Scotland* series, fulfill's Pevsner's desire that the series he originally envisaged solely for England, should be extended to Scotland and Northern Ireland. The Scottish series was originally unattractive to him until he looked more deeply at Scotland's architecture and the series began. Mile End Mill in Paisley is just one of the listings contained in the 82 pages devoted to Paisley. Designed by W J Morley of Bradford and constructed 1897-99, it is the largest surviving Paisley mill.

The gender of those giving their energies to the project on the table are once again predominately female. The women are quick though to defend and laud any stitches by a male hand, citing as support how it was men who were the first knitters as their innovative knot-work formed fishing nets. I check this later on the internet and discover the word 'knit' is derived from Old English 'cnyttan' — 'to knot'. And the women stress that the artist designer behind all the Scottish tapestries is Andrew Crummy. The fact remains though that it is women who are major players in the selecting, planning and stitching of the tapestry, while keeping within the designated boundary as laid down by Timothy Pont's 'Baronee of Renfrew' (c.1583 and 1596) as the boundary for the project. Pont's map, the first record of the county, incorporates in today's terms, Renfrewshire, East Renfrewshire, Inverclyde and part of modern day Glasgow.

The final outcome of many many hours spent stitching will undoubtedly be impressive but what is also worthy of admiration is the underlying philosophy of the group. All abilities are welcome. It doesn't matter where someone is from, which socio-economic background they belong to, what accent they have and if they count themselves as Scottish or not, what their back story is, how successful they are or have been in other areas of life. If you are interested in sewing then you are welcome. It is then a place of acceptance. A levelling place. A sacred space if you choose to name it so.

'There is something we call *the flow*,' someone says. 'It's hard to describe, but it happens when you are really quiet and focused on your sewing. It seems to come from the rhythm of what you are doing. The repetitive way of it, but also the concentration. Your thoughts slow down with your breath. I suppose it's just about being in the moment and stopping worrying about other stuff. If I haven't sewn for a few days I feel all out of synch.' I think of how I feel when I haven't been able to get out for a run for overly long, and smile.

Those who worry that their stitching is rusty, need not fear. The memory of how to do it is not far away. Some know this as 'muscle memory', and a woman nods her head when I say that when I was given a hand-cranked Singer sewing machine as a Christmas present and came to try to thread it, I felt that the only way to remember was to let my hands guide me. When I said this a woman sitting across from me, immediately closed her eyes and imitates the action.

'Exactly,' I said. 'That's what I did. Exactly.'

Liz says that she feels it has something to do with pathways laid down in early life which you can return to much later. What was familiar then, what was usual, can lie dormant unused for years, but return to the front of your mind very clearly when called upon.

We talk of how it was for many of us when we were younger. How our mums, our aunties — or in my case, my dad — made many of our clothes. Liz asks the group 'What was the first thing you can remember somebody making for you?'

'A wee red coat with a matching muff,' says one. 'Mind those. They were attached with a string round your shoulders inside your coat.'

'A crocheted poncho,' giggles someone else.

'A kilt,' says another.

'A skirt I called *my tuddle skirt*,' I add. 'I couldn't pronounce my Cs and the name stuck. It was made from a brushed wool fabric and had crossover straps attached to the waist with two big buttons.'

What we are sharing, without realising, is social history. In *The Button Box*, (2016), Lynn Knight, traces the changing mores of society as reflected in women's clothes. The weaves, the threads, the buttons, the rising and falling hem and waistlines, the iconic designs, the ever-prevalent question of how a garment washed and who or what did that washing, the statements clothes made about your class, occupation, age, significant moments or wider life experience, are illustrated in personal memory or family story and offset with a charting of women's shifting place from the Victorian era to the present day. It is, like her grandmother's wonderful button box, a treasure trove of curious gems worth careful rummage. Like Lynn Knight, and I presume like most of the tapestry stitchers, I still keep a button box. Not quite as large nor as fascinating though as the one kept in the hidden cupboard in our fold-up dining table in my childhood home, brought out on so many occasions to function not just as buttons but as counters, prizes, currency in our games. My sister and I had our favourites amidst the curved shell pinks, the velvet covered eyelets, the wooden toggles, the chocolate leather weaves, the bold penny shapes, the embossed steels and the plain but very pretty baby buttons. Each one stretched and attached our thoughts to garments and scenarios real or fabricated. Enchantment lies in button boxes.

So too does it lie in the tapestry panel being carefully created by the stitchers. They unfold the large piece of cotton linen, with the base design drawn by Andrew Crummy, for me to see. It is a whirlpool of sequential movement depicting mill workers reaching deep into the distinctive palm frond watermark from where vibrant green blades shoot, sending the first ribbons towards another figure who pulls them to her while two other figures release a rapture of ribbons upwards into a glorious sky or ocean. Each figure important in the process. Each figure adding their own particular effort — symbolised by the chain shape of the palm frond — in the creation of something painstaking but wondrous. But, unlike any rigid or severe corrective meted out to mill workers who failed to notice mistakes in their work, the tapestry group is strong in their charism of inclusivity.

'It doesn't matter if a stitch goes wrong,' Liz is saying. 'What does that mean anyway? Who's to say what perfection is? It's real. It's genuine. That's what matters. Our panel will tell a human story. There will be no picking out on ours.'

That said, the stitchers are their own regulators. They know when something looks right or when it doesn't. Today they are practising their personal tear-drop designs deciding which colours, which stitches, which patterning, will best honour part of Paisley's story. They are unhurried in this. Taking time to discuss their ideas and test them out. No-one is clock watching and every new arrival is greeted and welcomed. What strikes me as I watch the stitchers gather and work is that this is a collaborative project, from start to finish. No-one is getting ahead of another, and, while individual talent is duly noted, no-one seeks dominance. The women point out what others have done, what others are good at. They are creating something together. The process is as important as the end product. In fact, probably more so. They are leaning in. Leaning in to each other and an age-old craft while creating something both meaningful and magical.

Retour

They have come back. Flying, feeding, sleeping, flying, feeding, sleeping all that way. Miles and miles and miles from a far distant land. All that herculean effort just to come to the eaves under the old Ballachulish slate roofs in our street and the telephone wires strung outside our house. How many countries must they have flown over? Flying high high above cities and deserts and mountains and rivers. Flying above jostling politics, human borders, demarcations, disputed territories, taking no part in any of that. Paying heed only to weathers, temperatures and a deep draw north.

Late in the dwindling light of a May evening I sit at my old but still sweet piano and decode the dots and lines and squiggles that are *L'Hirondelle* by Burgmüller. I can't play it yet as it should be played. Burgmüller must have listened to the rise and fall of the bird's call and captured it in notes. Played correctly it reflects rapture and streams of elegance. I know this because I have heard proper pianists play it. Did Burgmüller sit like me one May evening and listen to the song of the returned swallows and feel amazement and gladness enter his heart? Amazement and gladness that these fragile creatures would wish to risk life and wing just to return to a remembered place. A remembered place that must offer them something. I muse on the Scottish Gaelic word *ceanalas*. A near untranslatable word that English language can only circle around. Similar, I am told by my friend, Peter, to the German word *sehnsucht* — a word suggestive of an ardent yearning for a homeland, a homeland which the body and the mind knows of even if it has never been there. The swallows understand the pull behind these related words.

Perhaps, I think to myself, all is not lost. All is not quite as dark as I sometimes fear it is. The natural world, hearing and moving to a different rhythm than ours, is continuing. Despite our stupidities and senselessness and our insane unthinking desire to wreck it. The swallows are still flying. Surely that is something to rejoice in. While the media is relentless in its focus on earthbound powerful people and tells us that the future is bleak and that we are all in a discordant state, it is so easy to forget that which continues to instill life-giving rhythm and beauty into our world if we but take a moment to notice.

The swallow has something to teach us too about embarking on a seemingly crazy project. As it is only by being brave enough to spread one's wings that you begin on a journey that could take you to a whole other place. I began this book when Colum was on the cusp of leaving his IT job. The job that had sustained us financially for many a year. There were good and rational reasons for him not to leave. The regular rhythm of familiar work was one of them. The knowledge of a steady income was another. These were both sustainable reasons while our son was young and I wanted to be able to watch the moon with him. They remained sustainable reasons while I went on to further academic study and part-time teaching. Then there came a time when those reasons slipped status and we began to wonder what could happen if we took our feet off the ground. The lesson to be learned, we discovered, was that it is only when you listen to an inward instinct, direct your energies elsewhere and lift towards it, that the next experience opens out. You can dream of it, ponder it, wonder about it, plan it, but it will not happen till you fling yourself at it. As the John Anster 1835 translation of some lines from Goethe's *Faust* counsels:

Lose this day loitering — 'twill be the same story
To-morrow – and the next more dilatory;
Then indecision brings its own delays,
And days are lost lamenting o'er lost days.
Are you in earnest? seize this very minute –
What you can do, or dream you can, begin it,
Boldness has genius, power, and magic in it,
Only engage, and then the mind grows heated —
Begin it, and the work will be completed!

Thus, two years on from that raw weathered evening when I spoke to the women's guild in rural Renfrewshire, we are in very different territory. Colum's dream to open an Amichien-based day care centre for dogs has not yet happened. Be not quick to castigate though, for other excellent and unexpected innovative things have happened – such as the scripting and running of courses which teaches young people how to care for and understand dogs; such as an excellent Reading to Dogs programme where our Jenna curls up amidst primary school children while they sit on plump floor cushions and read their favourite stories to her – thus forgetting their anxiety about reading aloud, too focused on the pretty dog with the silky fur who appears to be enjoying the experience. All of which is carried out by the professional team who currently composes Doggy Chillin CIC — a social enterprise company doing something to right the imbalance of power in the business world. A company which takes time to build meditative silence into its planning days, ensuring that all decisions and directions stem from right thinking and allowing trust and intuition to play its full part.

What has become key for both Colum and I, is the importance of keeping peace in the soul while striving to put flesh on a vision and simultaneously cope with the unexpected situations that life presents. I thought of this recently as I stood on the shoreline of the very southern tip of Kintyre. The light was fast fading but I had lingered behind while my friends headed off the beach towards our rented caravan, their thoughts focused on cosy sleeping bags, their limbs tired from their victorious road race held earlier that day in Campbeltown. I had had to scratch my entry because, of late, my leg muscles have been telling me they need a rest. A short swim in the local pool that morning was all that had filled the exercise gap, so I was happy to stay by the shore for a while longer, wander along its perimeter and watch and listen to the gentle wash of the waves as it rippled over my wellies. To the left of me were the lights of Northern Ireland, immediately in front was the island of Sanda, and far far to the left were the few visible lights of Ayrshire. The only sounds were the bleating of sheep from the farm behind me, the sporadic cry of a seagull or gannet, the soft slosh of the sea water and my own breathing.

I thought on all that had happened over the last two years. All that busyness. All that ferocity of doings, goings, leavings. And all that was still filling my usual life. On that tranquil shore, with no other human in sight, I reflected on how it was easy to be at peace in such surroundings, but the trick was to find that same peace in my usual places. In my usual places where the people I love best are. Places not as picturesque, granted, as where I am standing, staring out to a quiet sea and up to the first stars of the night. Not as quiet nor as cleansing of the skin or lungs. Precious places, nonetheless, because they are my reality and are where I play out my daily life.

My mind presented something Dominique Browning speaks of in her gracious memoir, *Slow Love,* (2010). Going through a period of sleeplessness she finds herself one night at her piano. She picks her way through a volume of music by Bach. It is a challenging piece and one that, in her much earlier years, she swept through without any thought for its emotional expression. Now she takes her time, reads the music as it was composed, and feels herself drawn into an attentive and far calmer state. Instead of ignoring the repeats she takes them, working back through notes she has just played again and again when directed. Unlike her impatient younger self, she now realises the profundity of the repeats, the necessity of them. In the next few days she notices that she is also taking the repeats in conversations. Listening more instead of talking or judging. And, as she walks, she observes more. Reading all around her as they are meant to be read. She becomes aware that the cadence of her life has changed. From an imperfect and irregular jarring it has moved to a more tranquil progression and fulfilment.

I sweep my eyes round the skyline for one last time then turn towards the caravan which is now lit and has sporadic laughter spilling out of it. My mind is quiet. Instead of refusing the repeats, all of those life notes needing attention, it is perhaps that I need to reappraise them. See them for the depth they offer, the profundity and gravitas they bring both to me as a person and me as a writer. Seeing it to the end. Just as it is. As also with the cadences of my life. Feeling the cadences, living the cadences, recognising the cadences and writing of the cadences is what I have to do. In doing so I will thus reach for the final form, the Plagal, the Amen cadence. Let It Be.

My Scots — English glossary

aebody:	everybody
aifter:	after
ashet:	small dish
aye:	yes
bairn:	child
bunnet:	cap
blether:	chat
brae:	hill
cairn:	pyramid of loose stones on top of a hill or mountain
caller:	fresh
canny:	shrewd / careful
carfuffle:	disorder
caul:	cold
chap	knock
clout:	piece of cloth / layer of clothing
coorie-in:	to snuggle together or lean-in
craig:	throat
craw:	throat
darg:	work
dee:	die
didnae:	did not
douce:	respectable
dreich:	miserable weather
dreepin:	dropping, hanging
drouthy:	thirsty
freend:	friend
flichterin:	fluttering
gie:	give
guid:	good

happed:	wrapped up
hen:	young woman
hoach:	large number
ithers:	others
jalouse:	suspect
joukit:	to bend, swerve
kenspeckle:	conspicuous / recognisable
lug:	ear
moothie:	harmonica
oot:	out
ower:	over
peesweep:	lapwing
purvey:	food and drink laid on after a wedding or funeral
roun:	round
sair fecht :	sore fight / hard struggle
scrudge:	scourge
shilpit:	thin / drawn-looking
shoogly:	loose
skoot:	move quickly
skint:	have no money
skive:	to avoid work or duty
sleekit:	cunning
sma:	small
smeddum:	strength / grit
stramash:	commotion
stravaiger:	idle walker
stooshie:	fuss
stour:	dust
tae:	to
thole:	put up with
thrawn:	perverse / obstinate
tummled-its-whulkies: do a somersault	
wan:	one
weans:	children
wee:	small / young
week:	wet
weel kent :	well known
welkin:	sky / heavens
wimplin:	winding / meandering

Lightning Source UK Ltd.
Milton Keynes UK
UKOW01f0008230917
309728UK00007B/135/P